INDUSTRIAL
MARKETING
MANAGEMENT

PRIORITIES IN MARKETING SERIES

Leonard L. Berry, General Editor

ROBERT W. HAAS *Industrial Marketing Management*

INDUSTRIAL MARKETING MANAGEMENT

Robert W. Haas
PROFESSOR OF MARKETING
SAN DIEGO STATE UNIVERSITY

FIRST EDITION

PETROCELLI / CHARTER   NEW YORK 1976

First Printing

Printed in the United States of America

Library of Congress Cataloging in Publication Data

Haas, Robert W
    Industrial marketing management.

    (Priorities in marketing series)
    Includes index.
    1. Marketing management. I. Title.
HF5415.13.H27   1976   658.8   76-9050
ISBN 0-88405-329-6 paperback
ISBN 0-88405-341-5 cloth bound

To Janet, Amie Lynne,
Chris, and Rob

CONTENTS

LIST OF FIGURES

LIST OF TABLES

PREFACE

Industrial marketing seems to be the forgotten child of the parent discipline of marketing. For reasons never fully explained, industrial marketing always seems to take a backseat to consumer marketing. To test this hypothesis, one has only to compare the number of textbooks in industrial marketing with the number of textbooks written in such areas as marketing principles, consumer behavior, advertising, sales management, marketing management, retailing, and other such areas of the parent discipline of marketing.

Another way of testing the hypothesis is to look at college and university marketing curricula. Research indicates that less than a third of U.S. collegiate schools of business offer courses in industrial marketing either at the graduate or the undergraduate level. In addition, most schools that do offer such a course typically consider it to be an elective course and one that is not required of their marketing majors. The result is that a great number of marketing majors graduate from the nation's business colleges with no more exposure to the area of industrial marketing management other than reading a chapter in a marketing principles textbook.

Much of the reason for the slighting of industrial marketing may be attributed to a lack of understanding of the industrial market. Many marketing professionals actually believe that industrial marketing is basically the same as consumer marketing except for the examples used. Anyone who has ever worked in both areas knows the folly of this assumption. Add to this the fact that the 1972 *Census of Manufactures* reported that over 10,500 separate products were manufactured by 420 manufacturing industries at a total value of over $700 billion, and this oversight of the industrial market, intended or accidental, makes little sense. The industrial market is large. Roughly one-half of all the goods produced in the United States can be defined as industrial goods, and this percentage is even larger in the overseas industrial market.

Within this background, the intent of this text is to develop an up-to-date, comprehensive source, focusing specifically on marketing management in the industrial market. The emphasis will be on the marketing management or decision-making implications in the industrial market as these apply to market segmentation, marketing planning, overall marketing strategy, and the substrategies of product, place, promotion, and price. It is hoped that the text will fill the gap that exists in contemporary marketing literature.

The author would like to thank all those who contributed in any way to the writing of this text. Particularly, the author wants to thank Dr. Leonard L. Berry of Virginia Commonwealth University for his very constructive help throughout the writing of the entire text and also Dr. Thomas R. Wotruba, whose insight and encouragement contributed greatly to the text's completion. Both contributed in no small way to this text, and the author is especially appreciative. In addition, thanks are due to the reviewers for their constructive comments.

1

THE INDUSTRIAL
MARKETING SYSTEM

The basis for defining industrial marketing appears to lie in the understanding of the industrial customer rather than in the products involved. In theory, this is not any different from the way it is in the consumer market. Products and services are want satisfiers and as such must fulfill the wants, needs, desires, and expectations of selected target customers if the companies producing those products and services are to survive and succeed. This is just as true in the industrial market as it is in the consumer market even though the products and services involved in the former are usually more complex and more expensive. But some big differences exist in the rationale behind buying motivations in the two markets, and the basic structures of the two markets contrast sharply. Unless these differences are understood and properly assessed as to their marketing importance, it is impossible to formulate and implement realistic and practical marketing decisions in the industrial market.

A DEFINITION OF MARKETING

Before an attempt is made to define the specific area of industrial marketing, it is first necessary to formulate a workable definition of the general discipline of marketing. One of the most encompassing definitions of marketing to be found is as follows:

Marketing is the process of discovering and translating consumer needs

1

and wants into product and service specifications, creating demand for these products and services, and then in turn expanding this demand.[1]

The value of this definition is that it illustrates that marketing takes place before the product is produced and that it continues after the sale is made. To illustrate, the "process of discovering and translating consumer needs into product and service specifications" implies market segmentation; marketing research into what the segments require in terms of products and/or services; and the conversion of intangible customer wants, needs, problems, expectations, and so on, into very specific product and service specifications, which form the basis for what will actually be produced or supplied. The phrase "creating demand for these products and services, and then in turn expanding this demand" implies the need for effective promotion of the products or services developed, appropriate channels of distribution, and proper pricing. Inherent also in this definition is the proper servicing of the customer after the sale to keep him satisfied, to encourage him to buy again, and to discourage him from switching to a competitor.

A DEFINITION OF INDUSTRIAL MARKETING

In a general sense, industrial marketing describes all marketing activities not directed at the household or the ultimate consumer. Used in this manner, the term *industrial marketing* applies to the marketing, as marketing was described in the general definition previously given, of all goods and services to businesses and other organizations for their use, either directly or indirectly, in the goods and services that they, in turn, produce. Their demand for industrial goods is derived from the demand for the goods that they, in turn, produce. In economic terms, industrial goods and services might be described as capital goods—those that are used to produce other goods and services! Within this context, industrial marketing may be defined as follows. It is the process of discovering and translating industrial customer wants, needs, expectations, and requirements into product and service specifications and then, in turn, through effective promotion, channeling, pricing, and after-sale servicing, convincing more and more of these customers to use and continue to use these goods and services.

This definition may be criticized on the basis that it is unrealistic in a period of recession and shortages when industrial marketing managers may use marketing to discourage sales to existing customers rather than encourage them. In the recent recession, many industrial companies did restrict sales to existing customers because of shortages of materials. For example, public utilities supplying energy to industrial customers implemented aggressive demarketing programs to help those customers reduce energy consumption as opposed to convincing them to consume more energy.

Yet the cold hard truth is that even in a recession the task of the industrial marketing manager is to market his company's goods and services and keep his company in business. When traditional markets are depressed, the manager does not attempt to convince customers in those markets to purchase more of his goods and services. Rather, he must seek out new markets, as all activity does not cease even in a recession. Viewed in this perspective, the definition is valid. The industrial marketing manager must locate those new markets, assess their requirements, convert those requirements into goods and services, and then market those same goods and services.

WHO ARE INDUSTRIAL CUSTOMERS?

Within the definition thus described, industrial customers are all customers other than the ultimate consumer. The latter term is generally used to describe the household buying unit in the marketplace. Industrial customers can be classified into three groups, which, at times, may overlap. These three classifications are (1) types of commercial enterprises buying goods and/or services, (2) governmental organizations purchasing goods and/or services, and (3) institutional customers in the market for various goods and/or services. A more detailed analysis of each of these three classifications is as follows.

Commercial Enterprises
The group known as commercial enterprises includes any type of commercial business enterprise purchasing industrial goods and/or services for use other than selling directly to the ultimate consumer. There are basically three types of this customer in the industrial market.

Original Equipment Manufacturers. The original equipment manufacturer, more commonly referred to as the OEM, is a commercial customer that buys products and sometimes services to incorporate into the products that it, in turn, produces and sells either into the industrial or ultimate consumer markets. Thus, an electronics company selling components to a manufacturer of television sets would consider the television firm as an original equipment manufacturer or OEM customer. The important point to realize with this type of customer is that the product of the industrial marketer (in this case, the electronics company) ends up in the product of the customer (in this case, the television manufacturer). The purchased product becomes an integral part of the final customer's product. OEM customers may also purchase services from subcontractors, but normally the term *OEM* refers to an industrial customer of products. In the following chapters, the importance of understanding the OEM customer will be emphasized; so it is important that the full meaning of OEM be understood as it relates to a specific type of industrial customer.

User Customers. A second type of commercial enterprise customer is known as the user. In the industrial market, this term refers to those commercial enterprises purchasing goods and/or services for use in producing, in turn, other goods and/or services, which are then sold into the industrial or consumer market or both. Examples of user customers are manufacturing companies purchasing lathes, drilling machines, gear-cutting machines, purching and shearing machines, bending and forming machines, and other similar pieces of machinery that they use in their production processes. In contrast to the OEM, the industrial products purchased by user customers never end up in the final product being produced by the industrial customer. In a purely economic sense, the user customer is a purchaser of capital goods—goods that are used to produce other goods and/or services. The user customer buys the product or service and uses it to produce the product or service that it, in turn, sells to its customers.

Industrial Distributors. The third type of commercial enterprise customer is the industrial distributor. Strictly speaking, distributors are not customers in the industrial market, but rather middlemen who purchase products from manufacturers or other distributors and then, in turn, sell these same products, often in the same form as purchased, to other distributors, OEMs, or to user customers. They are resellers rather than actual customers for industrial goods. In a loose sense, distributors are very similar to industrial wholesalers, and they may be highly specialized or very generalized in their product offerings. As stated, they are technically middlemen as opposed to customers, but because they take title to the products they purchase, many practicing industrial marketing managers treat them as customers. Examples of such distributors are plumbing supply houses, steel service centers, electronic supply houses, and the like. Although they are often thought of and treated as customers in the industrial market, they are technically middlemen reselling industrial goods to actual customers of the OEM or user variety. Throughout this text, distributors shall be considered as middlemen rather than as industrial customers.

It is important to realize that industrial customers of this commercial enterprise classification are not exclusively OEMs or users or distributors. To illustrate, a fabricating plant might be an OEM customer when purchasing component parts from some suppliers. At the same time, however, the machinery that the company purchases for its production line qualifies it as a user customer to the suppliers of such machinery. At the same time, a manufacturer might act as a distributor for another manufacturer, distributing products that are compatible with the products that the former manufacturer produces on its production line. This means that the same company can be an OEM, a user, and a distributor at the same time, but normally not for the same supplier! As might be expected, it is of critical importance that any marketing manager in the industrial market know whether customers are OEMs, users, or distributors. If this is not known, the industrial marketing manager can hardly market effectively, as the manager will be completely ignorant of the differences in buying motivations predominant with each type of customer. An OEM does not purchase for the same reasons as does a user customer. And, of course, the OEM does not normally buy the same product as the user.

GOVERNMENTAL ORGANIZATIONS

Industrial customers of the government variety can range all the way from the smallest township or village in the United States to the Department of Defense, which is sometimes considered to be the largest single concentration of economic power in the world. Great variations occur among governmental customers in their buying patterns, purchasing procedures, and volume of their buying; but basically they all fit into the general classification of governmental customers. Broadly defined, government customers fall into four basic classifications.

Municipalities. There are in excess of 18,000 municipal governments in the United States, and over one-half of their total expenditures are made in such areas as streets and highways, municipally owned water supply systems, police, sanitation, municipally owned electrical power systems, and fire protection.[2]

County Governments. There are a total of 3,043 counties in the United States, but 323 of these are metropolitan in nature, and their expenditures alone account for over one-half of all county government expenditures. This indicates great differences in their volume of purchasing and their buying practices. County government expenditures are mostly in such areas as highways, hospitals, police and fire, correction facilities, and sanitation and sewage. It is of interest to note that, when combined, the 18,000 municipalities and the 3,043 counties include over 56,000 local government buying units, which indicates that there may be any number of local government buying units within any one municipality or county. Of the total 56,000 combined buying units, however, about 7,600 are considered urban and account for over 80 percent of all local purchasing of equipment, services, and supplies.[3]

State Governments. The nation's 50 states are also customers for many industrial marketing firms. Collectively, their major expenditures are made in such areas as education, highways, hospitals and institutions, police and correction, and miscellaneous areas such as water, airports, community redevelopment, and other such projects.[4]

Federal Government. Name just about any industrial product in existence, and the chances are that someone, somewhere, at sometime in the federal government uses it. The many departments, administrations, agencies, boards, commissions, and other independent establishments of the federal government are often customers for many industrial companies.

Institutional Customers

The institutional market includes all those customers of the industrial variety not falling into commercial or governmental classifications. Examples of institutional customers are schools, colleges and universities, churches, hospitals, nursing homes, sanitariums, rest homes, medical clinics, trade schools, nonprofit foundations, and other such types of institutions. As can be seen by these examples, institutional customers can be public or private. A company could market products to both state universities and private universities, to both public and parochial schools, to both private and government sponsored vocational schools, and so on. From the point of view of the industrial marketing manager, the difference is not so much whether the institution is public or private, but rather how each institution purchases its goods and services. For example, a multicampus state university with autonomous purchasing authority on each of its campuses may be marketed to in the same manner as any private university. But a multicampus state university with centralized buying for all its campuses might be more properly considered a governmental customer. The point to remember is that institutions do not fall into a clear-cut classification, but are rather a hybrid of government and private organizations that must be considered on an individual basis according to their purchasing practices and policies.

Although all three types of industrial customers are dissimilar in many respects, they are generally considered to comprise the industrial market because they all purchase goods and/or services to use either directly or indirectly in providing goods and/or services to their own customers. They all differ from the ultimate consumer in that they all purchase goods and services only to satisfy the demand of their own customers, either directly or indirectly. In addition, they are often remarkably similar in their purchasing behavior. A hospital often buys in much the same manner as an industrial manufacturer, and, at times, they will both be purchasing the same products from the same suppliers. In a loose sense, the industrial market refers to all those companies marketing to industry and commerce, government, and the institutions. In this text, the emphasis throughout will be primarily on industrial customers of the commercial enterprise classification with particular attention to OEMs and user customers. Time and space do not permit an exhaustive analysis of the governmental or institutional markets, although many of the concepts covered in this text will apply to marketing into both of the latter markets.

CLASSIFICATIONS OF INDUSTRIAL PRODUCTS

Although there are many types of products that can be sold into the industrial market, they generally fit into one of the six following classifications.

Heavy Equipment
The heavy equipment classification of industrial products includes such as metal-cutting machine tools (lathes, boring mills, drilling machines, gear-cutting machines, grinders, and polishers), metal-forming machines (punching and shearing machines; hydraulic, mechanical, and forging presses; and forging machines), forklifts, overhead cranes, blast furnaces, electrical drive systems, and other such heavy capital goods. Heavy equipment products are basically capital goods, and, as such, their purchasers are normally user customers. But it is possible that situations can be found where such goods are purchased by a fabricator who purchases several pieces of heavy equipment and then integrates those into one overall package and, in turn, sells this package to a user customer. In this case, the first industrial purchaser would actually be an OEM customer. Generally, heavy equipment can be purchased outright, or it can be leased by industrial user customers, and each approach has its own marketing merits, of which the marketing manager should be aware. In cases where capital equipment is purchased, it is treated as an asset by the purchasing firm and depreciated for tax purposes. This cannot be done with some of the other types of industrial products.

Light Equipment
The light equipment classification of industrial products includes such as portable power tools like drills, saws, grinders, sanders, polishers, and so forth, measuring instruments, typewriters, calculators, and other similar prod-

ucts. The market for light equipment is also normally comprised of user customers, but transaction values are considerably lower than with heavy equipment, and the products purchased are not permanently affixed to the buyer's physical plant as is heavy equipment. Again, light equipment may also be leased or purchased outright by the industrial customer, and in the latter situation this classification can be treated as an asset and depreciated for tax purposes.

Consumable Supplies

The consumable supplies classification of industrial products includes any products that are used up or consumed by the purchasing company in the operation of its business. Typical of such products are cleaning compounds, business forms, soaps, cutting fluids, and small tools such as welding rods, drill bits, and so forth. The essential characteristic of this classification of product is that the product purchased is used up by the customer firm, either directly or indirectly, in the normal operation of its business. These products are considered expense items and cannot be depreciated by the industrial customer for tax purposes. Industrial customers of the consumable supplies variety are normally user customers.

Component Parts

The component parts classification of industrial products includes all those products that are purchased for the purpose of inclusion into the final product of an industrial company. Examples of this classification are switches, transistors, motors, gears, nuts, bolts, screws, and other such products of this type. When sold to industrial customers using them in their production processes, they are marketed as OEM products. Such products, however, are very often sold to distributors who, in turn, resell them to other distributors or to OEM customers, and in these cases the industrial marketing manager may not consider them to be OEM products. At other times, component parts are sold into the replacement market to repair and service facilities, distributors, and other such outlets. Thus, component parts may have two distinct markets—an OEM market and a replacement market. It is also important to realize that component parts may be marketed by their manufacturers as finished goods whereby the industrial customer uses them directly in its product with no modification whatsoever. They may at times also be marketed as semifinished goods, in which case the purchasing manufacturer modifies the component in some manner prior to using it in its product. The essential point to remember with this classification of industrial products is that it ends up within the product of the purchaser, oftentimes contributing to the salability of the customer's final product in the marketplace. As such, component parts are normally sold into OEM markets.

Raw Materials

The raw materials classification of industrial products includes all those products generated by the extractive industries that, in turn, sell those products to their customers with little or no alteration. Examples of this classification are coal, iron ore, bauxite, gypsum, crude oil, fish and other seafood, lumber, field crops, copper, lead and zinc ores, tungsten ores, and other such similar products. These products may at times be marketed as either user or OEM products. An example of the former is the purchase of coal by a manufacturer for heating purposes. An example of the latter is the purchase by a seafood processor of tuna from the fishing industry.

Processed Materials

The processed materials classification of industrial products includes all types of processed materials not considered component parts. Typical of the products in this classification are steel plate, chemicals, glass, coke, sheet metal, plastics, cold finished steel bars, leather, asphalt, plywood, and other similar products. In most cases, processed materials are marketed to OEM customers, but this is not a rule. A steel producer purchasing coke might well be considered a user customer rather than an OEM customer. In addition, processed materials may also be sold to distributors who, in turn, resell to the OEM or to the user market. A good example of the latter are steel service centers that purchase various types of steel products and then process them to specifications for their customers.

It is extremely important that the industrial marketing manager realize the classification or classifications of his products as they are purchased by his customers. This is because buying motivations differ within product classifications—processed materials are not purchased for the same reasons as are component parts—heavy equipment is not bought in the same manner as is light equipment—and the replacement market purchases component parts quite differently from the way the OEM market does for the same product. If the marketing manager sees the product being purchased as light equipment and customers perceive it as being heavy equipment, effective marketing can hardly take place, as buyer and seller are each operating on their own ground rules. It is incumbent upon the marketing manager to determine into what classification each product falls for each customer firm.

THE INDUSTRIAL MARKETING SYSTEM

Describing the industrial marketing system is relatively simple when it is viewed in terms of (1) who produces industrial goods, (2) who consumes industrial goods, and (3) who are involved as middlemen between producers

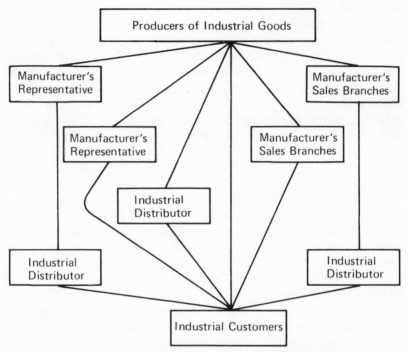

Fig. 1.1. The industrial marketing system. (Reprinted by permission from William M. Diamond, *Distribution Channels for Industrial Goods,* Columbus: Bureau of Business Research, College of Commerce and Administration, 1963.)

and consumers. Fig. 1.1 illustrates the industrial marketing system based on a survey of 156 industrial manufacturers in 220 product lines.[5]

Understanding Fig. 1.1 requires at least a cursory examination of the middlemen involved. Later in the text, these middlemen will be analyzed in great depth. At this point all that is required is a brief description to aid in the understanding of the middlemen involved and their respective functions in the industrial marketing system.

The Manufacturer's Sales Branch

Manufacturers' sales branches are wholly owned field operations of the manufacturers in the industrial market and, as such, are not independent middlemen. Nevertheless, they provide middlemen functions by the manufacturer. There are two basic types of this operation. The first is the manufacturer's branch, also called the branch house. The branch house is primarily a field warehouse owned and operated by the manufacturer and placed at strategic locations for serving the firm's customers. Branch houses are very close to company-owned warehouses found in the consumer market.

The second type is the branch office, which is essentially owned and operated by a manufacturer as a field sales office. In contrast to the branch house, branch offices ordinarily carry no inventory, but are rather strategically located offices from which the company's field sales personnel operate in their respective field territories. At times, branch houses and branch offices may be housed in the same physical facilities, whereas at other times they may be housed independently of one another. In other instances, a manufacturer may elect to use only a branch office for selling purposes and ship directly from the factory, thus performing no inventory function in the field and therefore requiring no branch house. Yet, in other instances, a manufacturer may use only branch houses to field inventory his product and use manufacturer's representatives to perform the selling function. In any case, the manufacturer's sales branch as shown in Fig. 1.1 indicates instances where manufacturers are performing middlemen functions of one type or another or both in the industrial market.

The Industrial Distributor

The industrial distributor was very briefly described in the section on types of industrial customers. As was stated at that time and as Fig. 1.1 illustrates, these are technically middlemen reselling goods in the industrial market. They are normally local and independently owned and operated, and they take title to and possession of the goods they handle. They stock goods, thus performing a field inventory function for the manufacturer. Industrial distributors will be analyzed in great depth later in this text. At this point, all that is needed is to understand that they are middlemen who take title to and stock goods in the industrial marketplace. They perform a function quite similar in some respects to that performed by the wholesaler in the consumer market. And as has also been described, industrial distributors can be highly specialized or widely diversified in their product line offerings and their sales and service capabilities.

The Manufacturer's Representative

The manufacturer's representative, also called the manufacturer's agent, is also an independent middleman, but is quite different from the distributor. Very common in the industrial market, the manufacturer's representatives are agents who sell on behalf of manufacturing principals. As such, they take no title to the goods involved, and they often do not even see or handle those goods. Basically, they are independent salesmen who sell on a commission basis for manufacturers, thus eliminating the need for those manufacturers to employ company salesmen. The manufacturers' representatives often represent a number of manufacturers whose products are complementary and not competitive. They are compensated on a commission basis and assigned to sales territories just as are company field salesmen. Simply viewed, they compare to company salesmen except that they are independent and usually represent a number of manufacturing principals. Their basic function as middlemen in the industrial marketing system is to sell, but in recent years there has been a trend toward what is called a "stocking representative." A stocking rep is basically a manufacturer's representative who also carries some field inventory and is a sort of hybrid between a distributor and a manufacturer's representative. In industry, this general classification of middleman may be called the manufacturer's representative, the manufacturer's agent, the manufacturer's rep, or simply the MR. In this text, the term *MR* shall be used in reference to this type of middleman. Later in the text, manufacturers' representatives shall be analyzed in great depth for their contribution toward effective industrial marketing.

In addition to the industrial distributor and the manufacturer's rep, such middlemen as brokers and sales agents may sometimes be found. Overall, these middlemen do not form a significant part of the industrial marketing system.

This, then, is the industrial marketing system. On one end are producers of industrial goods such as firms involved in manufacturing, mining, forestry, fishing, and agriculture. On the other end are the industrial customers of the commercial OEM or user variety, government, and the institutions. Linking the two together are the various methods by which industrial marketers market their goods and services to industrial customers as illustrated in Fig. 1.1.

BASIC DIFFERENCES BETWEEN
INDUSTRIAL AND CONSUMER MARKETING

Another way to gain a better understanding of the industrial marketing area is to contrast it with consumer marketing. There are many major differences, and they will be developed in depth throughout this text. At this point, however, it may be worthwhile to create an appreciation of these differences. These differences may be classified in terms of such criteria as (1) those related to market characteristics, (2) those related to characteristics of industrial buyers, (3) those related to characteristics of the products involved, (4) those related to characteristics of the channels of distribution involved, (5) those related to promotional characteristics, and (6) those related to pricing characteristics. The following sections discuss some of the major differences based on these criteria between industrial and consumer marketing and may help in understanding why industrial marketing is not just another type of consumer marketing with minor variations of basic principles.

Differences Related to the Characteristics of the Market

There are many differences between industrial and consumer marketing that can be traced to differences in the markets served by the two. The following illustrate some of these differences: (1) often a relatively small number of customers comprise the market for a particular industrial good—it is not uncommon to find instances where fewer than 25 companies comprise the entire market for a product; (2) although there may be relatively few industrial customers, they are normally large in size; (3) their purchase orders are often very large, and they engage in volume purchasing of goods and services on repeat bases; (4) industrial customers are not spread uniformly throughout the United States, but are rather concentrated in such areas as the Northeast, the Southeast, and the Pacific Coast; (5) the industrial market is characterized by derived demand, which means that the demand of industrial customers for goods and services is derived from the ultimate consumer demand for the products that they, in turn, produce—if the demand for their products falls off, they, in turn, require fewer industrial goods and services; and (6) the industrial market is characterized by joint demand, which means that industrial customers often purchase products that they combine with other purchased or manufactured products to form their final products, which are, in turn, sold into their markets. When this happens, industrial goods are demanded jointly with other goods, or they are not demanded at all.

Differences Related to the Characteristics of Industrial Buyers

Some of the major differences between industrial and consumer marketing occur because of differences in the buyers in the two markets. The following illustrate some of these differences: (1) the industrial market is normally characterized by more technically qualified and professional buyers; (2) their buying motives are usually more rational than those found in the consumer market—their buying decisions are often made on the basis of such factors as specifications, vendor analysis, and cost effectiveness as opposed to emotional or impulse purchasing motives; (3) multiple buying influences are involved in almost all industrial purchases; this means that decisions to buy are not made by one person, but rather by those individuals within a purchasing company who will have use for the product being bought either in a direct or an indirect manner; (4) committee buying is often found in the industrial market where a committee of people in various positions in the purchasing firm have the responsibility of making the buying decision and choosing the vendor; (5) there are very few women buyers in the industrial market in contrast to the large amount of purchasing by women in the consumer market; (6) industrial purchasing people often will select two or more suppliers from which to buy the same product just to protect themselves against the possibility of a single supplier's not being able to supply required amounts; (7) the industrial market is characterized by situations of reciprocity whereby buyers buy only from their own customers when the opportunity presents itself— two companies are both buyer and seller to each other; and (8) buyer expectations of future price changes often bring about situations of reverse elasticity of demand in short-run instances. What this means is that buyers buy more goods when suppliers increase price because they expect still further price increases, and they hope to protect themselves against these anticipated changes.

Differences Related to the Characteristics of the Products Involved

There are differences in the products sold into the consumer and industrial markets. Some of the major differences are as follows: (1) the products in the industrial market are usually of a more technical nature; (2) products in the industrial market are normally purchased on the basis of specifications; (3) there is multiuse of products in the industrial market as different buying influences within a purchasing company may use the same product for a different use; (4) industrial buyers purchase products for production inventories as opposed to immediate use; (5) there is a predominance of raw and semifinished goods found in the industrial market—these products are sold into the consumer market only on rare occasions; (6) there is tremendous emphasis on the importance of product service after the sale in the industrial market; (7) there is also tremendous importance placed in the industrial market on presale servicing and technical assistance in setting up and operating products in the customer's plant; (8) packaging in the industrial market is generally more protective in nature rather than promotional, although instances of the latter can be found, especially with distributor items; (9) there is tremendous emphasis placed in the industrial market on promptness and certainty of delivery of products owing to effects of delays on production line operations, and so forth; and (10) industrial customers do not always have to purchase the products they require, but can sometimes produce them with their own productive facilities—this is very rare in the consumer market.

Differences Related to the Characteristics of the Channels Involved

There are very distinct differences between the channels of distribution used in the two markets. Some of the major differences are as follows: (1) channels of distribution in the industrial market are generally shorter and more direct; (2) there is much more usage of the direct channel (no independent middlemen) in the industrial market than in the consumer market; (3) middlemen in the industrial market are different from those in the consumer market—industrial distributors and manufacturers' representatives are the primary middlemen found in the industrial market; (4) there is greater expectation of sales effort from industrial channel components than from those in the consumer market; (5) all told, there are fewer feasible channel alternatives in the industrial market than there are in the consumer market; and (6) physical distribution is extremely important in the industrial market because of production line inventory requirements.

Differences Related to Promotional Characteristics

Promotion also differs in the two markets. Some of the major differences are as follows: (1) there is generally a much heavier emphasis on personal selling in industrial marketing than there is in consumer marketing; (2) salesmen in the industrial market are more like consultants and technical problem solvers to their customers than salesmen in the consumer market; (3) the industrial market is characterized by the use of inside or phone salesmen; (4) there are relatively few saleswomen in the industrial market; (5) salesmen in the industrial market possess more technical backgrounds and are more likely to fall into the classification of sales engineers than those found in the consumer market; (6) advertising in the industrial market often plays a different role than advertising in the consumer market—it is often used to lay a foundation for the industrial salesmen's sales call; (7) advertising themes in the industrial market normally stress more factual and technical data and are generally less emotional; (8) advertising media in the industrial market differ from media in the consumer market—the two prime media in the former are trade journal publications and direct mail; and (9) sales promotion activities in the industrial market center around the catalog and the trade show.

Differences Related to Pricing Characteristics

There are also very distinct differences in pricing in the two markets. Some of the major differences are as follows: (1) price is less of a determining factor in industrial purchasing—it is often of much less importance than quality and uniformity of the products purchased, certainty of delivery of the products purchased, service, and technical assistance; (2) prices are often based on competitive bidding in the industrial market; (3) negotiated prices are very common in the industrial market; (4) in pricing their products, industrial marketing firms must provide financing arrangements for their customers owing to the high dollar amount of industrial sales; (5) there is wide usage of list and net pricing of industrial goods, which involves the use of trade and quantity discounts off published price lists; (6) leasing is often used as a price alternative to marketing capital goods in the industrial market; (7) penalty clauses for nonperformance affect the final prices paid in the industrial market; (8) there is little use of price as a promotional tool in the industrial market—rarely are loss leaders used; (9) stabilization of price is quite common in the industrial market particularly with manufacturers resulting in nonprice competition; (10) return on investment pricing is widely used in the industrial market; and (11) industry price elasticity of demand in the industrial market is generally inelastic owing to the derived demand aspect, whereas company price elasticity of demand is often quite elastic owing to product specifications making products almost identical.

There are other differences, but these make the desired point. There are enough fundamental differences between the consumer and industrial markets to make the job of marketing management in each market a separate area of specialization. The consumer marketing manager moving into the industrial market would have to learn these differences as they are manifested in the products to be produced, the prices that are to be charged, the channels that are to be used, and the promotional efforts that are to be employed. This text shall examine the function of the marketing manager in the industrial market as regards market segmentation, overall marketing strategy and planning, and the substrategies of product, channel, promotion, and price.

CHAPTER SUMMARY

The purpose of this initial chapter has been to lay a foundation for an understanding of the industrial market and the tasks of industrial marketing management. A general definition of marketing was given, and a more specialized definition of industrial marketing was developed. Industrial customers were classified into three basic groups: (1) commercial enterprises purchasing goods and/or services, (2) governmental organizations purchasing goods and/or services, and (3) institutions purchasing goods and/or services. Industrial products were classified as heavy equipment, light equipment, consumable supplies, component parts, raw materials, and processed materials. The industrial marketing system was described in terms of who produces industrial goods and services, who consumes these goods and services, and who are involved as middlemen between producers and users. Basic differences between industrial and consumer marketing were examined with emphasis on market characteristics, buyer characteristics, product characteristics, channel characteristics, promotional characteristics, and pricing characteristics. The central point of this chapter has been to emphasize that although marketing in the industrial market is similar in principle to marketing in the consumer market, there are distinct differences that must be understood if effective marketing management is to take place.

QUESTIONS FOR CHAPTER 1

1. Marketing is marketing whether it be in the consumer market or the industrial market. Do you agree or disagree with this statement? If you agree, why do you agree? If you disagree, why do you disagree?
2. If the same product could be purchased by an OEM customer and by a user customer, how does the purpose behind the OEM customer's purchasing the product differ from the purpose behind the user customer's purchasing that same product?
3. Although their operations differ considerably from those of pure industrial customers, there is logic in considering governmental organizations and institutions as part of the industrial market. Why do you feel that both of the latter qualify for inclusion in the industrial market?
4. In viewing his product mix, the industrial marketing manager should attempt to classify his products according to the manner in which his customers classify these same products. Do you agree or disagree with this statement? If you agree, why do you agree? If you disagree, why do you disagree?
5. There are many fundamental differences between consumer marketing and industrial marketing. If you had to choose five differences as being most important, which ones would you choose? Why would you choose each of them?

2

THE DEMAND FOR
INDUSTRIAL GOODS

To market effectively into the industrial market requires a thorough understanding of demand mechanisms in that market. As was pointed out in the preceding chapter, the industrial market differs appreciably from the consumer market, and many of the key differences can be traced to differences in demand in the two markets. There are a number of demand characteristics peculiar to the industrial market that must be understood by the marketing manager. These may be classified as follows: (1) those characteristics related to the concept of derived demand, (2) those characteristics related to the concept of joint demand, (3) those characteristics of demand related to the types of products sold into the industrial market, (4) those characteristics of demand related to the nature of the market, (5) those characteristics of demand related to the nature of industrial buyers, and (6) those characteristics of demand related to the geographic concentration of industrial customers. Each of these characteristics will be developed in depth in this chapter, but first some assessment of the total demand for all industrial goods and services will be made.

THE TOTAL DEMAND FOR INDUSTRIAL GOODS

Estimating the total demand for the producers of industrial goods and services in the United States is relatively difficult to accomplish. There is no single source that provides such data on the total market for industrial products, as reflected by commercial enterprises, governmental customers, and institutions. Data on the latter market are especially elusive owing to the lack of a clear-cut definition of what actually constitutes the institutional market. The combined government market (federal, state, and local buying units) purchased about $277 billion of goods and services in 1973.[1] Just how large the demand of private commercial enterprises for industrial goods and services is can only be estimated through the use of some representative industrial market indicators. Table 2.1 illustrates trends in selected industrial market indicators from 1970 to 1974. As can be seen, the data in the table do indicate the size of the industrial market viewed from several different aspects. For example, manufacturer's new net orders, which are part of the industrial market, amounted to almost $900 billion in 1973; and new plant and equipment expenditures, which reflect part of the user market, amounted to just under $100 billion in the same year. In addition, the book value of manufacturing inventories was about $120 billion at year end 1973. The 1972 *Census of Manufactures* reported data on over 10,500 separate products manufactured by 420 manufacturing industries and placed the value of these products in excess of $700 billion in 1972.[2] In addition, the 1972 *Census of Construction Industries* estimated the value of new construction put in place in 1972 in excess of $123 billion.[3] Although this is a form of piecemeal ap-

Table 2.1

INDUSTRIAL MARKET INDICATORS: ANNUAL SUMMARY, 1970–74

	1970	1971	1972	1973	1974
Industrial Production, Total (1967 = 100)	106.6	106.8	115.2	125.6	124.8
New Plant and Equipment Expenditures, All Industries, Total (Billion $)	79.7	81.2	88.4	99.7	111.9
Manufacturers' Orders New (net), Total (Billion $)	625.4	668.7	755.1	886.0	1000.0
Manufacturing Inventories, Book Value, End of Year, Unadjusted Total (Billion $)	101.3	102.1	107.4	120.3	149.4
Production Workers on Manufacturing Payrolls Monthly Average (Millions)	14.0	13.5	14.0	14.8	14.6

Source: *Survey of Current Business* 55 (February 1975).
Note: 1974 figures are based on preliminary data.

proach to estimating the size of the total industrial market, it does provide enough of a basis to conclude that the total industrial market is huge.

For the individual practicing industrial marketing manager, it is not so important to know the total demand in the industrial market as it is to understand the demand in that market for the company's products and/or services. Thus, although it is interesting to attempt to estimate the size of the total industrial market, it is more of an academic interest than it is a practical decision-making factor.

CHARACTERISTICS RELATED TO THE CONCEPT OF DERIVED DEMAND

Derived demand may possibly be the single most important point that must be understood by the industrial marketing manager. Basically, it is a simple concept, although many people are confused by the term. What is meant by the term *derived demand* is that industrial customers, including government and institutions, do not purchase goods and services because of their own personal needs or desires, but rather to produce other goods and/or services for their own customers. This is where the use of the word *derived* originates—the demand of industrial customers for the products and services they purchase is derived from the demand for their products by their customers.

A simple example may help to explain how derived demand works. A fertilizer company purchasing ingredients from a chemical manufacturer buys those ingredients not because of personal preferences, but because such ingredients are required to satisfy demand for fertilizer in the ultimate consumer household market or whatever market that fertilizer is sold into. Logically then, the demand of the fertilizer company for the chemical ingredients is derived from the demand of the ultimate consumer for the fertilizer produced from those ingredients. Should these purchased chemical ingredients be found ecologically harmful, or should a competitive fertilizer firm introduce a better fertilizer into the consumer market, the demand for the previously purchased chemical ingredients would drop off as ultimate consumers switch to competitive brands. When circumstances such as this occur, the demand of the fertilizer producer for the chemicals will also decrease because the latter's need for the ingredients is derived. The chemicals are not required if the product in which they are being used is not being purchased. A price decrease by the chemical firm to stimulate sales in this instance would make no sense; yet a marketing manager not fully understanding derived demand might well try to use such a method to stimulate demand for the sagging product.

In the actual business world, there are often many levels in the derived demand concept. For example, the demand for cotton is dependent upon the demand of the textile industry, which, in turn, is dependent upon the demand of the garment industry, which is ultimately dependent upon the demand of the ultimate consumer for clothing in general and for cotton products in particular. A shift in the preferences of the ultimate consumer from cotton to synthetic fibers, because of less wrinkling or some other such properties, would be felt all the way back to the cotton farmer. And if the switch were drastic enough, some firms could very well fail, even though they themselves never really came in contact with the ultimate consumer. In other words, even though the ultimate consumer buys no cotton per se, he or she is the driving force behind the production of cotton—the cotton producer's demand is derived from the consumer's demand for fabric preferences.

The Volatility of Derived Demand

Derived demand affects industrial firms whether they be selling to OEMs, to users, or to distributors. With OEM customers and distributors, it is fundamentally a one-to-one relationship, at least in the long run, although inventories will affect differently in short-run periods. For example, if an electronics company manufactures switches for a television producer and one switch goes into each TV set produced, then any percentage decrease in sales of TV sets will be matched by the same percentage decrease in the purchase of switches and thus in the sales of the electronics manufacturer. If TV sales dropped 20 percent in a year, then the demand for switches will also drop 20 percent. But if the TV manufacturer purchases switches for inventory rather than for immediate use in each set, which is much more realistic, short-run sales of the switches will fluctuate more drastically than the sales of the TV sets.

Inventory levels have an effect because when TV sales decrease, the TV firm will use up present inventory stocks first and thus reduce inventory purchase levels. What this means is that the 20 percent decrease annually in sales of switches may be even more pronounced on a monthly or bimonthly basis if inventoried stocks are used up in lieu of new purchases. If the TV customer decided to use up present stocks before purchasing any more, the result could be zero sales of switches in the short-run period of one or two months. Just how much of a short-run impact would take place would depend upon the sales decrease of TV sets and the normal inventory level of switches stocked.

It is in the user market, however, that derived demand is really volatile. Very often, relatively small fluctuations in ultimate consumer household demand bring about much larger fluctuations in the demand for capital goods used to produce the products sold into the consumer market. The classic example of this took place during the depression years of 1929 to 1932. During that time period, the physical production of consumer goods dropped 20 points from an index of 100 to 80. At the same time, capital spending for equipment dropped 65 points from an index of 100 to 35. The message for the industrial marketing manager in this example should be clear! Whereas a consumer marketing firm might be hurt by a 20 percent sales decline, it could survive. But the industrial company supplying that consumer marketing firm could scarcely hope to absorb an accompanying 65 percent decrease in its sales.

An Example of Derived Demand

Table 2.2 may help to explain the derived demand phenomenon in regard to user customers. Assume that the Premold Corporation produces premolded fiber glass shower stalls, which are sold to contractors for installation into new houses, apartment buildings, condominiums, and so on. To produce these stalls, Premold uses heavy equipment heat presses, each of which is capable of producing 200 stalls per year. Each machine has a 10-year life cycle, and the company replaces 10 percent of its machines each year. Premold purchases the heat presses from the ABC Company, and Table 2.2 shows the relationship between Premold's sales of stalls and the sales of the ABC Company supplying Premold.

If it is assumed that the six-year period in the table illustrates years in which 10 percent of the presses will wear out and that no new technological innovations will render the presses obsolete, the table shows the effects of changing consumer market demand on both the sales of Premold and the ABC Company. By the use of this table, the volatility of derived demand can easily be seen. In the second year, for example, a 10 percent increase in the consumer demand for shower stalls (from 100,000 to 110,000) brings about a 100 percent increase (from 50 to 100) in the demand for the presses to produce those stalls. In the third year, however, the demand for the stalls increases 4.5 percent (from 110,000 to 115,000), but the demand for the presses decreases 25 percent (from 100 to 75). A similar happening takes place in the fourth year. In the fifth year, the consumer demand decreases 15.2 percent (from 118,000 to 100,000), but the demand for presses ceases to exist and, in fact, becomes negative because Premold actually has 40 more presses than is required to fulfill its demand. And Premold can apply its excess machines to the replacement of worn-out machines in the sixth year, thus depressing demand for ABC in that year. With this admittedly oversimplified example, the volatility is easy to see and understand. Consumer demand for the shower stalls never fluctuated by more than 12.5 percent, but industrial demand fluctuated wildly as high as 400 percent in the sixth year and sometimes even in inverse relationship to consumer demand as in years two and four.

Derived demand has tremendous implications for the industrial marketing

Table 2.2

DERIVED DEMAND EXAMPLE

Time Period	Consumer Demand for Premolded Fiber Glass Stalls			Number of Machines in Use to Produce the Shower Stalls			Demand for the Machine		
Year	Previous Year	Current Year	Net Change	Previous Year	Current Year	Net Change	Replacement	New	Total
1	100,000	100,000	–	500	500	–	50	–	50
2	100,000	110,000	+10,000	500	550	+50	50	50	100
3	110,000	115,000	+ 5,000	550	575	+25	50	25	75
4	115,000	118,000	+ 3,000	575	590	+15	50	15	65
5	118,000	100,000	– 18,000	590	500	–90	–	–40	–40
6	100,000	100,000	–	500	500	–	10	–	10

Source: Adapted from Vaile, Grether, and Cox, *Marketing in the American Economy* (New York: Ronald Press, 1952), p. 16.

manager and will be referred to extensively throughout this text. The big point to understand is that the industrial marketing manager cannot simply let customers succeed or fail on their own. The manager may often have to be involved with stimulating demand in the marketplace of the industrial customers so that desired levels of derived demand are maintained. Thus, the industrial marketing manager still has to be consumer-oriented even though the company does not market directly into the consumer market.

CHARACTERISTICS RELATED TO THE
CONCEPT OF JOINT DEMAND

Another demand characteristic that must be understood by the industrial marketing manager is joint demand. Joint demand occurs when the demand for one product depends upon that product's being used in conjunction with another product or products. In such a situation, the products are demanded jointly, or they may not be demanded at all. For example, to produce pig iron, a producer requires both coke and iron ore. If, for some reason, that producer cannot obtain coke, it does not continue to purchase iron ore in the same quantities as before. Without coke, the firm has no need to keep buying iron ore—the two products share a joint demand.

Joint demand is very common in the industrial market, particularly with OEM customers. A fabricator purchasing 200 to 300 component parts for assembly into a finished product has a joint demand for all these components. For lack of a single component, no matter how large or small, the final product often cannot be assembled. This means that purchases of all others may be curtailed, at least in the short run, if the fabricator has delivery problems of any type with any of his suppliers. A good example of this took place in the auto industry in August 1974, when strikes at A. O. Smith Corporation and at Briggs & Stratton Corporation, both suppliers of critical auto parts, caused production cutbacks at General Motors and at Chrysler.[4] These production cutbacks, in turn, caused depressed sales of other GM and Chrysler suppliers because of the joint demand aspect. As can be realized, any industrial marketing manager selling products into this type of market had better well understand the reliability of all of the customer's other suppliers. Demand can also be affected in joint demand situations whenever the purchasing company changes specifications on a component with the result that previously purchased components may not be compatible with the new specifications. In cases such as this, the joint relationship may be dissolved, and the demand for many components may disappear if they do not fit into the new specification.

Joint demand may also occur in the case of user customers. For example, if a manufacturer is currently using a particular brand of machine in its production process, other pieces of peripheral equipment must be compatible with that machine if the production line is to function effectively. If, however, the manufacturer replaces the brand with a newer updated version or switches to another brand of another manufacturer and the replacement machine is not compatible with the peripheral equipment previously purchased, the demand for the latter may be depressed and even eliminated because the joint relationship is dissolved. New pieces of peripheral equipment would be purchased that would be compatible with the new machine, thus creating an entirely new series of joint relationships.

Still another aspect of joint demand can be seen in the product lines of many industrial marketing firms. This takes place when customers prefer to buy complete product lines from one manufacturer rather than purchase individual products from different manufacturers. If an industrial marketing manager has a gap in an otherwise complete product line, the industrial customer may buy none of the company's products and, in fact, purchase from a competitor who can supply the entire product line desired. In this case, the products in the product line are demanded jointly or in conjunction with one another. The individual products do not have individual demand, but rather are demanded jointly with the other products in the line.

The main point is that joint demand is very common in industrial marketing and it may take various forms. The astute industrial marketing manager must be aware of any such joint relationships with the products and/or services offered by the company. The manager must constantly be on the lookout for any changes taking place in these relationships that could affect the demand for those goods and/or services. In addition, the manager must be aware of any conditions regarding other suppliers that could have detrimental effects on the demand for those same goods and/or services.

CHARACTERISTICS RELATED TO THE TYPES OF PRODUCTS

Demand in the industrial market will also vary, depending upon the type of products being marketed. To illustrate, the demand for processed materials may differ considerably from the demand for capital equipment primarily because of the characteristics of the products themselves. Perhaps the best way to understand these differences is to review each type or classification of industrial product and discuss those factors that may influence an industrial customer to purchase from one supplier rather than another. At the same time, it must be recognized that derived demand and perhaps joint demand are in addition to demand implications caused by different product classifications. The following is a partial list of those factors affecting demand for each of the classifications of industrial products.

Heavy Equipment

When industrial customers purchase heavy or major equipment, their ultimate selection of suppliers may be influenced by factors such as the following: (1) strict conformance of the equipment to buyer specifications; (2) service capabilities of the supplier in case of breakdown or malfunction; (3) technical assistance provided by the supplier at the time of installation in the purchasing plant; (4) product warranties; (5) capability of the purchased equipment to supplement existing production line equipment; (6) degree of ease or difficulty of operation by the purchasing firm's employees (Will the new equipment require worker retraining?); (7) price, price conditions, and other financing arrangements; (8) certainty of delivery of the equipment by the supplier (Will the equipment be in the buyer's plant installed and operational when it is needed?); (9) past experience with the supplier and his equipment; (10) effects on manpower requirements or labor reductions of the new equipment (Will it do the same or a better job with less labor?); and (11) competitive alternatives open to the purchaser.

Light Equipment

The demand for light equipment in industry is often influenced by factors such as the following: (1) price and price considerations such as quantity and trade discounts, and so forth; (2) certainty and speed of delivery; (3) provisions for returning defective equipment; (4) personal preferences of those who will use the equipment—a foreman's preference for a Skil saw over a Black & Decker, not because of specifications or technical capabilities, but because of personal likes or dislikes; (5) competitive alternatives open to the purchaser; (6) product warranties; (7) service capabilities of the supplier and the speed of such service; (8) certainty and speed of delivery; (9) past experiences with the supplier and his equipment; and (10) whether the equipment is single or multiuse in nature. Since light equipment is often standardized and marketed into a wide spectrum of industries, its demand is influenced by factors different from heavy equipment which may be non-standardized and custom produced to individual buyer preferences and specifications.

Component Parts

The demand for component parts may be influenced by factors quite different from those affecting the demand for capital equipment, whether the latter be heavy or light equipment. One major difference is that heavy and light equipment is sold to user customers, whereas component parts are typically marketed to OEM customers. The impact of this difference on derived demand may be very important. To illustrate, although ultimate consumers may not care at all, if they even know, what drill press or boring mill was used to produce the products they are buying, they often care a great deal about what component parts are put into those same products. This is particularly true when they know, use, and understand those parts, such as tires on a car, turntables on a stereo hi-fi, and so on. At other times, however, the consumer does not even know what component parts are being used, let alone their reputation—nor does he or she even care! The point being made here is that component parts, by virtue of the derived demand mechanism, have a different demand influence from that of capital goods. The selection process by OEM customers among possible suppliers is often made on the basis of factors such as the following: (1) strict conformance to buyer specifications; (2) the quality and uniformity of the purchased components—this affects the quality of the OEM's product in his market; (3) certainty of delivery—delays in delivery can cause production line shutdowns and incur enormous costs; (4) price and price considerations such as quantity and trade discounts; (5) capability of the supplier to provide the quantity of parts required; (6) size of the replacement market—some component parts have more market potential as service replacements than in the OEM market; (7) the price of the purchased components compared to the cost of the purchaser producing the part in his own plant; (8) return provisions for defects, and the like; (9) past experience with the supplier and the component part; (10) competitive alternatives available to the purchaser; (11) specific derived demand considerations—the OEM's customers demand specific components in the products they buy; and (12) the capability of the component part to add to the marketability of the OEM's product—the component parts of one supplier may be better known and better accepted than similar component parts of competing suppliers.

Processed Materials

The demand for processed materials is also influenced by the OEM market, but this differs in two major ways from the demand for component parts. First, there is usually no replacement market for processed materials. Second, processed materials are usually not used in the same form by the purchasing OEM as are component parts. Normally, processed materials are cut or pressed into required shapes and forms by the OEM after buying the materials. Thus, derived demand may not be so brand-conscious with processed materials as it is with component parts. In choosing among suppliers of processed materials, industrial buyers are influenced by factors such as the following: (1) strict conformance to buyer specifications, (2) price and price considerations such as quantity and trade discounts, (3) quality and uniformity of the materials, (4) certainty of delivery, (5) capability of the supplier to provide the quantity required, (6) return provisions for faulty lots, defects, and so on, (7) freight differences among suppliers, (8) past experience with the supplier's materials, and (9) competitive alternatives open to the buyer.

Consumable Supplies

Consumable supplies have probably the simplest demand mechanism of all industrial goods. Normally, they are standardized products that can be sold to all different types of industrial customers. Often there are no specifications involved, and these products are marketed much like many consumer goods. In choosing among possible suppliers of consumable supplies, industrial customers base their decisions to purchase on such factors as the following: (1) price and price considerations such as quantity and trade discounts, (2) certainty of delivery, (3) brand name of the supplier, (4) capability of the supplier to provide the quantity required, (5) past experience with the supplier, and (6) competitive alternatives open to the purchaser.

Raw Materials

In choosing among suppliers of raw materials, industrial customers base their decisions on factors such as the following: (1) standards and grades of the material, (2) certainty of delivery, (3) capability of the supplier to provide the quantity required over time, (4) price and price considerations such as quantity and trade discounts, (6) freight rates and charges involved in buying from different suppliers, (7) past experience with the supplier, and (8) competitive alternatives open to the buyer.

This partial list may help make the desired point. In addition to understanding both derived and joint demand, the industrial marketing manager must understand fully those characteristics of demand peculiar to the particular products or product line of the company. It should be apparent that an industrial marketing company selling capital equipment via custom sales to user customers faces a completely different demand mechanism from that of the firm selling standardized component parts to a lot of different industries. In short, demand differs according to products involved, and the industrial marketing manager must realize these differences to market products effectively.

CHARACTERISTICS RELATED TO THE NATURE OF THE MARKET

In addition to the demand characteristics discussed thus far, another factor that must be considered by the industrial marketing manager is whether he is selling goods and/or services into a horizontal or a vertical market. A vertical market exists when a company sells its products and/or services to one specific industry, whereas a horizontal market exists when a firm is able to market its goods and/or services to a broad spectrum of industries. To illustrate, the market for manufacturers of blast furnaces is quite vertical, whereas the market for manufacturers of machine tools might be horizontal. Vertical or horizontal markets may exist for all types of products in the industrial market, and there are degrees of occurrence. An aerospace firm selling only to the Department of Defense is about as vertical a market as can be found—there is only one buyer for the product.

An understanding of this demand phenomenon is critical for an industrial marketing manager. Given the volatility of derived demand and the operation in a vertical market, what happens when ultimate demand decreases or ceases to exist? The aerospace industry in California learned the answer to this question the hard way after the end of the Korean War when government purchases of military aircraft decreased, and the firms had no other markets. The point here is that knowledge of the concept of vertical and horizontal markets with all their implications is a must if the marketing manager is to fully understand the demand for the company's products or product line or services.

CHARACTERISTICS RELATED TO THE NATURE OF INDUSTRIAL BUYERS

The two following chapters will develop in detail industrial buying behavior, but a general reference to the nature of industrial buyers is in order to understand fully demand in the industrial market. Because industrial goods and services are purchased by people, it is difficult to generalize about the nature of industrial buyers. Nevertheless, some generalizations will help us to understand what influences industrial purchasers in their buying with subsequent effects on demand.

In a broad sense, demand is influenced by buyers in the industrial market by such factors as the following: (1) price is often not the major determinant of demand, as buyers would be willing to pay more if certainty of delivery, quality, service, technical assistance, and so forth, were assured; to pay less for goods and be uncertain of their delivery or quality could result in huge losses in production delays overshadowing any savings in cost reductions; (2) buyers will often split purchases of products rather than buy from a single source of supply; they do this to assure themselves of always having at least one source of reliable supply and to pit one supplier against another to obtain the best deal; (3) many buyers prefer to purchase from those firms they perceive to hold positions of technical leadership in their own industries with the logic that this allows the buying firm to keep up-to-date with technological innovations in the supplier industry; and (4) instances of reverse elasticity of demand often occur in the short run owing to buyer expectations. As was related previously, occasions can be found where a price increase by a supplier brings about an increased quantity demanded as buyers expect even further price increases and thus purchase and stockpile goods to protect themselves against such further anticipated price increases. On the other hand, instances can be found where price decreases have little or no effect on quantity demanded because the company image of the supplier, the quality of his goods, and his service capabilities are not considered by the buyer to be up to those of competitors.

The main point in this discussion is that industrial buyers influence demand for the product or service of an industrial marketing manager regardless of the type of product involved, derived demand, joint demand, and horizontal or vertical aspects of demand. And in order to understand truly demand in the industrial market, the impact of industrial buyers must be considered, and this will be developed in great depth in the following chapters.

CHARACTERISTICS RELATED TO THE GEOGRAPHIC CONCENTRATION OF CUSTOMERS

The demand for industrial goods and services is not spread evenly throughout the United States, but is often concentrated in various regions for differing products. It is vital that the industrial marketing manager recognize the important locational demand characteristics for individual goods and/or services. Otherwise, effort may be expended in areas where no demand exists; and no effort, in other areas where demand potential is the greatest. This is not to imply that a single geographic demand factor exists for all industrial products, but a number of generalizations can be made about the locational demand for industrial goods based on characteristics compiled by the federal government.

Of the nation's 3,000 some counties, 294 are considered the major industrial counties when measured by manufacturing employment, a common method for assessing manufacturing concentration. It is estimated that these 294 counties account for about 80 percent of all industrial buying power. According to data provided by *County Business Patterns,* these 294 counties are those listing 10,000 or more in manufacturing employment, in addition to other counties with less than 10,000 manufacturing employment, but which are part of standard metropolitan statistical areas.[5]

Analysis of *County Business Patterns* also discloses that the northeast quarter of the United States (New England, Middle Atlantic, and East North Central areas) accounts for about 57 percent of all manufacturing employment in the country. This is followed by about 19 percent in the South (South Atlantic and East South Central areas) and by about 10 percent in the Pacific states. Collectively, over three-quarters of all U.S. manufacturing employment is concentrated in these three areas.[6]

Another method of assessing industrial demand concentration is to use the number of manufacturing establishments as criteria. Data from the 1967 *Census of Manufactures* shows that about 54 percent of all manufacturing establishments are located in the Northeast, followed by about 16 percent in the South, and by about 14 percent in the Pacific states. Again, these three areas show the most concentration, accounting for about 84 percent of all manufacturing firms in the country.

Collectively, then, the major demand concentrations for industrial goods and services are located in the Northeast, the South, and the Pacific Coast areas. This, of course, has general interest in attempting to determine geographic demand, but may have little meaning to individual industrial marketing managers whose market concentrations do not match the general pattern. To illustrate, if an industrial manufacturer produces component parts purchased by the auto industry, that firm would find its market to be concentrated in 47 establishments located in Michigan, Missouri, California, New Jersey, Wisconsin, and Ohio.[7] On the other hand, a manufacturing firm selling to the fabricated structural steel industry would find its market in 2,000 establishments located throughout the United States.[8] In other words, general geographic demand concentrations are interesting and give some insight into the demand picture, but they must be used as a general rule and not as a specific marketing tool. It is up to the individual industrial marketing manager to determine the geographic concentration of the customers for his particular products or services as opposed simply to applying the general concentrations. Table 2.3 illustrates the geographic concentration of demand for selected industrial products and points out clearly that the overall industrial concentration figures rarely apply to the producers of specific industrial products. The table shows also how easy it is to find data pertaining to the geographic concentration of demand for particular industrial products. Data such as those illustrated in Table 2.3 can be found in the U.S. Department of Commerce's *U.S. Industrial Outlook,* which is published annually.

CHAPTER SUMMARY

Understanding demand in the industrial market is critical for the marketing manager and is one of the first steps in formulating realistic and effective marketing strategy. As this chapter has shown, industrial demand involves the understanding of the various characteristics that combine to make the job of industrial marketing a formidable one. The industrial marketing manager must be able to integrate the characteristics of derived demand, joint demand, individual product demand, industrial concentrations, vertical or horizontal markets, and the peculiarities of individual buyers in assessing demand for the firms's products or product lines or services. Unless this task of integra-

Table 2.3

GEOGRAPHIC DEMAND FOR SELECTED INDUSTRIAL PRODUCTS

Product Group	SIC	Value of Industry Shipments ($ Millions)	Number of Establishments	Major Producing Areas	Annual Growth Rates 1967–71 Value of Shipments
Fabricated Structural Steel	3441	$ 3550	2,000	Throughout the entire U.S.	+ 4.6%
Glass Containers	3221	$ 1,930	120	Middle Atlantic & North Central Areas	+ 9.5%
Business Forms	2761	$ 1,311	580	Middle Atlantic & East North Central	+ 8.9%
Industrial Chemicals	281	$16,475	1,900	Middle & South Atlantic & West Central States	+ 4.9%
Synthetic Rubber	2822	$ 1,070	50	South	+ 4.5%
Metal Cutting Tools	35451	$ 596	365	East North Central & New England	– 5.7%
Oil Field Machinery	3533	$ 1,240	360	Texas, Oklahoma, & California	+11.6%
Electronic Systems and Equipment	3662	$ 8,200	630	California, New York, & Pennsylvania	+ 1.0%
Electronic Components	367	$ 6,885	1,400	Massachusetts, New York, New Jersey, Illinois, Pennsylvania & California	– 2.0%

Source: U.S. Department of Commerce, *U.S. Industrial Outlook 1972 with Projections to 1980* (Washington, D.C.: U.S. Government Printing Office, April 1972).

tion can be accomplished, the manager can scarcely hope to market effectively into the industrial market.

QUESTIONS FOR CHAPTER 2

1. The 1975 recession in the United States has been described as an "inventory" recession. In such a recession, which company's demand would be most seriously affected initially—an industrial company marketing OEM products or an industrial company marketing user products? Explain your answer.
2. Do you believe a price decrease would be an effective marketing tool if an industrial marketing manager found the demand for his product decreasing because of decreased demand for his customers' products in the ultimate consumer market?
3. The concept of joint demand is a concern only for manufacturers and marketers of capital equipment. Do you agree or disagree with this statement? If you agree, why do you agree? If you disagree, why do you disagree?
4. Do you believe the differences in demand attributable to characteristics of the products involved are sufficient to warrant separate marketing programs for each classification of product? Explain your answer.
5. Although the overall major concentrations of demand for industrial products are located in the northeastern, southern, and western parts of the United States, it may make little sense for an individual industrial marketing manager to establish sales territories to match these overall concentrations. Why is this a true statement?

3

THE INDUSTRIAL CUSTOMER

As was developed in the opening chapter, customers in the industrial market fall into three basic classifications: (1) commercial enterprises, (2) government, and (3) institutions. Although this classification has merit for descriptive purposes, it has little meaning in terms of practical marketing management. The reason for this is that the industrial marketing manager must know customers explicitly and must perform detailed research and analysis into market segmentation, organizational behavior, purchasing policies and procedures, and formal and informal buying influences appropriate for their customers. In addition, there are differences between the commercial, governmental, and institutional customers in regard to these factors. Because it is outside the scope of this text to cover the governmental and institutional customers, attention shall be given to an in-depth analysis of OEMs and user customers of the commercial variety as regards the job of the industrial marketing manager.

THE STANDARD INDUSTRIAL CLASSIFICATION (SIC)

The key to obtaining data in the industrial market is a thorough understanding of the standard industrial classification system, more commonly referred to as SIC. Basically, SIC is a uniform numbering system for classifying establishments in the United States according to the economic activity engaged in by those establishments. Establishments are classified by economic activity by the Office of Management and Budget and compiled in its *Stand-*

ard Industrial Classification Manual. This manual, which is published every five years (the latest one in 1972), contains all industries classified by a four-digit SIC number and can be purchased from the U.S. Government Printing Office in Washington, D.C.

The basis of the SIC manual is relatively easy to understand. The U.S. economy is divided into 11 divisions, including one for nonclassifiable establishments. Within each division, major industry groups are classified by two digit numbers. Table 3.1 illustrates the basis of the SIC system, showing the 11 divisions and the major industry groups within each division. For example, all manufacturing firms are in division *D*, and two digit numbers from 20 to 39 indicate major manufacturing industries. SIC 22 includes all manufacturers of textile mill products, SIC 25 includes all manufacturers of furniture and fixtures, and SIC 37 includes all manufacturers of transportation equipment. As can be seen by these descriptions, the two-digit SIC numbers describe major or basic industries. As will be shown, the major industries can be fur-

Table 3.1
THE STANDARD INDUSTRIAL CLASSIFICATION SYSTEM

Division	Industries Classified	First Two-digit SIC Numbers Involved for Major Industry Groups
A	Agriculture, Forestry, and Fishing	01, 02, 07, 08, 09
B	Mining	10–14
C	Construction	15–17
D	Manufacturing	20–39
E	Transportation, Communications, Electric, Gas, and Sanitary Services	40–49
F	Wholesale Trade	50–51
G	Retail Trade	52–59
H	Finance, Insurance, and Real Estate	60–67
I	Services	70, 72–73, 75–76, 78–86, 88–89
J	Public Administration	91–97
K	Nonclassifiable Establishments	99

Source: Office of Management and Budget, *1972 Standard Industrial Classification Manual* (Washington, D.C.: U.S. Government Printing Office, 1972), pp. 5–7.

ther subdivided more specifically into three-, four-, five-, and seven-digit SIC numbers.

As Table 3.1 shows, in each division there are major groups of industries, which can be identified by the first two numbers in a particular firm's SIC code. All firms having the number 22 as the first two digits in their SIC code are known to be manufacturers of textile mill products. Similarly, all firms having the number 37 as the first two digits in their SIC code are known to be manufacturers of some type of transportation equipment.

Then, within each major two-digit SIC industry group, industry subgroups are defined by a third digit, and detailed industries are defined by a fourth digit. This is the basis of the four-digit SIC system found in the *Standard Industrial Classification Manual*—the longer the number, the more detailed the industry being defined. It is also possible to supplement the four-digit SIC numbers with five- and seven-digit SIC numbers provided by the *Census of Manufactures*. An example of this can be seen in Table 3.2. As can be seen, the seven-digit SIC numbers are very specific, and the use of the seven-digit numbers provides good industrial market segmentation criteria. For example, note that SIC 3441121 defines fabricated structural metal for buildings—iron and steel for sale to other industrial companies. But SIC 3441125 defines the same products, but for sale to commercial, residential, and institutional customers rather than to industrial customers. And SIC 3441127 defines these same products for sale to public utilities. In this case, the seven-digit SIC numbers provide market segmentation data not available through the use of the four-digit SIC numbers provided by the *Standard Industrial Classification Manual.*

What this means to the industrial marketing manager is that a practical classification system for industrial customers already exists, and firms in practically every industry in the United States are already classified by appropriate SIC numbers. If the marketing manager knows enough about present and potential customers to classify them into at least four-digit SIC market segments, that manager is halfway home in regard to locating such customers, defining their sales volumes, and determining market potential and other such considerations. Without knowledge of the SIC classification, the industrial marketing manager is like a blind man trying to find his way in a strange city. As will be developed throughout this text, the SIC system is one of the keys to industrial marketing. It is absolutely essential in the industrial market to be able to understand and use the SIC system.

DEFINING THE CUSTOMERS TO BE REACHED

The standard industrial classification is only a tool for classifying those customers to be reached. By itself, SIC will not necessarily tell the industrial

Table 3.2

BREAKDOWN OF THE STANDARD INDUSTRIAL
CLASSIFICATION SYSTEM

Classification	SIC Number	Description
Division	D	Manufacturing
Major Group	34	Manufacturers of Fabricated Metal Products
Industry Subgroup	344	Manufacturers of Fabricated Structural Metal Products
Detailed Industry	3441	Manufacturers of Fabricated Structural Steel
Manufactured Products	34411	Manufacturers of Fabricated Structural Metal for Buildings
Manufactured Products	3441121	Manufacturers of Fabricated Structural Metal for Buildings —Iron & Steel (for sale to companies): Industrial

Source: Adapted from Office of Management and Budget, *1972 Standard Industrial Classification Manual* (Washington, D.C.: U.S. Government Printing Office, 1972); U.S. Bureau of the Census, *Census of Manufactures, 1967 Industry Series: Fabricated Structural Metal Products* (Washington, D.C.: U.S. Government Printing Office, 1970).

marketing manager who customers are or who they should be or where they are or how big they are, and so forth. There are ways, however, of finding out these things and then using the standard industrial classification system to refine market segments further. There are a number of approaches that might be used to accomplish this task, but lack of space precludes discussion of all of them in this book. Instead, the focus will be on the use of input-output analysis as one of the methods that might be used in defining industrial customers to be reached by the marketing manager.

Input-output Analysis

Input-output analysis is based on the relatively simple concept that the sales or output of one industry are the purchases or inputs of other industries. This has industrial marketing applications in that it can show what industries are purchasing the products of the manager's industry. National input-output models are published by the Commerce Department's Office of

Business Economics, and upgraded versions appear periodically in issues of the *Survey of Current Business,* a monthly periodical, which is published by the U.S. Department of Commerce.[1] Although regional and even local input-output models may occasionally be found, references here shall be to the national model of the Office of Business Economics because it is the one most readily accessible to most marketing managers.

The basic Office of Business Economics input-output table covers 83 basic industries in a grid or matrix. Each horizontal row shows how an industry's sales or output are distributed among its customer industries. Because each sale is a purchase, each vertical column shows how an industry's purchases or input are a percentage of the supplier's output. A second table, which converts the percentages to dollars, shows the value of the flow of goods and services between industries. In essence, this second table indicates an industry's potential in sales to other industries. A third table then details what the buying industry, for each dollar of output, requires from first-level or direct suppliers. This third table basically indicates the impact that a change in a buying industry will have on other industries. Each of the three tables has its own value, but in this chapter focus will be on the basic table and its use in defining appropriate segments in the industrial market.

Using the Input-output Model. Assume that a manufacturer of farm machinery wishes to know what potential customers exist for its products in addition to those customers it is already servicing. Who are the prime users of the products produced by this manufacturer? Is the market vertical or horizontal? One way to answer these questions is for the marketing manager in that firm to consult the input-output table. Referring to the basic table, the manager refers to row 44, which represents the farm machinery and equipment industry. Then, by following that row across the 83 columns in the table, the manager can find what industries buy such equipment as expressed in millions of dollars at producers' prices. In the case of row 44 (farm machinery and equipment), analysis will show that 30 of the 83 industries buy such products. Further analysis will reveal that seven industries account for 76.9 percent of the equipment purchased. Thus, the market concentration is relatively vertical, something that may have been previously assumed, but never known for certain. But who are these buying industries and what are their appropriate SIC numbers? The seven industries that purchase the bulk of farm equipment and machinery are found in columns 2, 44, 45, 73, 69, 37, and 61. These are illustrated in Table 3.3 along with the percentage of output purchased by each industry. As stated, these seven industries purchase 76.9 percent of the output of industry 44 (farm machinery and equipment). Twenty-three other industries purchase the remaining 23.1 percent of such machinery and equipment. Table 3.3 is quite meaningful in that it shows the

Table 3.3

CONVERTING INPUT-OUTPUT DATA TO THE STANDARD INDUSTRIAL CLASSIFICATION
FOR A MANUFACTURER OF FARM MACHINERY, INPUT-OUTPUT 44, SIC 3522

Major Customer Input-output Number	Input-output Industry Definition	Percent of Total Intermediate Outputs	Appropriate SIC Numbers	Number of SIC Establishments in the U.S.
2	Other Agricultural Products	31.2	0112 Cotton Growers 0113 Cash Grain Growers 0114 Tobacco Growers 0119 Field Crops 0123 Vegetable Growers 0141 General Farms	363 568 68 664 889 2,263
44	Farm Machinery & Equipment	23.8	3522 Farm Machinery & Equipment	2,371
45	Construction, Mining & Oil Field Machinery	6.0	3531 Construction Machinery 3532 Mining Machinery 3533 Oil Field Machinery	1,021 335 604
73	Business Services	5.8	7394 Equipment Rental & Leasing Services	11,232
69	Wholesale & Retail Trade	3.5	5083 Wholesale Distributors of Farm Machinery 5252 Farm Equipment Dealers	1,869 21,801
37	Primary Iron & Steel Manufacturing	3.4	In SIC's 331, 332, 339	Too Broad to define
61	Other Transportation Equipment	3.2	3799 Transportation Equipment, Not Elsewhere Classified	917

marketing manager who is purchasing the products of the industry in which the company is a member. And it gives the manager an estimate of what markets should be reached and in what proportions. For example, is the manager's company selling 31 percent of its output to agricultural customers? In other words, the manager now has a barometer to compare company sales to industry sales.

Converting Input-output to SIC Numbers. At this point, it is necessary to convert the industries found in input-output analysis to appropriate SIC numbered classifications. This is a necessary step if further data are to be obtained regarding the purchasing industries. The fitting of four-digit SIC numbers to input-output industry numbers is not always easy owing to the general nature of input-output industry classifications. Generally, however, such conversion is possible, as is also shown in Table 3.3. In this table, the conversion from input-output industries to SIC numbers was accomplished with the help of tables prepared by the federal government.[2] As is shown in the table, some conversions are simpler than others. For example, the SIC numbers appropriate for defining input-output industry number 37 can only be defined in three digits because of the general nature of the input-output industry classification. It is questionable whether this particular conversion is of any managerial value whatsoever, but because this industry accounts for only 3.4 percent of industry sales, it may be acceptable. In the cases of the other input-output industries, more precise matching to SIC is possible, as the table illustrates.

The marketing manager now knows a great deal more than before applying the input-output analysis. It is now known what industries are major customers and what SIC numbers are appropriate for potential target customer markets. The manager is also now in position to compare company market segments with industry market segments in terms of sales percentages. From this the manager can determine where the company is doing well and where it is doing poorly. For example, if 10 percent of the company's sales are to the farm machinery industry and if the industry is selling 23.8 percent of its output to the same industry, the company is not keeping pace with the industry, and an area of underdeveloped potential may exist. The next question is how to use the SIC numbers to locate specific customers for the company's products. Input-output analysis has not done this, but conversion to SIC will permit it.

LOCATING SPECIFIC CUSTOMERS

Once major customer market segments are found via input-output analysis and classified into appropriate SIC numbers, the marketing manager must go one step further. Specific customers must now be located, and marketing effort be directed toward them. It is one thing to know what industries are purchasing the types of goods and services produced, but that is not enough for the marketing manager. Specific customer firms within those industries must be sought out if the manager is to market to them. Referring again to Table 3.3, the manager in this case now knows that about 5.8 percent of the industry's sales are to equipment rental and leasing companies. Through conversion it is also known that this industry is classified by SIC 7394. The problem now is to locate specific firms with the SIC number of 7394 because companies with that number should be prime potential customers for the products involved. The question to be answered is how are these companies found?

There are a number of ways of locating specific industrial customers once appropriate market segments are defined in terms of their SIC numbers. To illustrate, in the case of SIC 7394, reference to Dun & Bradstreet's *Market Identifiers* reveals that Dun & Bradstreet has data on 11,232 such firms in the United States with the SIC classification of 7394.[3] The industrial marketing manager now has a number of options open in locating specific customers in SIC 7394. One method would be to go to some outside organization such as Dun & Bradstreet's Marketing Services Division and have it provide data on each and every firm of SIC 7394 in its file. In the case of Dun & Bradstreet, that company has on file 11,232 firms in the United States with the SIC of 7394 and could provide such data on each firm as its mailing address, telephone number, name and title of the chief executive, line of business/primary SIC, up to five secondary SICs, number of employees, company sales volume, whether the unit is a branch location, whether the unit manufactures or not, and other such relevant data. With such data, the marketing manager is now in position to plot geographic concentrations, determine market sales potentials, and so on. This method is quick and reliable as long as the four-digit SIC numbers adequately relate to specific customers in the market segment. The marketing manager must pay for this service, but for many managers the savings in time and effort are well worth the funds expended. The biggest problem with this approach is that for many managers the four-digit SIC classification is not explicit enough to locate their customers.

The other option is for the marketing manager to compile the customer list himself after the SIC numbers have been assigned. This is not as difficult as it appears although it may take considerable time and effort to research all the appropriate sources. For example, if the marketing manager knew that all firms in the United States classified by the SIC number 7394 were prospective customers, reference could be made to the many directories that contain information on business firms based on SIC numbers. Examples include such directories as Dun & Bradstreet's *Million Dollar Directory,* their *Middle Market Directory,* and their *Metalworking Directory* as well as Standard &

Poor's *Poors Register.* All of these are good sources of information on national data based on the SIC system. In addition, every state has a state industrial directory of one type or another that will provide data by SIC in its own respective state. Most of these sources can be found in the reference sections of public and university libraries and are readily accessible. Through the use of these sources, it is possible to obtain information on each firm listed under each SIC number such as the following: (1) firm name, address, and phone numbers; (2) corporate officers by name, title, and position; (3) areas of responsibility of those officers; (4) directors by name; (5) annual sales volumes; (6) number of employees; (7) appropriate SIC numbers, primary and secondary; and (8) products or services produced. If the marketing manager could locate information such as this on each and every prospective customer in SIC 7394, that manager would have come a long way from where he was prior to implementing the use of input-output analysis and the standard industrial classification system.

There are other sources of information available to the industrial marketing manager once target markets are defined in terms of SIC numbers, and reference to some of these sources is worthwhile.

The Survey of Industrial Purchasing Power. Sales Management magazine publishes an annual survey of industrial purchasing power, which provides information based on four-digit SIC numbers by state and county. Table 3.4 shows the type of information that is available from this survey, and *Sales Management's* guide to using the survey follows shortly. As can be seen in the table, data are provided in this survey according to the size of the potential customers, based on the number of plants and total shipments broken down by state and county. The value of the *Sales Management* survey is that it supplies updated information and allows the marketing manager to tell where the larger buyers are located and where the larger potential markets lie. The survey will be referred to again in the chapter on selling and sales management, but, at this point, it is only necessary to know the survey is available and can be used in conjunction with the other sources that have been cited. The survey of industrial purchasing power is especially useful for locating potential markets and determining the size of those markets once the SIC definition has been made. The guide that follows shortly illustrates how the *Sales Management* survey should be used.

Federal Government Data. The federal government publishes an almost unbelievable amount of data based on the SIC system that has application to industrial marketing. As stated earlier in this chapter, the *Census of Manufactures,* which is published every five years (the last one in 1972), provides data down to seven-digit SIC numbers, which is about as specific as can be found.

Table 3.4

EXAMPLE OF DATA AVAILABLE FROM SALES MANAGEMENT'S
SURVEY OF INDUSTRIAL PURCHASING POWER

STATE County SIC	Industry	No. of Plants Total Plants	No. of Plants Large Plants	Total Shipments $ Mil.	% of U.S.	% In Large Plants
CALI- FORNIA						
Los Angeles	All Manu- facturing	6,648	1,458	23,799.7	3.7741	72
3312	Blast furn. & steel mill	14	4	173.2	–	84
3317	Steel pipe & tubes	5	4	55.1	–	97
3321	Gray iron foundries	28	11	53.2	–	61
3351	Copper rolling, drawing	6	4	88.0	–	93
3352	Alum. rolling & drawing	14	6	232.6	–	91
3361	Aluminum castings	47	4	47.4	–	29
3369	Nonferr. castings, n.e.c.	25	4	31.9	–	39
3391	Iron & steel forgings	11	2	33.2	–	54
3399	Prim. metals indus., n.e.c.	31	1	35.1	–	14

Source: "*Sales Management's* First Annual Survey of Industrial Purchasing Power," *Sales Management* 112 (April 22, 1974), 32.

Note: Reprinted by permission from *Sales Management, The Marketing Magazine,* *Copyright 1974.*

Exhibit 1

GUIDE TO USING *SALES MANAGEMENT'S* SURVEY OF
INDUSTRIAL PURCHASING POWER

STATE County SIC	Industry	Total Plants	Large Plants	Total Shipments $ Mil.	% of U.S.	% in Large Plants
A	B	C	D	E	F	G

A. All of the 2,802 counties with at least one manufacturing establishment of 20 or more employees are included. In each county, individual industries with at least 1,000 employees are listed. Such industries are at the four-digit level of the standard industrial classification (SIC) system used by the federal government.

B. "All mfg" refers to the overall totals for all manufacturing plants. Because of space limitations, the wording of the qualifying four-digit industries is shortened in some cases. A complete listing of all SIC-coded industry titles is in the *1972 Standard Industrial Classification Manual,* U.S. Government Printing Office, Washington, D.C. 20402; $6.95.

C. The total number of manufacturing plants with at least 20 employees.

D. Because large plants (with 100 or more employees) account for a significant share of a county's manufacturing activity, a separate total is provided for such facilities. They can be considered key prospects—the ones that merit the most selling attention.

E. The dollar value of all goods produced by the manufacturing plants. It is an effective indicator of buying potential because, generally, half of the dollar amount represented by shipments is spent for equipment, supplies, and materials. This figure includes interplant shipments between establishments of a common ownership; however, such shipments are a very small percent of the overall total. Where the four-digit SIC industries are concerned, if a plant produces goods that fall into more than one industry, all its output is credited to the "primary" industry that describes the largest share of its output.

F. The county's share of U.S. shipments indicates its importance relative to other counties. This ratio is not provided for the four-digit
industries. However, forthcoming reports from the *1972 Census of
Manufactures,* which will include U.S. totals for all four-digit industries, will enable you to calculate such ratios.

G. That portion of a county's manufacturing output produced by the
large plants will suggest the level of sales coverage required in the
county. The higher the ratio, the fewer salesmen will be needed
because there will be proportionately fewer prospects to call on.

Source: "Guide to Using *Sales Management's* Survey of Industrial Purchasing Power,"
Sales Management 112 (April 22, 1974), 28. Reprinted by permission from
Sales Management, The Marketing Magazine. Copyright 1974.

The major problem with the data in the *Census of Manufactures* is that the
census is not as current as most marketing managers would prefer—the data
are updated every five years, with the 1972 census replacing the 1967 census.
Nevertheless, the census can be a very useful source of SIC-related data pertaining to industrial customers. There is also an *Annual Survey of Manufactures,* which is conducted for those years not covered by the *Census of Manufactures.* Although the *Survey of Manufactures* does not have the depth of
coverage of the *Census of Manufactures,* it can be used in conjunction with
the latter for updating purposes. Another good source of data is the U.S. Department of Commerce's *U.S. Industrial Outlook.* This book is published annually, is classified according to four-digit SIC numbers, and contains projections that are useful to the marketing manager. Referring back to Table 3.3,
one will recall that SICs 3522 and 3532 were considered potential markets
for the farm machinery producer in the example. Table 3.5 shows the type
of information that can be obtained from the *U.S. Industrial Outlook* once
market targets are defined in terms of appropriate SIC numbers. As has also
been mentioned, *County Business Patterns* can be used by the industrial marketing manager as a source of data on the industrial market. In addition to
these federal government sources, state and county governments often provide good data pertaining to industrial concentrations in their areas.

This brief discussion is certainly not exhaustive in any manner, but it does
show the type of information that is available to the industrial marketing
manager once markets are segmented by SIC numbers. As was shown in this
discussion, through the use of input-output analysis, SIC, and appropriate
sources of market data, the marketing manager now knows exactly who customers are, where they are, their sales volumes, what other products they
produce, who some of their key officers are, and other such pieces of infor-

Table 3.5

SIC-BASED DATA AVAILABLE FROM FEDERAL GOVERNMENT SOURCES

	Farm Machinery and Equipment	Mining Machinery Industry
SIC Code	3522	3532
Value of industry shipments (millions)	$4,965	$927
Number of establishments	1,473	212
Total employment (thousands)	116	23.6
Exports as a percent of product shipments	10	25.3
Imports as a percent of apparent consumption	9.0	2.3
Compound annual average rate of growth 1967–72 (percent):	2.9	
Value of product shipments (current dollars)	2.9	8.3
Value of exports (current dollars)	0.0	7.5
Value of imports (current dollars)	2.8	16.4
Employment	–2.8	1.7
Major producing areas	Ohio, Indiana, Illinois, Iowa, Wisconsin, and Minnesota	Pennsylvania, Ohio, and Colorado

Source: U.S. Department of Commerce, *U.S. Industrial Outlook With Projections to 1980* (Washington, D.C.: U.S. Government Printing Office, January 1973), pp. 231, 235.

mation. With such data, the manager can now begin his marketing strategy to reach those customer firms. The manager has been able to start with but a general idea of what markets should be addressed and then refine that idea down to individual companies in those markets. And all this can be accomplished at minimum cost with the manager perhaps never leaving his office to do it. The main point here is that information is available if the standard industrial classification is used to classify customers.

UNDERSTANDING ORGANIZATIONAL CHARACTERISTICS

Once industrial customers have been defined and located, each must be further analyzed in terms of characteristics that will have an effect on its purchasing. Typically, this involves researching each of the customers located in the preceding section with regard initially to the purchasing functions of the particular firms in question. Purchasing functions differ among industries and among companies in the same industry. Thus, it is important that the marketing manager gain insight into the purchasing behavior of each and every present and prospective customer firm. It is generally conceded that the first step in understanding the very complex area of corporate industrial purchasing behavior is to understand the organization of the particular firm involved. From the point of view of the industrial marketing manager, the following characteristics are very important in attempting to understand customer purchasing behavior.

Size of the Customer Firm and Specialization of Purchasing

Although there are no hard-and-fast rules, the size of the company generally has an effect on the way in which it purchases goods and services, and thus size has an effect on the marketing approach to be used. For example, in smaller firms (fewer than 20 employees), purchasing is often a part-time responsibility held by someone such as the shop foreman or office manager or owner/manager. This implies that the purchaser is normally not a specialist, and educational selling on the part of the marketing manager is required. The part-time purchasing individual seeks help in his buying and often looks to his suppliers as a prime source of such help. In medium-sized firms (20 to 100 employees), formal purchasing departments are commonly found, often being relatively small in size with perhaps one or two on the staff. Although these people are normally purchasing professionals, they may be spread thin in their knowledge of all the products they purchase and thus lack the specialization often found in purchasing departments in large firms. But the marketing manager would be wise not simply to assume this lack of specialization, for a great deal of specialized technical knowledge can be found in purchasing agents and other purchasing professionals in medium-sized firms. In the larger industrial firms (over 100 employees), it is very common to find a great deal of purchasing specialization in very formalized departments. There are definite lines of authority and responsibility, and highly specialized buyers are the rule. It should be apparent that marketing into this type of purchasing department would differ from marketing into the smaller companies. It is imperative that the industrial marketing manager understand the differences involved and classify each and every present and prospective customer according to the specialization of its purchasing activities.

Purchasing's Position in the Customer Organization

Another extremely important characteristic that must be determined for each and every customer is the position of the purchasing department in the formal organization of each customer firm. This is not to imply that the formal organization necessarily reflects actual buying practices in all firms, but it is the most logical place for the marketing manager to start because it is usually the most accessible criterion available to outsiders. In most instances, it is next to impossible for the marketing firm to market initially to a customer firm without having some contact with that firm's purchasing department or individual responsible for purchasing if no formal department exists. Therefore, some knowledge of where purchasing is in the formal organization chart of the customer is a very useful piece of marketing information. In attempting to determine the position of purchasing in the customer organization, the marketing manager should look at points such as the following: Is the purchasing department a line or staff department? Where is the level of the purchasing department in the organization? Are purchasing responsibilities split between headquarters and operating divisions? What purchasing policies are involved? Because these are extremely important questions in formulating a marketing strategy, it is well worthwhile to examine these areas in some detail.

Is the Purchasing Department Line or Staff? In some companies, purchasing is a line position, whereas in others it may be a staff position. The importance of this to the industrial marketing manager is vital. Line purchasing departments possess the authority to decide what will be purchased and from whom it will be bought. Staff purchasing departments, on the other hand, usually operate in an advisory capacity, advising such other departments as production, engineering, and so on, on what they might buy and from whom; but the authority is vested in the other departments. Obviously, this is a very important factor in effective industrial marketing! If the marketing firm is spending its time cultivating a staff purchasing department when the decisions are actually made elsewhere, that firm will lose orders if the recommendations of purchasing are not followed. The inverse is also true—if purchasing has authority and the marketing manager is devoting efforts toward the using departments, that manager may be bypassing the actual decision maker and thus losing orders to competition. In other instances, purchasing may possess both line and staff authority. It is quite common to find situations where the purchasing department does not decide what will be purchased, although it may advise; but once a decision is made to buy certain equipment, the purchasing department has the authority to choose the supplier. As can be realized, it is imperative that the marketing manager attempt to define purchasing within each of his customer firms on the basis of their line or staff authority.

Where Is the Level of the Purchasing Department in the Organization? In addition to determining whether purchasing is a line or staff position, the industrial marketing manager must also discover how high or low the purchasing department is in each buyer firm's organization. This is the kind of information that shows on formal organization charts, and it can be found with some effort, although the manager must not simply assume that the formal organization reflects actual operations.

What is meant by the level of the purchasing department concerns where that department is on the organization chart and to whom it reports. To illustrate, if a customer firm has a vice-president of purchasing reporting directly to a president or general manager at the same level as other officers such as the vice-president of production, vice-president of marketing, the comptroller, and so forth, then that is line authority very high in the organization. On the other hand, if the purchasing director is responsible to and reports to the vice-president of production, he is lower down in the organization, and his authority is tempered, even though he may still hold a line position.

The difference between these two cases is important. In the former, the VP of purchasing may have the authority to make a decision and even override the VP of production because both are at the same level. In the latter case, however, the VP of production has the authority to overrule the purchasing director's decision because he is the director's superior. These examples are both line in nature, but their authorities are quite different.

The same concern over the level in the organization applies to staff purchasing departments. The point here is that the level of the purchasing department in each customer firm must be known if those firms are to be marketed to effectively. Without such knowledge, the marketing manager will never know if he is selling the person with the authority to buy. Again, there are few rules here—the level of purchasing differs among companies even in the same industry. Regardless, the level of purchasing must be determined, and the most logical place to start is the individual customer firm's formal organization chart.

Are Purchasing Responsibilities Split between Headquarters and Operating Divisions? In many industrial companies where multiunit plants and/or divisions are found, there are split purchasing responsibilities. The divisions or plants have the authority to purchase operationally, but overall purchasing policy may be determined at the corporate level at the home office or headquarters. This can take many forms. To illustrate, the authorization to purchase capital equipment may have to be obtained from central headquarters purchasing, but the actual decision as to which specific machines will be purchased may be made by personnel in the divisions. In other instances, both decisions may be made at headquarters, or both may be made in the divisions with true autonomous buying being found.

The marketing implications of this are easy to see! If the purchasing functions are split, marketing must hit both levels, but with different approaches— the company salesmen may contact the divisional buyers whereas an executive salesman, such as a corporate vice-president, might be directed to sell policy changes at the headquarters administrative level. For instance, if a prospective customer firm has buying authority at the divisional level, but a policy of buying locally dictated at the corporate level, it may be impossible for company salesmen who are not locally based to sell to the company unless the buy-local policy is changed at the corporate level; and this involves an entirely different type of selling. To market effectively, one must know this type of purchasing behavior before it can be handled. Sometimes it is relatively easy to find out such information, as companies make it known to potential suppliers. At other times, it must be discovered through diligent effort by field salesmen and the marketing department. Either way, it must be determined!

What Purchasing Policies Are Involved? Another essential characteristic that must be known about each customer firm is that firm's purchasing policies. Different companies, even in the same industry, have different policies governing their purchasing, and these policies must be understood and adapted to if the firm is to be sold. Sometimes these policies are relatively easy to discover, as the companies make such policies known to all possible suppliers. At other times, discovering such policies involves much time and effort by company field salesmen and marketing managers and their departments. Often customer purchasing policies may make little sense to the industrial marketing manager, but if he cannot change them, he must adapt to them. To do this, however, he must first determine what those policies are.

Some typical purchasing policies found in the industrial market are as follows: (1) buying from local suppliers whenever possible, (2) buying only American-made products or from domestic suppliers, (3) centralized purchasing from the home office when purchases exceed certain dollar amounts, (4) requiring bids when purchases exceed certain dollar amounts, (5) reciprocal agreements with customers by which an industrial firm buys from its own customers whenever feasible, and (6) buying from at least two suppliers on every purchase.

These are just a few of the policies that can be found in the industrial market. It is imperative that the marketing manager discover such policies when they exist and adapt to them! If these policies are not determined, complete customer orientation will never be achieved. A good example of what such policies mean to the marketing manager took place when Cities Service Corporation considered entering the market for sales of processing oils to rubber companies and found that each of the big four rubber companies had reciprocal agreements with each of the four major oil companies.[4] Because of such purchasing policy, Cities Service was unable to penetrate the market and gave up the attempt. It would be interesting to know how much time and effort were expended before the firm found out why it was not penetrating the market! The problem is that some policies such as reciprocity are not published, and thus may not even be cited by the customer as the reason for refusing to purchase. Nevertheless, if it exists, it must be determined, just as any other purchasing policy must be determined. Purchasing policy determines purchasing behavior and thus must be determined and understood if effective marketing is to take place.

OBTAINING INFORMATION ON PURCHASING BEHAVIOR OF INDUSTRIAL COMPANIES

As has been stated, it is often relatively easy to find out characteristics related to the purchasing by industrial companies because many such companies provide this type of information to their suppliers. They do this because it makes the suppliers more knowledgeable about their purchasing practices, and this saves time and effort by the company's purchasing people. A good example of this is American Cyanamid Company, which publishes a booklet entitled *Calling on Cyanamid,* which is distributed to present and potential suppliers.[5] This booklet contains a great deal of information that would help the industrial marketing manager to understand better Cyanamid's purchasing behavior. Included in this booklet is such information as (1) what Cyanamid expects from salesmen calling on their purchasing departments; (2) how Cyanamid's purchasing organization is divided into three groups—central purchasing, operating division purchasing, and plant purchasing—and what the function of each purchasing group is; (3) how materials, supplies, and services are purchased within the three groups; (4) how capital purchases are made within the three groups; (5) who in the firm is responsible for purchasing various types of products by name and position in the purchasing division headquarters; and (6) who is responsible for purchasing in the various divisions and subsidiaries, also by name and position. The booklet contains much more information, but the desired point is made. It is possible to determine a great deal about a customer's purchasing prior to calling for the first time. This, of course, is why companies like American Cyanamid provide such materials to their suppliers. They also profit when the marketing firms calling on them know enough about their purchasing operations to call on the right departments or divisions and on the right buyers. The point here is that information is available, and the industrial marketing manager would be well advised to contact any prospective companies prior to first calling on them and see if they can provide information pertaining to their purchasing behavior. This information can later be refined by salesmen in the field, but initially any information peculiar to a particular company's purchasing behavior is of marketing value as it permits the manager insight into the customer and how it will affect marketing to that customer.

CHAPTER SUMMARY

This chapter has been devoted to understanding the industrial customer. A method for using input-output analysis and the standard industrial classification to define specific target markets has been illustrated. To market to the industrial customer involves first discovering who that customer is, finding out how many of those customers exist, finding out where they are located, and determining how big they are in terms of sales volume and value of shipments. In many cases, this can be accomplished through secondary source data published by governmental organizations and private firms. Once this is accomplished, a better understanding of each customer and its purchasing behavior must be undertaken. Initially, this involves analyzing each customer firm's purchasing behavior in terms of its formal organization. The differences that size of the customer company makes in purchasing behavior was discussed, and the implications in line and staff purchasing functions were developed. The level of purchasing in the organization chart was discussed along with split purchasing responsibilities and purchasing policies as they affect the industrial marketing manager. By itself such knowledge is not sufficient for understanding industrial buying behavior, and the following chapter will go into industrial purchasing in depth. On the other hand, if the industrial marketing manager does not accomplish the points outlined in this chapter, it is highly unlikely that a full understanding of his customers will ever be determined.

QUESTIONS FOR CHAPTER 3

1. From an industrial marketing viewpoint, the main problem with using the SIC system in delineating markets is that the system is based primarily on theoretical data and is difficult to apply to real world situations. Do you agree or disagree with this statement? If you agree, why do you agree? If you disagree, why do you disagree?
2. If an industrial marketing manager wanted to determine appropriate markets for the company's products, how could that manager use input-output analysis to do so?
3. Although there are probably no rules to follow, the size of an industrial customer's firm affects the manner in which that firm purchases goods and services. What are the industrial marketing implications in this statement?
4. For the most part, it is irrelevant to the industrial marketing manager whether that manager is marketing to a line or staff purchasing department in a customer firm. Do you agree or disagree with this statement? If you agree, why do you agree? If you disagree, why do you disagree?
5. For an industrial customer to purchase the same product from two or more suppliers is totally inconsistent purchasing behavior if the product in question could be purchased cheaper from any one particular supplier. Do you agree or disagree with this statement? If you agree, why do you agree? If you disagree, why do you disagree?

4

UNDERSTANDING
INDUSTRIAL BUYING

Once the industrial customers have been defined, located, and analyzed from an organizational characteristic's point of view, each customer firm must then be analyzed in greater depth to determine those characteristics peculiar to its individual buying of goods and services. This is no easy task and sometimes takes years, even with experienced field sales personnel, to discover the intricate operations at work in the purchasing of each particular firm. Unless this is accomplished, however, effective marketing can never take place. As was developed in the preceding chapter, the first step in understanding an industrial customer is to gain as much knowledge as possible about its purchasing department as can be obtained through analysis of its formal organization. Yet this knowledge is rarely sufficient to sell goods and services into the industrial market. The manner in which the formal organization claims that a company purchases may not at all be the manner in which that company actually does purchase. To illustrate, it is common to find circumstances where the purchasing department has line authority according to the formal organization structure. In actual buying situations, however, it may be just as common to find that the department buys only those products that are requested by the originating department. For example, a production supervisor wishes to buy some new pieces of light equipment, for which he has budget allowances, and he desires that equipment to be of a particular brand. The purchasing department simply rubber-stamps his request, and the purchase order is issued for that particular brand of product. In other instances, the purchasing department may be staff and advisory in the formal organization, but it is so well respected that its recommendations are followed explicitly even though formal purchasing authority does not exist in the department. These are simple examples that in actual business situations become much more complex, particularly in the larger firms. There are a lot of informal factors that influence industrial purchasing decisions, and if the marketing manager does not understand these factors, orders will be lost to competitors who do understand them!

There are no shortcuts or simple rule-of-thumb approaches that can be employed to discover individual customer buying behavior. This must be learned over time by marketing departments and field sales personnel who make concentrated efforts to discover how each and every customer buys. It requires insight and stamina to ferret out such information and keep track of it for future use. In fact, this is the forte of any successful industrial salesman—knowledge of who affects the purchasing of his products in each of his customer firms and reaching each of these people with a sales message relevant to their interests, problems, expectations, and desires. Normally, the salesman reaches this stage through years of diligent effort with each customer firm by knowing what to look for in the beginning. The same is true for the successful industrial marketing manager—unless it is known how each of the customers purchases its goods and services and who in each firm makes or contributes to the decision to purchase, the company can never effectively market to them.

There are a number of factors that the industrial marketing manager and the industrial field salesman must seek out and understand for each customer firm if buyer behavior is to be fully understood. These are the following: (1) a thorough understanding of the industrial buying process—the process by which industrial firms actually purchase goods and services; (2) a thorough understanding of who in each customer firm is actually involved in this buying process—at what stages in the process is each person involved and how much influence does each person have in deciding what is actually to be purchased; and (3) a thorough understanding of those factors motivating each of the people involved in the process—both rational and emotional factors. Once these types of things are known and understood, the industrial marketing manager is in position to implement the marketing strategy. Therefore, an analysis of each of these factors is in order.

THE INDUSTRIAL BUYING PROCESS

Although there is no single format dictating how industrial companies actually purchase goods and services, there is a relatively standard process that is followed in most cases. This process is as follows: (1) a department discovers or anticipates a problem in its operation that it believes can be overcome with the addition of a certain product or service; (2) the department head then draws up a requisition form describing the desired specifications he feels the product or service must have to solve his problem; (3) the requisition form is then sent by the department head to the firm's purchasing department; (4) based on the specifications required, the purchasing department then conducts a search for qualified sources of supply; (5) once sources have been located, proposals based on the specifications are solicited, received, and analyzed for price, delivery, service, and so on; (6) proposals are then compared with the cost of producing the product in-house in a make or buy decision: if it is decided that the buying firm can produce the product more economically, the buying process for the product in question is terminated; however, if the inverse is true, the process continues; (7) a source or sources of supply is selected from those who have submitted proposals; (8) the order is placed, and copies of the purchase order are sent to the originating department, accounting, credit, and any other interested departments within the company; and (9) after the product is shipped, received, and used, a follow-up with the originating department is conducted to determine that department's level of satisfaction or dissatisfaction with the purchased product in terms of the problem faced for which the product was purchased.

Although there are many variations of this process in actual operation, this is typical of the process by which industrial goods and services are purchased. It must be understood that in actual practice these are not separate steps, but, in fact, are often combined. Nevertheless, the process described in the preceding section is probably a good illustration of the operation of the industrial purchasing process.

Marketing Implications in the Buying Process

The real importance of the buying process to the industrial marketing manager is that it shows how customers make a purchasing decision, and it also shows what must be done if the company's product or service is to be considered and ultimately purchased. Two considerations are most important! First, the manager must recognize that such a process does exist in each and every industrial customer. Secondly, the manager must get the company's marketing efforts involved in the process as early as possible if it is to be considered as a supplier of the required product or service. As will be developed throughout this text, the marketing firm has a better chance of getting the order if its salesmen are involved in the first step of the process than if they were to get involved later in the process, such as in steps four or five. The reason for this is not difficult to understand! If the marketing manager or the company salesman or both can get involved in the first step, it is possible that they could solve the purchasing company's problem around the specifications of their product. When this happens, their specifications become the basis for the product to be purchased, and these specs go right through the entire process. Unless competitors can match these specifications exactly, they may not be considered, unless, of course, they can convince the buying firm to change specifications later. In most cases, however, there is an edge to be gained from getting involved early in the process at the point where specifications are established.

Another way in which the marketing manager should view the purchasing process of customer firms is in relation to the types of purchases being made. To illustrate, what is the difference in the process if the company is purchasing a new product for the very first time as opposed to the company's purchasing on a repeat basis a product it has bought numerous times previously? Table 4.1 is an excellent marketing tool for analyzing this aspect of industrial purchasing. Purchases in the table are classified into three basic types: (1) new task purchases, where the buying firm is buying a new product for the first time for the purpose of accomplishing a new task, solving a new problem, and so forth; (2) straight rebuy purchases, where the buying firm simply buys on a repeat routine basis those products it has always bought; and (3) modified rebuy purchases, where, for one reason or another, the purchasing company modifies a new task purchase the second or third time through or modifies a straight rebuy purchase, looking for lower price, better service, better delivery, or some other such factor. New task and straight rebuy situations are easy to understand, but the modified rebuy situations confuse many marketing managers. An example may help to show what is meant by a modified rebuy. In the economic crunch of the early and mid-1970s, shortages of supplies and rising prices were the two most pressing problems facing industrial purchasers according to the National Association of Purchasing Management.[1] The effect of this was to force professional purchasers in industry to review what had traditionally been straight rebuy situations, seeking better prices and adequate supplies. This is what is known as a modified rebuy for a purchasing industrial customer.

With reference again to Table 4.1, in the case of a new product being purchased for the first time, all eight buyphases or steps in the buying process are important, but the first few phases are critical. If the industrial salesman can point out the problem to the originating department and then solve that problem around the specifications of his product or products, it is very difficult for a competing salesman to get those specifications changed at a later stage in the process. Most effective industrial salesmen and marketing managers understand this very well and attempt to get their products specified as the solution to the buyer's problem. They then follow their customer through each stage of its buying process to make sure nothing goes wrong. This is necessary because it is a new experience for the buyer, and a great deal of communication is necessary between purchaser and seller. And new task pur-

Table 4.1
THE BUYGRID FRAMEWORK

		BUYCLASSES		
		New Task	Modified Rebuy	Straight Rebuy
B	1. Anticipation or Recognition of a Problem (Need) and a General Solution			
U	2. Determination of Characteristics and Quantity of Needed Item			
Y	3. Description of Characteristics and Quantity of Needed Item			
P	4. Search for and Qualification of Potential Sources			
H				
·	5. Acquisition and Analysis of Proposals			
A				
S	6. Evaluation of Proposals and Selection of Supplier(s)			
E	7. Selection of an Order Routine			
S	8. Performance Feedback and Evaluation			

Source: From Marketing Science Institute Series, *Industrial Buying and Creative Marketing* by Robinson, Faris, and Wind. Copyright 1967 by Allyn and Bacon, Inc. Used with permission.

chases are important to the marketing manager because, if properly handled, they can lead to repeat purchases and ultimately to straight rebuy situations, which are ideal marketing conditions.

Again with reference to Table 4.1, a straight rebuy situation would be handled quite differently. The early stages of the process are probably of little importance because buyers are purchasing products they are familiar with and feel that they know most of what they need to know. The major emphasis for the industrial marketing manager should be placed in the latter stages of the process, for as long as that manager can get the products to the customer when the latter needs them and in the required quantity and up to specifications, that is all the purchaser looks for. The real danger to the marketing manager in straight rebuy situations is tending to become complacent and take customers for granted and thus may not pay them much attention at all. When this happens, the marketing manager may be unwittingly setting up a modified rebuy situation if deliveries are late or service is poor or some other such happening takes place to irritate customers. Straight rebuys can be looked at from two points of view. With the company's straight rebuy customers, the marketing manager should pay very close attention to stages seven and eight to make sure no opportunities are created for competing firms to come in and take them over. With the competitors' straight rebuy customers, the marketing manager should be looking into the process for ways in which to find areas of dissatisfaction or unrest to switch them to modified rebuys and create sales opportunities. Satisfied straight rebuy situations are almost the ideal in industrial marketing when they involve the firm's own customers. When they involve the customers of competitors, straight rebuying by satisfied customers probably creates the single most difficult task in the areas of industrial selling and marketing.

In modified rebuy situations, emphasis on the buystages will again differ from the other two instances. The early stages are again important, and so are the latter stages. In some manner, industrial buyers must be convinced to look elsewhere if modified situations are to be created. Then it is the job of the industrial marketing manager and company field salesmen to provide information that will encourage the buyer to switch. Once this is accomplished, the marketing job involves taking care to see that all goes right and that the customer is not irritated by any problems or delays. Again the job of the marketing manager in the modified rebuy situation is to change it into a straight rebuy situation.

These are very important points for any industrial marketing manager if the company is to market that manager's goods and services effectively. But they cannot be put to use by the manager who does not understand the process involved or know what is to be gained by getting involved as early as possible in the process. The marketing manager can use tools such as the buy-grid framework illustrated in Table 4.1 to great advantage by analyzing each of the customer firms in terms of this process and then assessing where marketing emphasis should be placed within the process. The next thing the manager must know in addition to the buying process itself is who is involved in that process in each of the customer firms.

WHO IS INVOLVED IN THE BUYING PROCESS?

Although the purchasing process found in the buying practices of industrial corporations may be relatively standardized, each company will differ in regard to what people and positions are involved in the process. Another way of saying this is that two firms may be in the same industry and have need for the same equipment even from the same supplier. In addition, both firms may be following the same basic buying process. But the people who influence the purchase and their respective positions can differ in each firm. Understanding who is involved in each customer firm is a very important consideration in industrial marketing. It is also a very difficult undertaking, for rarely does a single person decide what will be purchased and from whom. This means that the industrial marketing manager and the field salesmen must discover who in each customer firm are the influencers of the decision to buy or not to buy their products. Once these people are defined and located, marketing approaches can be directed specifically toward them via personal selling and advertising. If these people are not known, it is virtually impossible to communicate with them, and yet they will continue to make their decisions and buy those products they are aware of and prefer. In short, effective marketing requires a knowledge of who in each customer firm has an effect on products and services that are purchased. These people or positions involved are what are known as *buying influences.*

Multiple Buying Influences
Because the purchasing of goods and services affects virtually every other function of the industrial firm and because other departments use what is being bought, it is only logical that the departments that will use the products may in some way influence what is being purchased. This is the concept of the buying influence—those personnel within the purchasing company who in one way or the other actually have an influence on what is or is not purchased. Because, as has been stated, there is rarely one such person involved, most industrial marketing firms face multiple buying influences. This is where a number of people in the purchasing firm have the power, either formally or informally, to influence the decision being made. A good definition of a buying influence is anyone within the purchasing firm who not only has the power to make a decision in favor of the product involved, but who may also be able to cast a negative vote for that product. Thus, buying influences can be positive, or they can be negative, and there can be any number involved, depending upon the product involved and the buying firm.

The actual number of buying influences for any particular industrial product or service differs among purchasing firms and is determined by factors such as the following: (1) the size of the purchasing firm in terms of the number of departments, number of employees, and so forth; (2) the breadth of usage of the product involved—the more departments that can use the product, the larger the number of potential buying influences; (3) the dollar volume of the product being purchased—the higher the unit value of the product involved, the higher the likelihood of more buying influences; (4) the technical sophistication of the company's purchasing personnel—the less its sophistication, the more likely it is to rely on other departments and, therefore, the more buying influences that may be involved; and (5) the technical background of the product involved—the more technical the product involved, the fewer people who understand it, with the result that fewer buying influences may be involved. The number of buying influences could range from a single influence to over 20 influences, depending upon factors such as the above. Typical buying influences in an industrial firm are the company's plant engineers; production engineers; production personnel such as supervisors, foremen, and even production line workers; field sales representatives of the buying company; quality control personnel; purchasing; the comptroller's office; logistics and transportation; and so forth.

It is also important to realize that such buying influences may be formal or informal or both, depending upon the individual customer firm. To illustrate, an industrial company's decision to purchase a new drill press might be influenced in some instances by the machinist who will actually operate the unit. He may have no formal authority, but his suggestion regarding what manufacture of unit he prefers may have considerable impact on what is ultimately purchased. In other firms, the machinist's thoughts and preferences would not even be solicited or listened to, even for identical equipment. Therefore, the importance of defining buying influences in customer firms cannot be overstressed if effective marketing is to take place. In some industries, this is a very difficult undertaking, but there is no escaping it—if the industrial marketing manager does not know the buying influences for each customer firm, that manager cannot possibly communicate with them. And they will continue to influence purchasing decisions whether they are known or not.

Examples of Buying Influences

To give a better understanding of what is involved in multiple buying influences, some examples will be illustrated.

A *Purchasing Magazine* survey of 603 chemical industry purchasing executives disclosed that in only 13 percent of the cases, the purchasing agent alone chose the source of supply for the purchased products. And in 10 percent of the cases, buying influences other than the purchasing agent chose the source of supply. In the remaining 77 percent of the cases, the purchasing department and the other departments agreed upon the approved sources of supply, and then the purchasing department selected the particular supplier. In this survey, the average number of buying influences involved in the purchase of bulk chemicals was five, but the range ran from one to over 50 in a few cases.[2]

Viewed in terms of the type of transaction, the number of buying influences may also vary. For example, a *Business Week* study showed that an average of 3.5 buying influences are involved in a typical nonrepetitive type purchase, and this increased to 4.4 persons when such purchases were repetitive in nature.[3] *Factory* magazine, however, determined that 11.9 buying influences, not including purchasing personnel, are involved in the average industrial purchase.[4]

An in-depth study of the purchasing practices in a typical pulp and paper mill disclosed that 40 persons in that mill could influence the purchase of chemical products, 26 persons could influence the decision to buy instrumentation equipment, and 45 persons could influence the decision to purchase stock of paper preparation or conversion equipment.[5]

These examples are sufficient to make the desired point. Industrial purchasing involves a number of people in a number of positions, and industrial marketing involves discovering these people and their purchasing motivations. Although the task is difficult, there is no alternative, and this fact is recognized by every successful industrial marketing manager and industrial field salesman.

The Key Buying Influence

Complicating the multiple buying influence phenomenon is what is commonly referred to as the *key buying influence*. Basically, all this term means is that all buying influences in a customer firm are not equal in the influence they can exert. Some have more influence than others, and some have less, even though they all do have some influence on the particular product being purchased. The key buying influences are those who for some reason are able to sway other influences to their way of thinking, sometimes by design and sometimes without even realizing it. For example, there may be ten buying influences involved in the purchase of a piece of equipment, but perhaps two or three are able to influence the others. Obviously, the ability to pick out the key buying influences and sell them on the product in question is an integral part of industrial marketing. Equally obvious is the fact that this is not an easy task to accomplish.

There are few rules to apply in finding the key buying influences. Experience and diligence seem to be the major factors in locating such influences. Generally, it is the field salesman who ferrets out such information, but this does not have to be the case. The marketing manager can also exert concentrated efforts to locate the key buying influences through marketing research. To quote the marketing vice-president of FMC's Link Belt Division, "the guy who's good at locating the key buying influence has an innate curiosity and drive to get at the bottom of things."[6] Again it is important for the industrial marketing manager to realize that key buying influences exist in almost every case and to alert company personnel, particularly the field sales people, to the need to discover these people in each customer firm. It is then up to the field salesman to listen and observe in every buying situation encountered so as to determine who is most influential in the purchases made. Following such discoveries, records should be kept so that such knowledge, once discovered, is not lost when a salesman quits, dies, or retires. Locating key buying influences is a tough job that requires constant attention because customer firm personnel change jobs, retire, are promoted, and so on. When these things happen, buying influences are shuffled, with the result that purchasing decisions often change. Thus, keeping track of key buying influences is a constant job that must be done if the manager is to continue to market effectively to customer firms.

THE PURCHASING PROFESSIONAL

The typical buyer is a man past middle-life, sparse, wrinkled, intelligent, cold, passive, noncommittal with eyes like a codfish, polite in contact, but at the same time, unresponsive, cool, calm, and damnably composed as a concrete post or a plaster of paris cat; a human petrification with a heart of feldspar and without charm; or the friendly germ, minus bowels, passions, or a sense of humor. Happily, they never reproduce, and all of them finally go to hell.[7]

The preceding quotation probably summarizes well the feelings of many industrial field salesmen and marketing managers about the purchasing people in customer firms with whom they must deal in selling goods and services. The purchasing professional is considered by many to be the protagonist of the industrial salesman and the marketing manager.

For many industrial marketing managers, however, the purchasing professional must be considered a prime buying influence. He may not always make the decision, but is almost always involved in some way with what is being purchased. This professional may be known by a number of titles and may be specialized or generalized in his product knowledge, but he is the person most normally involved in the actual process of purchasing in industry. As stated earlier in this chapter, the specialization of the purchasing man often depends on the size of the firm, but there are no rules here, for product knowledge differs among individuals. The purchasing professional may be found working under a number of different titles, the most common of which are purchasing agent, purchasing manager, director of purchasing, vice-president of purchasing, buyer, senior buyer, procurement manager, procurement officer, materials procurement manager, and others. These titles differ among firms, and the jobs are not equal in rank, status, or compensation. For example, a buyer may be anyone within the purchasing department who has the responsibility of purchasing specific products, whereas the vice-president of purchasing may be the top purchasing officer in a corporation and actually responsible for purchasing policy and thus performing no actual buying himself. Yet all of these people are professional as regards industrial purchasing, and as such they are instrumental in their company's buying.

The Importance of the Purchasing Professional in Industrial Marketing

The purchasing professional is important to the industrial marketing manager as regards buying influences for a number of reasons. These are as follows: (1) the purchasing professional may have the actual line authority to purchase goods and services in some customer firms and thus must be considered a key buying influence; (2) in other instances, although he may not have the line authority to make the decision to buy or not to buy the products, he does have the authority to choose among suppliers the particular brand that will be purchased once someone else makes the decision to buy— here again, he must be considered a key buying influence; (3) in some instances, he may make recommendations regarding what brands will be purchased, and, in this position, he can and does influence purchases even though he possesses no line authority; (4) in cases where new industrial customers are being approached for the first time, the purchasing professional may be the only buying influence that can be initially determined, and thus he is important in gaining entrance to that company; and (5) the purchasing professional may often be that individual within the customer's firm who can refer the industrial field salesman and the marketing manager to those in his firm who actually make the decision.

What all this adds up to is that the purchasing professionals are important in industrial marketing, and they must be taken seriously. Although many industrial marketing people may be in sympathy with the opinion of the purchasing professional as expressed in the quotation at the beginning of this section, they would do well not to let their feelings be known when dealing with a purchasing agent. To quote a sales vice-president at Latrobe Steel, "We think it's important to work through the purchasing agent as the initial contact. If he's good, he can steer your salesmen in the right direction."[8] And a vice-president at Honeywell Test Instruments says, "You don't under any circumstances want to incur the wrath of the purchasing agent because often he is the one who holds the purse strings and has to approve the orders after the buying influence decides he wants your product."[9] These two quotations illustrate well the importance that most industrial marketing managers place on the purchasing professional. The purchasing professional should almost always be considered a buying influence and in some instances must be treated as a key buying influence.

Profile of the Purchasing Professional

Because the purchasing professional plays such a prominent role in the purchasing of industrial goods and services, it is critical that the marketing manager understand fully the role of the purchasing agent in each customer firm. In the actual business world, this would involve research and analysis, both demographically and psychographically, of each purchasing professional with whom the marketing manager must deal. What are the person's likes, dislikes, preferences, attitudes, opinions, prejudices, and so forth. In other words, he must be known well enough to communicate with. In a text such as this, such individual analysis is impossible, but a composite profile of the average purchasing professional may be helpful in determining what characteristics are involved and what functions are involved. A survey by *Purchasing Magazine* of more than 2,000 of its readers disclosed the following profile of the purchasing man.[10]

1. The average purchasing professional is 42 years old.
2. He has been a purchasing man for 13 years, has worked for two companies, and has held his present position for eight years.
3. His previous experience before achieving his present purchasing post was either in purchasing, accounting, or sales. Forty-two percent came from purchasing; 35 percent, from production; 18 percent, from sales.
4. He is well educated, with 77 percent having attended college and 38 percent receiving degrees. In addition, 12 percent attended graduate school, with five percent receiving advanced degrees. Majors in college were primarily in business administration, engineering, and accounting. Seventy-eight percent have continued to take college courses since leaving school.
5. He makes buying decisions that involve annual purchases of $18,745,000, with a range from three percent spending less than $1,000 and five percent spending more than $250,000,000.
6. He is usually a member of a company or plantwide committee that analyzes, reviews, or approves proposals for the purchase of goods and services. In such committees, he works closely with other departments such as top management, production, design engineering, maintenance engineering, sales, traffic, packaging, and accounting. Of all these departments, he works closest with top management and production.
7. The average purchasing man is involved in buying several or all of the following products or services: component parts; electrical equipment; maintenance, repair, and operating (MRO) supplies;

materials handling equipment; metals; chemicals; nonmetallic materials; office equipment; packaging; production tools; and transportation.

8. In addition to straightforward purchasing responsibilities, the average purchasing professional is involved with the following: evaluating and selecting suppliers and contractors (91 percent of those surveyed), evaluating capabilities of suppliers and contractors (86 percent of those surveyed), taking part in make-or-buy decisions (78 percent of those surveyed), specifying mode or carrier for incoming shipments (70 percent of those surveyed), being responsible for value analysis programs (56 percent of those surveyed), participating in the establishment or modification of specifications (57 percent of those surveyed), taking part in leasing decisions (41 percent of those surveyed), and recommending mode or carrier for outgoing shipments (25 percent of those surveyed).

9. What the average purchasing professional likes best about his job is trying to buy the best products at reasonable prices so that he can improve his firm's profits. What he likes least about his job is poor delivery by suppliers and people in other departments telling him how to purchase.

These are, of course, average statistics and do not apply to any one particular buyer. Collectively, however, they do tell an industrial marketing manager what to expect when encountering purchasing professionals. In summary, it can be said that the purchasing professional is a knowledgeable buyer who is well educated, very experienced, busy, probably underpaid in his own estimation, and probably impressed by his position and the amount of money he is responsible for spending and the ultimate authority in the buying of many products for his company. In addition, this person is often the initial contact for any new marketing endeavor, and he maintains daily contact with other departments within his firm. Thus, his ability to aid the industrial marketing manager and field salesman must be fully appreciated. At the same time, it is imperative that the two latter realize that there may be many more buying influences in a customer firm than the purchasing agent and that sometimes the professional purchaser is not an influence at all, but rather a person who rubber-stamps what is ordered by the key buying influences. In most cases, simply studying the purchasing man is not enough, but not to study him at all could be disastrous! The marketing manager should attempt to construct a profile such as the average profile shown in the *Purchasing Magazine* survey for each purchasing professional with whom the company must deal in its present and prospective customer firms.

UNDERSTANDING BUYER MOTIVATIONS

In addition to understanding the industrial buying process and defining the buying influences operating within that process, the industrial marketing manager must seek out and understand the buying motivations involved in each case. For instance, assume that a drill press is being marketed to an industrial user customer for use in the customer's production line. The main buying influences are located and found to be the purchasing agent, the foreman of the using department, the production supervisor, and the comptroller. Although each is interested in the same product—in this case the drill press— they may not all be looking for the same things in that drill press. The purchasing agent may make the decision among suppliers on the basis of price and certainty of delivery, the foreman may be choosing on the basis of ease of operation for the workers, the supervisor may make his decision on the basis of how well the drill press integrates into the entire production process, and the comptroller may choose on the basis of return on investment or laborsaving reductions or some other such financial factors.

The point is that although all four are buying influences for the same product, their buying motivations differ; and unless the industrial marketing manager and the field salesman address themselves to these differences, they may not communicate at all with their buying influences. If they are talking to the purchasing agent about ease of operation when that is not at all the basis of his decision, their marketing messages will have little effect. And, of course, it is imperative that the marketing manager address the motivations of the key buying influences if that manager is to sell the company's products or services. All this implies the need to analyze further the buying influences once they are defined and located. In the actual business world, this takes time, but effective industrial field salesmen are masters at the art. Through repeat calls and conversations and by keeping their eyes and ears open, they find out who in each customer firm is influenced by what, who is interested in what, and so forth. They then make a concentrated effort to discover what motivates each buying influence for their company's products or services.

Rational versus Emotional Motivations

Industrial buying influences may be motivated by both rational and emotional factors in choosing among suppliers of required goods and services. Rational motivating factors are those based primarily on economic considerations such as lowest price, reciprocity, technical assistance, service, certainty of delivery, and demands by customers and middlemen for certain brands. Emotional motivating factors, on the other hand, are more subjective in nature and may best be explained by such things as the image of a supplier or a brand, the size of a supplier's operation, the reputation of a supplier for prompt delivery, the reputation of a supplier for providing good technical assistance and service, and whether or not a company is a present supplier or a new supplier. Emotional motivating factors are based more on buyer impressions, attitudes, opinions, feelings, personal likes and dislikes, and so on, than on hard economic realities.

It is only in rare instances that both sets of factors are not found in the purchasing decision, and, therefore, both sets must be known and understood. Although it is generally conceded that industrial buyers are more rational in their purchasing than are ultimate consumers, those buyers are still people, and, as such, they are influenced by some degrees of emotion almost every time they purchase, even though they themselves do not realize it and will deny it vehemently. Much has been written about the lack of emotion in the buying of industrial goods and services, but this is not to imply that there is no emotion involved. An example may help to understand the point being made here. A purchasing agent who wants to buy a needed product at the best price may send out requests for proposals (RFPs) to qualified suppliers and then accept the lowest bid provided it is reasonable. The buyer will most likely claim that his decision is rational, being based on obtaining the lowest possible cost from screened suppliers. Upon analysis, however, it may be discovered he subjectively selected which suppliers were "qualified" and thus which ones would receive the RFPs. Selection of such suppliers might very well have been based on their size, brand name, image, hearsay from other buyers, and so forth. In this case, the buyer probably does not even realize the emotional characteristics involved. He honestly believes he made the decision based on the rational factor of lowest price and may never realize that subjectively he screened out other suppliers that might have given an even lower price and still met specifications and delivery dates. This is important—the buyer often does not realize the totality of his purchasing motivations. But the industrial marketing manager and the field salesman had better realize what factors really triggered the decision.

Motivations of Purchasing Professionals

Although all the buying influences have individual motivations, it is impossible to discuss all possible buying influences and their individual motivations. Therefore, attention will be focused on the purchasing agent or the other purchasing professionals and their motivations. These may then be related to the other buying influences.

Rational Motivations. The rational motives behind the buying of industrial purchasing professionals are relatively easy to understand. Basically, they are influenced by factors such as the following: (1) quality and uniformity of the products in relation to specifications; (2) lowest cost when the quality and uniformity are acceptable; (3) competency of the service accompanying the product; (4) competency of the technical assistance offered by suppliers in setting up the equipment, training the workers, and so forth; (5) certainty that the supplier can deliver in the desired quantities and at the required times; (6) reciprocity when buying elsewhere would violate the reciprocal agreement and have adverse economic repercussions; (7) buying locally or buying American when it is believed that economic benefits will accrue to the firm either in the short or the long run; (8) buying OEM component parts that have better consumer appeal and will increase the marketability of the buyer's own products; (9) buying capital equipment that will reduce labor costs; and (10) purchasing capital equipment that does not require worker re-training. These are just examples of what buyers look for on the rational side when judging suppliers in the buying process. These are all rational in nature because they are all based on economic considerations.

These rational motivations are important as they affect purchasing behavior in individual companies. For the marketing manager, it is well worth the effort to take time to evaluate individual customer companies and their purchasing professionals in terms of establishing the relative importance of such rational factors. Although most industrial customers and their purchasing people are interested in all forms of rational considerations leading to increased sales or profitability, they do not all rank such considerations equally. For example, some buyers are strongly motivated by lower costs, whereas others are much more concerned with quality and uniformity and will pay more for these considerations. The marketing manager can capitalize on such motivations if their existence is known. The key to this is as follows: (1) know what rational considerations are prevalent in industrial purchasing; (2) define which considerations exist in each customer firm and in their purchasing professionals; (3) rank these rational considerations for each firm and its buyers in terms of their relative importance; (4) maintain a file of these motivations so that company salesmen can call upon that file and use the appropriate considerations in their sales calls; and (5) build the marketing approach in terms of personal selling, advertising, product design, service, and so on, to match appropriate characteristics desired by each customer firm.

Emotional Motivations. In addition to the rational considerations, purchasing professionals are people and as such are also influenced by some very common emotional considerations. This is not to imply that all purchasing agents are motivated by the same emotional factors, but only that certain emotional characteristics appear to be common in purchasing professionals. Because such characteristics do appear commonly, they are important to the industrial marketing manager. Some of the more common characteristics are fear of the purchasing decision and possible personal repercussions, habit and complacency, desire for security, preservation of status, a gambling instinct to get ahead personally, and fear of the buying company's falling behind competitors because of faulty purchasing by the agent.[11] These factors are of great import to the industrial marketing manager and the field salesman. The purchasing agent primarily motivated by the preservation of his own job will purchase quite differently from the agent who is a gambler and intends to use his present purchasing job to make an impression and move ahead in his company. The former will be very conservative in purchasing and will show great reluctance in buying new products or buying from new suppliers or from new salesmen or getting involved in anything unknown because of fear of something backfiring and having adverse effects on his personal position. On the other hand, the gambler might welcome any new contact that might enable him to purchase something better or cheaper or both and thus make an impression on his superiors. Obviously, the industrial marketing manager could address efforts to these traits if their existence were known. Inversely, he could be destroyed by them if unaware of their existence. The key to all of this is as follows: (1) know what emotional characteristics are prevalent in industrial buyers; (2) define each purchasing professional in each customer firm to be reached in terms of those characteristics that apply; (3) rank the appropriate characteristics for each buyer in terms of what is most important to him, second most important, and so on; (4) maintain a file of these motivations that the salesman can call upon and use on each call and that advertising themes can be formulated upon; and (5) build the marketing approach in terms of personal selling, advertising, product design, service, and so forth, around the appropriate characteristics for each buyer. The rational and emotional motivational rankings can then be combined for a total ranking of priorities of each customer firm.

Another way of understanding the importance of these emotional factors is to integrate them into the industrial buying process previously discussed. For example, a buyer motivated highly by habit in the purchasing of a particular product would simply continue to buy that same product almost automatically on a repeat basis as long as nothing happened to disrupt his satisfaction. This is an almost perfect example of the straight rebuy situation explained earlier in this chapter. Attempts by a new supplier to sell this purchasing agent would be very difficult, if not impossible. On the other hand, the marketing manager who is fortunate enough to have habitual buyers in customer firms must concentrate on preserving the straight rebuy situation and keeping competitors away.

If the example is reversed with a purchasing agent who is a gambler, the picture changes radically. There are few straight rebuys with gambling purchasing agents, for they are constantly on the lookout for new approaches and have little allegiance to present suppliers. With this type of purchaser, modified rebuy and new task situations are commonplace, and nothing can be taken for granted by existing suppliers. This means that the marketing manager must concentrate efforts throughout the entire buying process if the company is going to keep such customers. On the other hand, new suppliers have an opportunity with this type of purchasing agent if they get into the buying process early and get the agent to switch, being able, of course, to prove the benefits from such switching. These examples show that emotional motivations can play a part in the actual buying process itself, and, therefore, they play a very large part in industrial competitive marketing strategy, which is often where the industrial marketing game is won or lost.

Cognitive Consonance. Still another way of conceptually understanding the emotional motivation of the purchasing professional is to look at his buying performance from a behavioral point of view. When is a purchasing agent psychologically pleased with his own personal professional performance? The chances are that he believes he has done a good job when he has accomplished the following: (1) purchased the right product—it meets specifications, and the using department is pleased; (2) purchased it at the right price; (3) purchased it at the right time—not too early to incur inventory costs and not too late to incur production line stoppages; (4) purchased it in the right quantity—not too much or too little; and (5) purchased the product from the right supplier or vendor—one with the image or reputation for delivering what is promised. When all of these factors are "right" in the mind of the individual purchasing agent, he is psychologically pleased with his buying and will not spend time looking for new products, new vendors, and the like.

This is what is known as cognitive consonance. As Shelby D. Hunt points out, "Cognitions are bits of knowledge one has about himself, about his behavior, and about his surroundings." He adds, "Two cognitions are consonant if one cognition follows from another."[12] This is what is happening with the purchasing agent who is psychologically satisfied that he is doing all the right things in his purchasing—he continues to purchase in the same manner! But if he becomes dissatisfied with any particular aspect of the purchase, cognitive dissonance sets in. In Hunt's words, "Two cognitions are in a dissonant state if, considering these two alone, the obverse of one cognition would follow from the other."[13] What this means is that if all factors are not "right" in the mind of the purchasing agent, dissonance is created, and he will look for other products or other suppliers. The latter can take place when the using department complains about the product purchased because of poor quality or late delivery or when excess inventories are discovered and the agent finds that he has been sold too much. When things like this happen, the purchaser will look past present suppliers to new sources that may alleviate his dissonance.

In a simplistic way, much of the success in industrial marketing can be explained in these terms. Industrial salesmen take away a competitor's customers by convincing the latter that all these things are not "right" and thus getting them to switch. Once the switch is made, the salesman's emphasis changes and he now convinces these same buyers that he is providing these "right" factors and that there is no need to consider other suppliers. Conversely, industrial marketing managers and field salesmen lose customers by getting complacent and not making efforts to ensure that all these factors are "right." In short, attempts are made to create dissonance in competitors' customers and to create consonance in the company's own customers. This is not as simple as it sounds. What is "right" to one purchasing agent is not necessarily what is "right" to another, as basic purchasing motivations will differ among buyers. Thus, the cognitive consonance approach does not relieve the industrial marketing manager of the problem of truly understanding buyers. On the contrary, it only reinforces the importance of such knowledge.

It should be apparent at this point that, contrary to popular opinion, emotional characteristics play quite a role in industrial purchasing even though such purchasing is more rational than that found in the ultimate consumer market. Rarely does an industrial purchase take place without some type of emotion being involved. In addition, as specifications force products to become almost identical and price competition is avoided, the decisions to purchase are often made on the basis of emotional factors, as the rational factors have been neutralized. Emotion is a big factor in a great deal of industrial purchasing, and the industrial marketing manager must recognize this and integrate it into the industrial buying process along with the better understood rational factors. Most of what has been discussed here applies to the purchasing professional, but it is just as applicable to all the buying influences. To market effectively into any particular company requires that these motivations of all buying influences be understood and considered in formulating appropriate marketing strategy.

CHAPTER SUMMARY

Understanding how industrial corporations purchase goods and services is imperative for effective industrial marketing, as industrial purchasing is the other side of the coin, and it is highly unlikely any manager can effectively market without a thorough understanding of how such firms actually buy. It must be understood that there is an industrial purchasing process and that people, not companies, actually do the purchasing. Those people in each company who have an effect on what is purchased are called buying influences, and those buying influences differ among firms, even firms in the same industry buying essentially the same goods and services. In fact, it is very possible that buying influences can change in the same company on subsequent purchases of the same product, as people are promoted, are demoted, are transferred, are fired, quit, or retire. In addition, all buying influences are not equal in the influence they exert and some are considered key buying influences. Moreover, each buying influence may be motivated by different factors, and these must be understood if they are to be addressed in the marketing strategy. Some of these factors are rational or economic in nature, and some are emotionally derived. In summary, the task of the industrial marketing manager is to view each customer firm as being unique and to attempt to discover how the buying process is used, who is involved, and what motivates those who are involved. With this base, the actual job of industrial marketing can take place.

QUESTIONS FOR CHAPTER 4

1. Is there a standard industrial buying process common to companies in the industrial market?

2. How does marketing to a straight rebuy situation differ from marketing to a new task situation in the industrial market?

3. The term buying influences refers to economic, social, legal, technological, and political considerations in the economy that affect industrial purchasing practices. Do you agree or disagree with this statement? If you agree, why do you agree? If you disagree, why do you disagree?

4. If you were given the assignment, how would you go about locating the buying influences in a business firm that is a potential customer for the products of your company?

5. In most cases, the purchasing agent is more of a hindrance than a help to the industrial marketing manager, and, as such, he should be avoided or evaded at all costs. Do you agree or disagree with this statement? If you agree, why do you agree? If you disagree, why do you disagree?

5

PLANNING THE INDUSTRIAL MARKETING STRATEGY

Once target customers have been defined, located, and analyzed, the actual task of marketing decision making begins. This basically involves the formulation of a marketing strategy to reach those target customers. Products and services must be developed that relate to the needs of those customers. In turn, those products and services must be promoted so that the customers are exposed to them. Those same products and services must be distributed properly so that they are physically accessible to the target customers. And they must be priced in a manner that these customers will relate to. In addition, the decisions involved in the strategy must consider competition and competitive reactions, changes in the marketplace, return on investment requirements, the physical and financial capabilities of the marketing firm, government regulations, and many other such factors.

MARKETING STRATEGY

As might be expected, the ability to design, implement, and control marketing strategy often means success or failure for the marketing manager. This is no less true in industrial marketing than it is in consumer marketing. Strategy can be defined as a plan of action created to achieve predetermined objectives. For the industrial marketing manager, designing the marketing strategy involves a number of steps that should be taken if that strategy is to have the best chance for being effective. These steps are as follows: (1) conduct a situational analysis of the present market situation, (2) identify the target market to be reached in the strategy, (3) establish marketing objectives that are to be attained in the strategy, (4) select and implement the proper marketing mix that will permit attainment of the objectives in the defined market target, and (5) control the strategy to determine if the strategy did attain the desired objectives. These are very important considerations and it is imperative that any industrial marketing manager understand fully what is involved in each of these steps. As will be shown later in this chapter, these considerations will become an integral part of the manager's formal marketing plan. Therefore, each of these steps will be analyzed in detail.

Analysis of the Present Market Situation

This involves a thorough analysis of the present market situation, both within and without the company, through the use of marketing intelligence, The industrial marketing manager would be analyzing such factors as (1) the performance of the firm's industry relative to the growth and fluctuations in the general economy with special emphasis on the derived demand aspects; (2) the firm's sales volume and market share; (3) the company's product and/ or service mix; (4) the composition of present and potential specifically defined markets; (5) the buying practices in corporations in those defined markets; (6) production technologies and distribution patterns affecting the company; (7) pricing trends and the emphasis on price competition; (8) the philosophy, goals, and corporate structure of the company's business organization; (9) the capabilities of the company's production, engineering, financial, and sales facilities; (10) competition, both from competing firms in the same industries and from competing firms in other industry, both foreign and domestic; (11) the social, legal, and political environment in which the company operates; (12) the major marketing problems that have confronted the company in the past or are now confronting it; (13) the relative emphasis on all aspects of the firm's promotional strategy including advertising, personal selling, sales promotion, publicity, and public relations; (14) distribution capabilities of the company; and (15) pricing capabilities of the company with emphasis on relevant costs and competition. There are many other factors that might be included in such a situational analysis. The idea here is for the marketing manager to view and review every possible factor that could be involved in the final marketing strategy to ensure that decisions are not made where data are not known.

Identification of the Target Markets

As was developed in detail in the third chapter of this text, identification of the target markets involves the careful definition of markets in terms of the standard industrial classification system and then clearly locating customers within this SIC system. Once this is done, the marketing manager must objectively appraise what resistances will be encountered and what difficulties will have to be overcome in marketing to these customers. The fact that potential market targets exist is not enough! The manager must realize that competitors will also be looking at these markets and that penetrating these markets will not be easy. Thus, it is important that the manager attempt to define the areas of difficulty that will be encountered in the attempt to penetrate those markets. The company's capabilities of overcoming these difficulties must be objectively evaluated if effective marketing is to take place. This step shows the importance of a sound situational analysis such as was described in the first step. Ideally, these assessments should be performed before products are produced, and such assessment should take place for each product in each market segment. In addition, these assessments should be viewed by the marketing manager as go–no go situations. To illustrate, if the market potential is not sufficient to support the costs involved, the market should not be entered, and perhaps the product should be dropped from consideration. Similarly, if the manager's firm does not have the financial, technical, or managerial capabilities to overcome anticipated competition and buyer resistances, then the decision to market the product should be abandoned. In other words, when the assessments of market potential, resistances and difficulties, and the company's capabilities are favorable, it is a "go" situation. But when any or all of these same assessments are unfavorable, it may very well be a "no go" situation, and other marketing opportunities should be sought. The major point in this step is that the identification of a market target means much more than just the definition and location of that target— it also means an objective assessment of the company's ability to penetrate that same target.

Establishment of Marketing Objectives

If the "go" decision has been reached in the previous step, the marketing manager must then set specific realistic objectives that the strategy is to achieve. In addition to being specific and realistic, these objectives must be consistent with overall corporate goals and objectives, and they must be capable of measurement. If the objectives cannot be measured, the marketing manager will never know if the strategy accomplished what it was intended to accomplish. And if this is not known, corrective action can hardly be taken. This step then involves the determination of objectives reflecting corporate philosophies and objectives and market capacities in such categories as (1) sales volume—by product line—by market area—by customer type—by time period; (2) sales growth rates and market shares; (3) penetration of present and potential market targets; (4) product mix—number and breadth of lines—standard and custom offerings; (5) profitability or return on investment—by product lines—by sales districts—by market segments—by time periods; (6) social responsibility and contribution to the community; (7) company image; and (8) innovation in all aspects of marketing strategy. The real point in this step is to stipulate specific realistic objectives that are capable of accomplishment and capable of measurement, at the same time being consistent with corporate goals and objectives.

Corporate goals and objectives comprise the overall business directions the company plans to take. Because many companies are very complex organizations, no single set of objectives can represent the entire company and its personnel. Therefore, top managements often formulate statements of the company's general mission and its particular aims. They then require the various departments within the company to define their own more specific objectives within the constraints of the overall corporate or business objectives. Typical of the types of statements found in a company's corporate objectives are "maximize revenue," "continue to be a good corporate citizen," and "stay one step ahead of competitors through a thorough understanding of the market and customer needs." These examples, taken from a list of corporate objectives of a large industrial corporation, are typical corporate or business objectives. They are generally very broad and relate to many functions of the company and not just to marketing. In addition, some corporate objectives relate to the marketing function, and some do not. But it is important that the manager know the company's overall business or corporate objectives well enough to ensure that marketing objectives are consistent with their general corporate direction.

Again the value of sound thinking in the situational analysis and the market assessments in the first two steps becomes apparent. If the marketing manager has not made an honest and objective effort to determine where the company is now, that manager can hardly define realistic objectives as to where it is to go in the future.

Selection and Implementation of the Appropriate Marketing Mix

Once objectives have been established, the industrial marketing manager must find the proper marketing mixes for accomplishing those objectives. The mix is that combination of product, promotion, channels, and price that is correct for his respective firm in the defined market targets. Selection of the right combination of marketing mixes comes from correctly covering the three previous steps, and the intelligent industrial marketing manager will have made good use of marketing information, experience, and personal judgment in selecting and implementing his marketing mix. This is a complicated step and involves the formulation of substrategies in product, promotion, channels, and price. The product substrategy would consider such factors as additions to the product line, deletions, alterations, expansions, as well as service and technical assistance offerings, and so forth. The distribution substrategy would be concerned with formulation of channels and methods for more effectively moving products and title to the market targets. The promotion substrategy would consider the proper combination of personal selling, advertising, and sales promotion to communicate the desired messages to the target customers and their buying influences. The pricing substrategy would be involved with the formulation of list prices, discounts from those list prices, rebates, special deals, handling of transportation charges, and nonprice competition. In addition, research substrategy would be developed to uncover new market segments, refine knowledge of customer firm characteristics, and understand better the buying behavior of customer firms. Included also in this step would be the tactical scheduling of activities within each of these substrategies to form the overall marketing strategy. This would involve such things as detailing activities that are to be performed, assigning of responsibilities for performing these activities, and the determining of time frames for completion of these activities. These latter activities are extremely important if the substrategies are to complement one another and contribute effectively to the effectiveness of the overall strategy. To illustrate, if new product development is not coordinated with the advertising of those products involved, an integrated overall marketing strategy cannot result. The task of the industrial marketing manager in this step is to decide what activities must be performed in the areas of product, promotion, channels, and price and then implement these activities in a coordinated manner. It is in this area of strategy formulation that such techniques as PERT (program evaluation and review technique) and CPM (critical path method) have been found useful by industrial marketing managers. Such techniques as these permit integration of the various substrategies over time periods.

The term *marketing mix* has two different meanings, both of which should be understood by the marketing manager. One meaning is that the manager needs to develop a marketing mix to serve the needs of a specific target market. It is in that context that the term is used in the preceding paragraph. At the same time, however, it should be understood that the marketing mix can be viewed as a blending or mixing of the four elements of product, promotion, distribution, and price to maximize impact in the target market. In other words, the term *marketing mix* refers to more than the four elements themselves—in short, to the optimum blending or coordinating of these same elements by the marketing manager.

Control of the Marketing Strategy

After the marketing mix has been selected and implemented, the task of the marketing manager is to plan the control of the strategy to determine if it is succeeding or not. Is it or is it not achieving the desired objectives? If it is, the manager should attempt to find out why—what is he doing correctly that he can apply elsewhere? In this manner, the manager can capitalize on correct moves and continue to do what works. If, however, the strategy is not achieving the desired objectives, the manager should determine why it is not! In this manner, corrections can be made either in reevaluating objectives that may have been unrealistic or in reworking various aspects of the marketing strategy, which may have been in error. The latter may dictate product changes, pricing alterations, switching channels, or revising promotional efforts. Regardless of what has to be changed, a marketing strategy without a control effort is virtually meaningless to the industrial marketing manager. This final step can also be complicated, as it involves a development of measures or criteria whereby the performance in each area of the strategy can be evaluated and controlled and whereby the feasibility of the objectives in each area can be assessed.

Criteria that can be used here include such as (1) the predetermined objectives in the strategy, (2) historical trends in performance, (3) industry averages in performance, (4) budget considerations, (5) industry ratios, and (6) adherence to predetermined time schedules.

Once measurement criteria are defined, questions such as the following must be considered for each area of the strategy: Who is responsible for each area of the strategy? What routine control reports should be required, and from whom? How often and when should such control checks be made? How much deviation from criteria standards will be permitted, and for how long? If unacceptable deviation does occur, how is the cause of such deviation to be pinpointed? Who is responsible for overall control and evaluation of the marketing strategy? Are the plans and substrategies properly coordinated among all areas of the marketing mix? How are the results of each period's evaluation to be used in the marketing strategy for the coming period?

It is much easier to describe these marketing activities in concept than it is to carry them out in the practical world of industrial marketing management. Nevertheless, these activities must be undertaken by every marketing manager if the decisions made in product, promotion, channels, and price are to have any continuity. In this regard, marketing managers have turned to the marketing plan as a way of integrating all the various areas of marketing responsibility. The marketing plan is the tool that allows the manager to integrate all marketing activities to a central theme and to keep track of all of strategy activities once they interrelate.

THE MARKETING PLAN

A marketing plan is a systematic anticipation and analysis of future changes coupled with the methodology for adapting to such changes—methodology that will allow the industrial marketing manager to capitalize on the changes in order to meet objectives and to gain an edge over competitors. Thus, the marketing plan is future-oriented and can relate to the immediate, intermediate, or long-run futures. It is imperative that any realistic marketing plan be defined in terms of the industrial company's corporate goals and philosophies and also with regard to where that company hopes to go in terms of its market share, its product mix, its profits and return on investment, and its legal and social responsibilities. The immediate marketing plan should be a coordination of parts dealing with industrial customers to be reached, products or services to be marketed, prices to be charged, advertising themes and media to be used, personal selling efforts to be expended, distribution methods to be used, and so on, through the entire marketing strategy as was previously described in detail. In short, the marketing plan is the formal written documentation of the marketing strategy—it is composed of a series of subplans in the functional areas of marketing that allow the company to adapt to anticipated and even unanticipated changes in accordance with carefully defined objectives over a specified period of time in the future.

Essential Characteristics of the Marketing Plan

There is no single marketing plan that is correct for all industrial firms. On the contrary, the best plan for one industrial marketing company may be unique, even within that company's particular industry. But there are basic characteristics that are essential to the effectiveness of any marketing plan. These characteristics are incorporated into the seven-step planning illustrated in Fig. 5.1. Although the procedure illustrated in Fig. 5.1 is not intended to be all inclusive, it should suggest to the industrial marketing manager areas where planning efforts should be expended. As applied to the industrial market, the marketing planning process in Fig. 5.1 should follow a step-by-step process such as was outlined earlier in this chapter in the discussion of marketing strategy. Note should be taken of the circular flow of the illustrated process indicating that marketing planning is a continuous process and in need of constant supervision and updating. It is not a one-shot endeavor that is undertaken once every year or every five years whether it is needed or not! Again it must be realized that the marketing plan is the written formal documentation of the manager's marketing strategy.

The Reasons for Marketing Planning

The marketing plan is not a luxury item for the industrial marketing manager. Indeed, it is an absolute necessity if the manager is to implement marketing strategy with any degree of effectiveness. The reasons for marketing planning can be summarized as follows: (1) without such a plan, the marketing manager has no basis upon which to carry out the other managerial functions of staffing, motivating, and controlling; (2) without such a plan, the manager loses control over the future of the firm—he has no ability to react in a logical and well-reasoned manner; (3) without such a plan, the manager

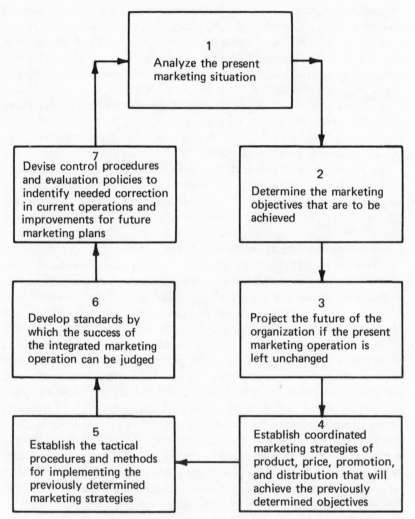

Fig. 5.1. Model of the industrial marketing planning process. (Reprinted by permission from Robert W. Haas and Thomas R. Wotruba, "The Marketing Attack Plan," *Bank Marketing* 3, September 1971, 60.)

inevitably ends up managing by crisis rather than by design; (4) without such a plan, the manager is forced to remain on the defense with marketing, constantly making decisions to counteract the well-timed, well-planned offensive thrusts of competitors; (5) without such a plan, it is difficult for the manager to make sure that short-run decisions have long-run continuity; and (6) without such a plan, it is almost impossible for the marketing manager to keep track of all of responsibilities in a systematic and orderly manner. As the scope and complexity of responsibilities expand, it is more difficult to keep reins on all the activities and to coordinate them into one overall integrated marketing effort, which is the ultimate responsibility of the marketing manager. In short, a marketing plan is necessary to implement a marketing strategy effectively.

Marketing planning in the industrial market differs little in principle from marketing planning in the consumer market. The same basic principles apply. In practice, however, they may not be the same because of the many basic differences such as were described in the first chapter of this text. It is the task of the industrial marketing manager to take the basics of sound marketing planning, such as have been discussed here, and adapt them to the specific requirements of the industrial market and the respective industry or industries involved.

MATRIX MODELS IN INDUSTRIAL MARKETING PLANNING

The use of matrix models has proved quite beneficial for many industrial marketing managers in the implementation of their marketing plans and strategies. Matrix models can be integrated very easily into the general process of industrial marketing planning such as was illustrated in Fig. 5.1. Simply defined, a matrix model is but a rectangular array of mathematical elements. Applied to industrial marketing, this approach may be used to form a grid or matrix showing the relationships between customers to be reached and products and/or services to be marketed. Table 5.1 illustrates the basic matrix used in marketing strategy formulation and planning and shows the interrelationships between products and/or services and present and potential customer segments.

The logic of this matrix, in relation to marketing strategy and planning, is irrefutable. Whether realized or not, the industrial marketing manager must make decisions pertaining to specific products and specific markets. It then logically follows that to make such decisions, the manager must know how each of the company products is performing in each of its target market segments. This is the essence of the basic matrix illustrated in Table 5.1. Its real value is that it forces the manager to look at the relationship of each product or service and each customer target market via a grid or matrix approach.

After the marketing manager has identified, analyzed, and classified customers and products in some meaningful manner, he undertakes a form of cell analysis on each and every cell in the basic matrix. One such method of analysis is illustrated in Table 5.2. It is recommended that such a cell analysis be conducted for each and every cell, or customer/product relationship, in the basic matrix illustrated back in Table 5.1. This analysis would show the manager the trend in each cell of total industry sales, the company's sales, and the company's market share over time. From such analysis, the manager can determine where the company is losing on the industry, where it is gaining on the industry, and where it is holding its own for each product or product group and each target market. If the manager then plugs such cell analyses back into the basic matrix, the manager can see at a glance where the company is doing well and where it is doing poorly—where things are OK and where marketing attention is needed.

A simple illustration may help to show the value of this matrix in planning industrial marketing strategy. Assume that (1) the letters *UP* indicate a favorable cell analysis—industry sales are rising as are company sales, and the company's market share is increasing; (2) the letters *DOWN* indicate an unfavorable cell analysis—company sales are not keeping up with industry sales, and the market share is decreasing; and (3) the letters *NC* indicate no change or a

Table 5.1
BASIC CUSTOMER/PRODUCT MATRIX

		Customer-Prospect Mix				
		1	2	3	4	i
Product-Service Mix	1					
	2					
	3					
	4					
	i					

Source: William J. E. Crissy and Robert M. Kaplan, "Matrix Models for Marketing Planning," *MSU Business Topics* 11 (Summer 1963), 53.

Note: Reprinted by permission of the author and the publisher, Division of Research, Graduate School of Business Administration, Michigan State University.

Table 5.2
SEGMENT ANALYSIS

	Past	Future	Trend
Industry Sales	Market $	Potential Market $	Increase, Decrease, or No Change
Company Sales	Sales $	Potential Sales $	Increase, Decrease, or No Change
Company Share of Market	Market Share %	Potential Market Share %	Increase, Decrease, or No Change

Source: William J. E. Crissy and Robert M. Kaplan, "Matrix Models for Marketing Planning," *MSU Business Topics* 11 (Summer 1963), 53.

Note: Reprinted by permission of the author and the publisher, Division of Research, Graduate School of Business Administration, Michigan State University.

static cell analysis, where the company's performance approximates industry performance, and its market share is relatively unchanged. Assume now that such cell analyses as those illustrated in Table 5.2 have been conducted and that the cells in the basic matrix are evaluated in terms of favorable, unfavorable, or static situations and that these findings are then plugged back into the basic matrix and the results shown in Table 5.3.

In situation 1, there is a definite customer problem, as the cell analyses show an unfavorable picture only for customer 2, and the analysis is unfavorable in three of the four cells in the basic matrix relating to this customer. Thus, it appears that the problem is not a product-oriented one, but rather poor marketing in some matter to customer 2.

In situation 2, however, a different picture presents itself. Here, a distinct product problem is in evidence, as the trend is definitely unfavorable for product 2, but not for the other products, nor can it be traced to any particular classification of customer.

In situation 3, a completely different phenomenon is observed, as no particular product or customer problem can be identified. Product 2 is down with customer 1, and product 3 is down with customer 3, whereas all other cells appear favorable on the basis of the analyses. In the implementation of these types of matrix analyses, there is no telling what combinations will occur; but there is also no doubt that by using such analyses, the market-

Table 5.3

SITUATIONS ARISING FROM MATRIX ANALYSES

Situation 1

Products	Customers			
	1	2	3	4
1	UP	DOWN	UP	NC
2	UP	NC	UP	UP
3	UP	DOWN	NC	UP
4	UP	DOWN	UP	UP

Situation 2

Products	Customers			
	1	2	3	4
1	UP	NC	UP	UP
2	DOWN	NC	DOWN	DOWN
3	UP	UP	UP	NC
4	NC	UP	UP	UP

Situation 3

Products	Customers			
	1	2	3	4
1	UP	NC	UP	UP
2	DOWN	UP	UP	UP
3	UP	UP	DOWN	UP
4	UP	UP	UP	NC

ing manager knows much more than would be known without it. And marketing strategy will differ according to what is discovered. For example, what is the corrective action that the marketing manager would take in situation 1 to alleviate the customer problems with customer 2? What action would be taken to correct the product problem found in situation 2? His marketing strategy will differ according to what is discovered in his matrix analysis. This is the real value of such matrices. They do not solve marketing problems in and of themselves, but rather give marketing direction to the manager, and thus their contribution to industrial marketing planning and strategy formulation is invaluable, particularly in the situational analysis stage of the marketing planning process. In the three situations just illustrated, the marketing manager in each instance would apply a different marketing strategy to correct what is wrong and thus the basic strategy hinges on what is revealed by the matrix analysis.

Application of the Matrix Model

The discussion of matrix models as they apply to industrial marketing planning and strategy formulation has thus far been of a general nature. It may be worthwhile, for practical purposes, to show how the model can be applied in an actual marketing management situation.

As stated earlier, such models are very easily adapted to the industrial market where customers are relatively few in number and where they can be identified by SIC number. What then is involved is that the marketing manager code company sales in some manner so that products sold can be identified with customer groups. And, of course, some source of industry data must be available to plot the appropriate industry figures. But all these things are possible once the marketing manager begins to think in terms of the matrix approach and what it offers.

An example of how to use the matrix analysis may be helpful. Let us refer back to the manufacturer of farm machinery discussed in chapter three and illustrated in Table 3.3. It will be recalled that such a manufacturer would be classified by the SIC number 3522, and specific target markets were determined through the use of input-output analysis and then also identified by SIC numbers. If one assumes that this manufacturer's product mix consists of farm tractors, balers, combines, harvesting machines, and mowers, the major or basic matrix can be developed as is illustrated in Table 5.4. This basic matrix allows the marketing manager in the company to cross-relate products and major markets located by input-output analysis and the standard industrial classification system. Now it is the task of the industrial marketing manager to analyze each cell in a manner similar to that previously illustrated in Table 5.2. For the sake of illustration, the cell depicting tractor sales to SIC 5083 wholesale distributors of farm machinery and equipment will be

Table 5.4

BASIC MATRIX OF A MANUFACTURER OF FARM MACHINERY SIC 3522

Product Mix	SIC 0112 Cotton Growers	SIC 0113 Cash Grain Growers	SIC 0114 Tobacco Growers	SIC 0119 Field Crops	SIC 3522 Manufacturers of Farm Machinery & Equipment	SIC 5083 Wholesale Distributors of Farm Machinery & Equipment	SIC 5252 Farm Equipment Dealers	Other Markets
Farm Tractors								
Balers								
Combines								
Harvesting Machines								
Mowers								

analyzed. In this illustration, the cell analysis will be expanded to include past, present, and future industry and company sales figures, and this revised cell analysis is shown in Table 5.5.

Finding the data to plug into this cell analysis may not always be easy to accomplish, especially with regard to industry data, but it can be done if the marketing manager is willing to expend some effort and imagination. Past and present company sales figures are relatively easy to determine because they are a matter of company sales records. This is true, however, only where the company has made efforts to determine what products were sold into what markets. Potential company sales are obtained from the company's own sales forecasts, which must be performed regardless of whether matrix models are used or not. Just how far back in the past to go and how far into the future to forecast are decisions that must be determined by the individual marketing manager and depend upon such factors as product life cycles and market development rates. For products with long life cycles and relatively static market development rates, 20 or 30 years of data might be available. For other products with short life cycles in highly volatile industries, six months might be as far back as the manager could go and still obtain meaningful data.

Industry data for particular products in particular market segments may

Table 5.5
SEGMENT ANALYSIS

		SIC 5083 Wholesale Distributors of Farm Machinery & Equipment			
F a r m T r a c t o r s	Industry Sales	Past Market $	Present Market $	Potential Market $	Increase, Decrease, or No Change
	Company Sales	Past Sales $	Present Sales $	Potential Sales $	Increase, Decrease, or No Change
	Company Share of Market	Past Market Share %	Present Market Share %	Potential Market Share %	Increase, Decrease, or No Change

Source: Adapted from William J. E. Crissy and Robert M. Kaplan, "Matrix Models for Marketing Planning," *MSU Business Topics* 11 (Summer 1963).

be more difficult to obtain, depending upon the particular industry involved. In most cases, though, reasonable estimates can be made from data published in trade publications, trade association materials, industrial directories, governmental sources, and other such sources such as were discussed in the third chapter of this text. In this instance, data could be found via input-output analysis to show what percentage of farm machinery sales are made to SIC 5083, as well as to all the other SIC classified markets in the basic matrix.

Then the marketing manager would have to estimate, on the basis of past sales data or trade association data or trade publication data, and so on, how much of total farm machinery sales is in tractors and in balers, combines, harvesting machines, and mowers. This would allow him to plug in past and present industry estimates with which to compare company sales figures. Potential sales for the industry group could be developed from projections published in such sources as the *U.S. Industrial Outlook 1972 With Projections to 1980.*[1] Using this approach, the cell analysis could be completed in a manner such as is shown in Table 5.6. The data shown in the table are derived from two assumptions: (1) that tractor sales are 10 percent of all farm machinery sales; and (2) SIC 5083 sales are 15 percent of all SIC 508 sales, which are those projected in the *U.S. Industrial Outlook 1972.* In an actual situation, the marketing manager would not be able to assume such percentages, but rather would have to make estimates based on past data.

As Table 5.6 illustrates, this analysis is very revealing to the company's marketing manager. It shows exactly what is taking place in the distributor market in regard to sales of farm tractors. It also forces the manager to look at industry sales, which that manager might not otherwise do, and to make comparisons with sales of the company. In this example, although the company's sales are increasing, they are not keeping pace with industry sales, with the result that the market share is steadily decreasing and the trend is not favorable. Armed with this knowledge, the marketing manager is now in the position to determine why the trend is unfavorable and also to determine what actions must be taken in the marketing substrategies of product, promotion, distribution or channels, and price in attempting to reverse the trend. Without such matrix analysis, it is highly doubtful that sales of particular products such as farm tractors into specific markets such as distributors would be analyzed in such detail.

This same procedure would then be repeated for each cell of the basic matrix, thereby providing such data for each product and each market target. Then the basic matrix would be completed in terms of favorable or unfavorable cell trends similar to the manner described earlier in the chapter with the three examples. This would show the industrial marketing manager where the company stands with each of its products in each of its defined markets and would provide the foundation for corrective marketing action to be taken

Table 5.6

SEGMENT ANALYSIS

		SIC 5083 Wholesale Distributors of Farm Machinery & Equipment			
		Past Market $ (1967)	Present Market $ (1972)	Potential Market $ (1975)	Trend
F a r m	Industry Sales	$35,754,000	$50,325,000	$62,250,000	Up
T r a c t o r s	Company Sales	$ 6,274,000	$ 7,369,000	$ 8,004,000	Up
	Company Share of Market	17.5%	14.6%	12.9%	Down

in the unfavorable cells and maintenance marketing in the cells that are found favorable. In other words, this type of analysis would point out to the manager areas of decision making in product, promotion, channels, and price that would have to be incorporated into the marketing plan and overall marketing strategy.

Matrix modeling is very appropriate in the industrial market owing to the types of products that are produced and the relatively small number of customer classifications that can be defined in terms of SIC. Matrix models are not a substitute for decision making, but rather should be used as a method for isolating problem areas that then can be incorporated into the situational analysis stage of the formal marketing planning process for the formulation of effective industrial marketing strategy.

CHAPTER SUMMARY

The intent of this chapter has been to create the impression of the importance of marketing planning and marketing strategy formulation. Without such an approach, the individual marketing manager will forever be on the defensive with all its accompanying disadvantages that usually lead to management by crisis. A marketing planning model and format were illustrated to show the scope and complexity of such planning and to give insight into what should be included in a realistic and effective marketing plan. The concept of matrix modeling was then introduced because of the easy adaptation of such models to industrial marketing planning and their capability to pinpoint marketing problem areas for strategy considerations. The logic behind the matrix model was examined, as well as sources of data available to make the model operational. Then a practical application of the matrix model was shown, using a manufacturer of farm machinery and equipment as an example. Finally, the value of the marketing planning model and the matrix models was developed to show how they could be used to advantage by the industrial marketing manager in making decisions in products, promotion, channels, and prices. The real value of the models in terms of practical industrial marketing management is that they allow the manager to focus attention on particular products and specific market segments as opposed to trying to make decisions pertaining to all products in all markets at the same time, which is virtually an impossible undertaking. The approach taken in this chapter will permit the manager to formulate marketing strategy in regard to products and customers individually instead of to all of them collectively. By doing so, the manager will find it easier to formulate substrategies in product, promotion, channels, and price that will comprise the overall marketing strategy.

QUESTIONS FOR CHAPTER 5

1. Some industrial marketing managers contend that marketing planning is something they do before they start to make decisions and take action and that, whether they planned or not, the actions they take and the decisions they make would be the same. Do you agree or disagree with these managers? Explain your reasons.
2. Should the first step in formulating a realistic marketing plan be the systematic gathering of information, or should it be the establishment of realistic quantifiable objectives? Explain your answer.
3. What do you believe are the major benefits to be obtained from marketing planning in the industrial market?
4. Why are matrix models so applicable for effective marketing planning in the industrial market? Explain your reasons.
5. If an industrial marketing plan is to be effective, what essential components must that plan contain?

6

INDUSTRIAL
MARKETING INTELLIGENCE

As the preceding chapter has indicated, effective marketing strategy formulation is dependent upon sound information from the marketplace. Without such information, the industrial marketing manager must base decisions on hunch and speculation, two factors often contributing to marketing failure. It should be recognized that product decisions made without the benefit of market input from those who will purchase and use that product may easily be in error or irrelevant. The same logic applies to the areas of promotion, distribution, and price and, of course, to the overall marketing plan and strategy. Information must be obtained from the marketplace if sound decisions are to be made. From a marketing strategy perspective, such information is called marketing intelligence.

MARKETING INTELLIGENCE

Marketing intelligence refers to any useful information that could be used by the marketing manager to enhance the competitive position of the company. This is a broad encompassing definition that could include almost any information that the marketing manager could use to make more effective decisions in market segmentation; in overall marketing strategy formulation and marketing planning; and in the marketing substrategies of product, promotion, channels, and price. Such information could vary all the way from complaints by distributors about packaging to data provided by the company's own accounting department regarding increasing costs of raw materials, and so forth. In addition, marketing intelligence can be both internal (that obtained from within the marketing firm) or external (that obtained outside of the firm). Examples of the former are reports by the production department of production capabilities that must be considered in sales forecasting, cost analysis data provided by the company's accounting department, credit ratings of potential customers as reported by the company's credit department, estimates of engineering capabilities as supplied by the firm's engineering department, cash flow data provided by the comptroller's office, and other such types of internal information that have marketing applications.

All of these can be termed a form of marketing intelligence, for they can have definite effects on marketing decisions being made by the marketing manager. To illustrate, adding new products to the company's product line to fill a market demand may make little sense if the company lacks production, engineering, or financial capabilities. Therefore, any internally generated bits of information pertaining to such capabilities would be useful to the manager and should be considered as marketing intelligence.

Marketing intelligence can also be external or from outside the company. Some examples of this are complaints about products or services, service parts, and so on, by customers or middlemen; feedback from sales personnel or manufacturers' reps regarding customer preferences or buying habits; information obtained from trade publications and trade associations and other such sources of secondary data; analysis of competitive reactions; and any forms of formal marketing research surveys, studies, and reports. To illustrate again, adding new products to the company's product line is foolish if customer buying habits and preferences, competitive reactions, and so forth, are ignored or overlooked.

Sources of Industrial Marketing Intelligence

The sources of marketing intelligence are as numerous as the types of information sought by marketing managers in the industrial market. Categorized into internal and external classifications, some of the more basic sources of industrial marketing intelligence are as follows.

Internal Marketing Intelligence. Internal marketing intelligence could be any type of useful information obtained from such sources within the company as (1) production, (2) production control, (3) purchasing, (4) quality control, (5) research and development, (6) credit, (7) accounting, (8) data processing, (9) personnel, (10) logistics and shipping, and (11) legal department.

External Marketing Intelligence. External marketing intelligence could be any type of useful information obtained from sources outside the company such as (1) company salesmen in the field, (2) manufacturers' representatives if used, (3) distributors if used, (4) formal marketing research projects, (5) customers both in terms of direct and derived demand, (6) analysis of competitors, (7) trade shows, (8) trade journal publications, (9) trade associations, (10) government publications, and (11) outside consultants employed by the company.

These lists are not intended to be complete, but only to illustrate the sources of intelligence in the industrial market. As can be seen, the sources are just about as varied as the types of information sought. There are many sources of marketing intelligence open to the industrial marketing manager. But no marketing manager can simply start collecting information from all possible sources on the pretense that sooner or later it will all have some marketing application. When this does happen, the information can rarely contribute to more effective decision making because the manager will be overwhelmed by bits and pieces that may never interrelate. The collection of marketing intelligence must be selective, and it must be collected by design if it is to be used to advantage. It should be selective in terms of the specific objectives in the marketing plan, and it should be selective in terms of choosing those sources of intelligence most likely to produce valid information. The preceding may be stated in another manner. The marketing manager should ideally refer to the specific objectives in the marketing plan and attempt to define the types of information that will best help to achieve those objectives. Then the manager should analyze all of the various sources that could provide such information, in full or in part, and finally choose those sources that offer the best material. After this, some form of marketing information system (MIS) should be developed to ensure the flow of desired information.

Unless a procedure similar to this is followed, the marketing manager will find that he is collecting all kinds of interesting bits and pieces of information, but that these have little collective value in terms of making sound marketing decisions. This procedure is what normally provides the basis of a marketing information system, more commonly referred to as the MIS.

Basically, marketing intelligence plays the same role in industrial marketing that it does in consumer marketing. It is the basis of all sound marketing strategies and marketing plans. What differs, however, are the types of information desired and the types of sources available in each market.

THE MARKETING INFORMATION SYSTEM

Fig. 6.1 illustrates the conceptual framework of the marketing information system as applied to a company in the industrial market. The rationale behind the model illustrated in Fig. 6.1 can be described as follows. The com-

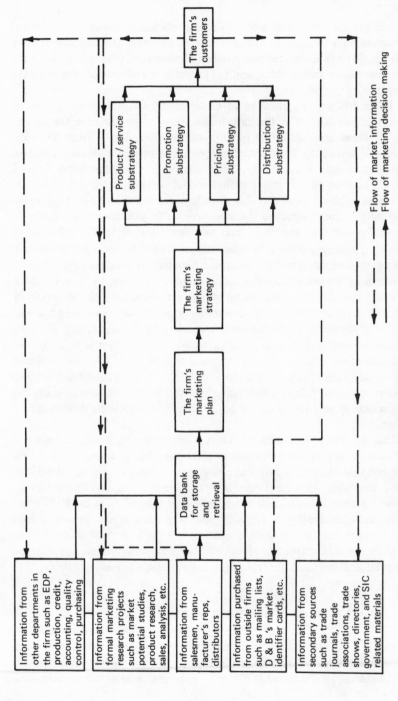

Fig. 6.1. Model of the industrial marketing information system.

pany collects information continuously regarding its marketplace from a variety of sources such as those shown in the illustration. Some of this information is primary in nature, and some of it is secondary—some of it is internal, and some is external. The marketing department then classifies this information, using immediately that which is needed at the present time and storing that data that cannot be used immediately, but that are known to have future marketing applications. This information is then fed directly, as needed, into the company's formal marketing plan and, therefore, becomes an integral part of the firm's overall marketing strategy. Finally, the data that have been collected and used have an input into the products and services to be offered, the prices to be charged, the promotional methods to be used, and the distribution changes to be enacted. Once such decisions have been made, the process starts all over again in terms of customer reaction to the decisions that have been made and competitive reactions to those decisions. The MIS never ceases to collect monitoring data from the marketplace, thereby providing the marketing manager with the continuous flow of marketing intelligence that is required for intelligent decision making.

In its simplest form, the concept of the marketing information system or MIS is to provide sound reliable market data on a continuous basis—data that can be incorporated into marketing decision making wherever possible to avoid decisions being made on such bases as rumor or speculation. Properly implemented, the MIS could enable the industrial marketing manager to make more effective decisions in overall marketing strategy and in respective substrategies. The logic of the MIS is hard to refute—if the marketplace has the ultimate ability to accept or reject a product or service or an advertising campaign or whatever (which it does), then it is imperative that attitudes, opinions, impressions, and feelings in that marketplace be considered prior to whatever decision is being made. To make industrial marketing decisions without input from the industrial marketplace appears illogical and dangerous considering the degree of competition faced by most U.S. industrial firms. The MIS is intended to provide information about customer problems and dissatisfactions, middlemen concerns, competitive moves, and so forth, before crisis situations are reached. The MIS, if properly formulated, can be preventative as well as curative for the practicing industrial marketing manager.

Under this definition of the MIS, the concept differs appreciably from what is commonly called marketing research, although marketing research certainly must be considered a part of the MIS. The MIS is an attempt to collect, analyze, and distribute to those who will use it market data on a continuous basis, whereas marketing research normally attempts to collect data pertaining to individual problems that are encountered either at periodical or irregular intervals. To collect data via marketing research on a continuous basis would involve tremendous costs in terms of time, money, and manpower. Yet continuous information is precisely what is required to make intelligent marketing decisions in the face of a constantly changing industrial marketplace. Circumstances forcing the requirement of continuous data have helped facilitate an increasing reliance on the MIS as a source of such market data.

One of the basic functions of the MIS is to get the right data to the right people at the right time. If this is not accomplished, it is questionable whether or not the MIS is managerially useful. Thus, the properly formulated MIS can provide data from the system on both regular and irregular bases. Executives can obtain data from the MIS at irregular times when they have decisions to make. In addition, a sound MIS is one that has the capability of providing typically different types of reports and other data on regularized and pre-determined schedules when such reports and data are required by company executives.

An Example of an Industrial Marketing Information System in Operation

To understand fully the marketing importance of the MIS, it may be worthwhile to work an example into the discussion. Assume that a steel manufacturer produces and markets steel used primarily in the production of automobiles. The marketing manager of this steel company wishes to set up a system that will allow a continuous flow of information regarding auto manu-facturing, so that he may adjust the marketing strategy to adapt to changes in the market. For this manager, there are a number of types of information that are required to make intelligent decisions. Some of these are as follows: (1) changes in the present and predicted demand for automobiles—these are the derived demand aspects of industrial marketing, and the demand for steel is derived in this case from the consumer demand for new cars; (2) changes in the auto manufacturing processes that affect the demand for steel—this might involve buyers in the auto firms switching to plastics or other materials instead of steel or changes in manufacturing processes that result in less scrap, and so forth; (3) changes in models produced by the auto manufacturers that could affect the demand for steel—this might involve the manufacturers pro-ducing small compact cars in place of luxury models and requiring less steel in the process; and (4) changes in the supply of steel that could affect the demand for the steel company's products—this might relate to changes in steel imports, changes in domestic steel production processes such as electric steel minimills being used to produce steel from scrapped autos, and so on.

This is not intended to be a complete list, but only to illustrate the types of information the marketing manager desires. If there were a continuous flow of information pertinent to the previously listed factors and others of a similar nature, it is obvious that the manager could make more realistic sales forecasts and thus more realistic marketing decisions. For example, the company could switch to other markets if demand were to drop off, or it could pull from other sources if demand were to increase. In short, if the marketing manager implemented a MIS to provide information pertaining to points of concern on a continuous basis, the company could keep current with changing market conditions and thus make more realistic decisions than if such information were not obtained.

The sources of information available to the marketing manager in this steel company are varied. For instances, changes in the demand for automobiles are published regularly in trade publications and in various government publications. To illustrate, auto sales of U.S. car manufacturers for the first six months of 1974 were 28.4 percent below sales for the same time period in 1973, and much of this could be attributed to the energy crisis during that time period. Data pertaining to individual American auto manufacturers are available for that same time period. To illustrate, comparisons made between U.S. auto sales during the first ten days of July 1974 and the first ten days of July 1973 showed that Ford's sales were off 41.8 percent, General Motors' sales were off 15.8 percent, Chrysler's sales were off 22.6 percent, and American Motors' sales were down 4.9 percent.[1] The point being made here is not to analyze the reasons for these decreases, but rather to make the impression that it is possible to obtain data if the manager knows where to look and makes a conscientious effort to get such data into the MIS. Similarly, individual auto manufacturers' estimates of auto production in September 1974 compared to 1973 September production figures showed that Ford's output would be 13 percent higher, General Motors' output would be 25 percent lower, Chrysler's output would be 39 percent higher, and American Motors' output would be about 2 percent higher.[2] Again these are only shown to indicate that data are available and can be found if the manager looks for it. In this case, if the marketing manager knew of the expected output of autos by each of the company's customer firms, as was shown here, demand for the company's steel could be estimated accordingly. And if the manager could get such data in advance for each month, the company would be in a much better position than if it did not know what was happening until it took place. The opposite of this would be the marketing manager of the company selling steel to General Motors who finds out after the fact that the customer's auto output was down 25 percent from the previous year, with the result that the demand for steel is also down 25 percent that month.

Other forecasts of auto production can also be found and followed over time. For example, the U.S. Department of Commerce's *U.S. Industrial Outlook* contains detailed forecasts for the auto industry in general. In the 1973 edition, their predictions are for U.S. auto production in passenger cars to increase by 3 percent annually to about 11 million units by 1980.[3] Again, for the sake of this discussion, it is not the actual figures that are so important as it is to know that such information does exist and that it can be incorporated into the MIS, then into the marketing plan, and subsequently into the marketing strategy.

In addition, it is possible to obtain data on consumer intentions to buy automobiles from such sources as the University of Michigan Survey Research Center and the Conference Board, among others. Fig. 6.2 illustrates this type of data and shows consumer expectations and plans to buy automobiles from January through May 1974 as compared with such expectations in 1973. Notice that consumer expectations and plans to buy were considerably down from 1973 and predicted that U.S. auto sales and production would also be down. This type of information is good for the industrial marketing manager to know because it gives insight into the derived demand implications involved in selling steel to the U.S. auto industry.

In terms of primary sources of information, feedback from company salesmen and manufacturers' reps and from distributors' salesmen could also

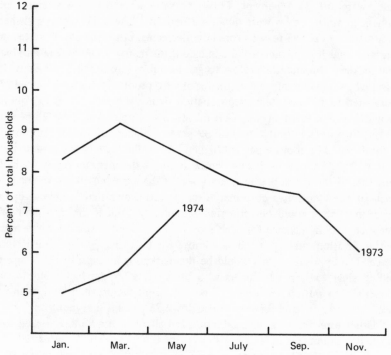

Fig. 6.2. Consumer expectations and plans to buy automobiles (expectations for six months hence). (Source: The Conference Board, "Customer Expectations and Plans to Buy," *Finance Facts*, September 1974, 3.)

be of benefit. These people call on the purchasing departments in the automobile industry and should be encouraged to seek out buyer impressions, opinions, feelings, and so on, about the demand for autos and, consequently, for steel. Formal and informal surveys of representative auto dealers might also provide such feedback regarding customer buying patterns, expectations to buy, and the like.

Information relating to customer preferences in models is also available and should be plugged into the information system. Company field sales personnel in contact with purchasing people in the auto firms can often discover predicted production model changes. In addition, secondary sources have been published and continue to publish data on buyer preferences. For example, between 1967 and 1972, the percentage of customers purchasing domestic compacts and intermediates increased from 28 percent to 40 percent, whereas the percentage purchasing medium and luxury cars decreased from 47 percent to 34 percent.[4] Again these data are cited only to show that it is possible to obtain information on model preferences that will have definite effects on the amount of steel consumed by the auto manufacturers, which, in turn, affects the demand for the product of the steel company's marketing manager.

Data regarding changes in steel requirements in auto manufacturing can also be obtained from both primary and secondary sources. Field sales personnel in contact with buyers, production, and engineering people in the auto firms often can turn up such information. Another way of obtaining this information might be through the use of the national input-output analysis as was described back in the third chapter of this text. For example, in the 1963 tables, direct requirements of steel in auto manufacturing was .085.[5] This meant that a one-dollar increase in auto output meant a direct 8.5-cent increase in steel sales. In the 1967 tables, however, this figure dropped to .071, indicating that a one-dollar increase in auto output now meant a direct increase in steel sales of only 7.1 cents. This represents a 16.5 percent decrease in the use of steel by auto manufacturers in producing their automobiles. If these same 1963 and 1967 tables are used, total requirements (direct requirements + indirect requirements) dropped from .203 to .181, amounting to a decrease of 10.8 percent. What this means is that in 1963, a one-dollar increase in the final deliveries of automobiles meant a total (direct and indirect) 20.3 percent boost in steel sales, whereas in 1967, this same one-dollar increase meant an 18.1 percent boost in steel sales. Although it is difficult to work with data such as these because they are normally nor current enough, it is a source of marketing intelligence that implies less steel in auto manufacturing, and it can be followed over time and trends established on its basis.

These examples are more than sufficient to make the desired point. There is a great deal of information available to the marketing manager in the industrial market that could be used in a marketing information system to bring about more effective decision making. In this steel and automobile example, there is certainly enough information available to ensure that a steel manufacturer is not caught unaware of decreasing auto demand and the subsequent effect on the demand for its steel. No industrial marketing manager should be unaware of what a properly constructed MIS can do in terms of sharpening decision making processes. But the manager must know what he wants from the MIS and must know what sources can best provide the desired intelligence. To collect data simply for the sake of data collection contributes little to effective decision making. Thus, to function properly, the MIS must tie into the company's marketing plan and marketing strategy and the various substrategies. It is important to realize that basically the MIS in the industrial market serves the same purpose as the MIS in the consumer market—the difference lies only in the data desired and the sources available.

The marketing manager must realize that the marketing information system is not a panacea for all problems. It is only a tool to sharpen the decision-making process by providing better information about various aspects of the marketplace. The marketing manager who assumes that the MIS will, in fact, make his decisions for him will be disappointed in its performance and err in doing so. In addition, it is rare when the MIS contains all the necessary data required by the manager, and it is unrealistic to think that the perfect MIS can be constructed. This is due to constant change in the marketplace, which, in turn, can originate from many various sources.

An example may help to explain what is meant here. In the steel manufacturer–auto manufacturers illustration in this chapter, it was shown that production output in the U.S. auto industry was down in 1974 from 1973. In August 1974, U.S. auto manufacturers built 4 percent fewer cars than they built in August 1973 and 11 percent fewer cars than they had planned for the month of August 1974. But one of the major reasons for the decrease at General Motors and Chrysler was the strikes causing work stoppages at A. O. Smith Corporation and Briggs & Stratton Corporation, two suppliers of required auto parts.[7] Shortages of OEM parts forced production cutbacks at both General Motors and Chrysler and would have naturally affected the demand for steel during the same time period. The point here is that it is doubtful that the marketing manager in any steel firm supplying the auto industry had this type of contingency built into the MIS because there are so many suppliers to the auto industry that it would be almost impossible to keep tabs on joint demand aspects of problems with any single supplier. This type of thing would be very difficult to incorporate into a MIS, although it could conceivably be done by a truly foresighted manager. Therefore, it is important that the industrial marketing manager understand the limitations of the MIS as well as its many contributions to more effective marketing decision making.

INDUSTRIAL MARKETING RESEARCH

Marketing research is defined as "the systematic gathering, recording, and analyzing of data about problems relating to the marketing of goods and services."[8] If this definition is compared with that given earlier for marketing intelligence, it is apparent that the two are not the same. Marketing research is more confined in scope and generally considered as a part of overall marketing intelligence. Moreover, marketing research normally involves projects of a single or nonrepetitive nature, whereas marketing intelligence gathering is more of a continuous process. In addition, marketing research is conducted to build a data base for individual marketing problems such as in the product, promotion, pricing, or channel areas, whereas marketing intelligence is broader and may encompass many problems at the same time. Viewed in its proper perspective, formal marketing research should be considered but one input into a total marketing information system designed to collect marketplace data, as was illustrated in Fig. 6.1.

The definition of marketing research given in the preceding paragraph applies to both the consumer and the industrial market. Perhaps the addition of the word *industrial* to the definition is all that is required to derive an acceptable definition of industrial marketing research. Industrial marketing research would then be defined as the systematic gathering, recording, and analyzing of data about problems relating to the marketing of industrial goods and services. This implies that marketing research is marketing research whether it be in the consumer or the industrial market and that there are probably more similarities between the two types than there are differences. It has been argued that a well-trained, competent marketing researcher could switch from a consumer marketing firm to an industrial marketing company, although that marketing researcher would not probably be truly effective until acquainted with the unique aspects of the industry or industries involved. There are differences, and it often takes considerable time and effort to adapt to these differences. What this means is that an individual performing marketing research for Procter and Gamble could not move to American Cyanamid without first attaining a knowledge of the chemical industry and the organizational behavior of firms in the marketplace of American Cyanamid.

Basic Differences between Industrial and Consumer Marketing Research

Though the basic objectives of marketing research do not differ between the industrial and consumer markets and though the same basic principles apply to each market, there are certain differences that must be understood. These may be summarized as follows: (1) there is a difference in the amount of technical knowledge required to research the industrial market; (2) in industrial marketing research, knowledge of organizational behavior is a necessity; (3) a knowledge of buying influences is required in the industrial market; (4) in industrial marketing research, derived as well as direct demand must be understood; (5) market structures differ in the two markets; (6) there are sampling differences in the two markets; and (7) there are differences in secondary sources of data in the two markets. Because these are of considerable importance to effective marketing management, a brief discussion of each of these differences is in order.

Technical Knowledge. The industrial marketing researcher must be more technically oriented than his consumer marketing counterpart. Often, the researcher must obtain data pertaining to exotic metals, electronics, nuclear physics, and so forth, from very technically trained respondents such as engineers, purchasing agents, production and production control personnel, quality assurance specialists, and the like. If the researcher does not understand the pertinent technology and principles, data collection may be superficial or irrelevant. And if reports are to be read by technical people within the company, he must know enough to write in their language and terminology. It is generally possible to team the marketing researcher with technically oriented counterparts such as in-house engineers to ensure the desired level of technical validity, but the point is there! Industrial marketing research requires a higher level of technical sophistication than does consumer marketing research. This is not so much because of increased product complexity as it is because of the backgrounds of people with whom the researcher must work both as respondents to survey efforts and as recipients of reports once the survey work is completed. Ideally, the industrial marketing researcher would have an engineering or production background in addition to marketing research training.

Knowledge of Organizational Behavior. Where the consumer marketing researcher deals with individual consumers and households, the industrial marketing researcher is concerned with business, institutional, and governmental organizations. Therefore, to perform the job effectively, the researcher must understand the behavior of the organizations involved in terms of formal and informal buying influences, purchasing processes, key buying influences, budget considerations governing buying, corporate purchasing policies, and so on. As might be suspected, this involves a knowledge of factors not normally considered by the consumer marketing researcher in surveying the ultimate consumer.

Knowledge of Buying Influences. As was discussed in depth in the fourth chapter of this text, buying influences are much more complex in the industrial market than they are in the consumer market. This does not mean to imply that buying influences do not exist in the consumer market, as they do, and sometimes they exert great influence over what is purchased by the household. Everyone is familiar with the child influencing his or her mother to buy a certain brand of breakfast cereal. In the consumer market, however, the number of buying influences for a particular product is normally small, and their motives are relatively easy to determine. For the industrial marketing researcher, a thorough knowledge of buying influences, both in general in the industry involved and in particular with specific firms in that industry, is imperative if the researcher is to collect valid and representative data. If the industrial marketing researcher does not reach those influences who can and will affect buying decisions in their respective firms, the research is basically worthless. The researcher must know the buying influences and how to reach them. In addition, their interests must be known well enough to communicate with them in their research design.

Knowledge of Derived Demand. For the most part, the consumer marketing researcher is concerned only with the direct consumer demand for the products or services produced by that researcher's company. The industrial marketing researcher must not only understand the direct demand of industrial customers, but also the derived demand of customers' customers. In short, there may be need to collect data in both the industrial and the consumer markets. In other words, the researcher may have to be a consumer marketing researcher in addition to being an industrial marketing researcher.

Knowledge of Market Structure Differences. Market structures are different in the two markets. In the consumer market, there are often many customers, and a single interview may be sufficient to collect the required data from such customers. For example, if General Electric wished to determine the level of satisfaction or dissatisfaction with a certain model of toaster, it might have a population of millions to interview, and its research could be accomplished with a single interview with selected sample customers. There would be no need to survey everyone in the sampled households to collect the necessary information. But if a ceramic manufacturer sold products to manufacturers of spark plugs, it would find a few large customers account for the vast majority of plugs produced. At the same time, however, it would find the need to interview in depth a larger number of people within each firm, each with differing backgrounds and concerns. Rarely would there be but one buying influence in each firm, and, as has already been developed earlier in this text, the researcher may not have the same buying influences in each firm. In short, the industrial marketing researcher has fewer customer firms to interview in most cases, but there are more in-depth interviews in each of those firms. The market structures differ considerably, and the researcher would have to adapt to those differences to switch between the two markets.

Sampling Differences. As the preceding section on market structures suggests, there are sampling differences involved in researching the two markets. In the consumer market, where large numbers of customers are involved, sampling is widely used to reduce costs in time, effort, and money. In the industrial market, however, relatively few customers are normally involved, and a census rather than a sample may be common. To illustrate, at one time nine companies made 100 percent of all piston-type fire extinguishers.[9] Obviously, a random sample drawn from a population of nine makes little sense. For any manufacturer producing parts for such extinguishers, a research effort would have to include all nine customer firms and not just a selected few customers, no matter how sophisticated the selection process. This is a rather extreme example, but many industrial firms do market their goods and services to a relatively small number of customers, and the point does apply. In other instances where industrial products are sold into horizontal markets, very large customer segments may exist, and sampling will occur. And, of course, where the industrial marketing researcher is interested in obtaining derived demand data, sampling techniques may be the same as those used by consumer marketing counterparts. In general, however, there are sampling differences between the two markets.

Differences in Secondary Data Sources. Source data, particularly that of a secondary nature, is quite different in the two markets. The consumer marketing researcher moving into the industrial market will have to turn to entirely different sources of secondary data, and until the sources are learned, effectiveness will be impaired. For example, the consumer marketing researcher accustomed to using census data, *Sales Management*'s "Survey of Buying Power," and other such sources of good ultimate consumer data would find these sources quite inappropriate if he switched to the industrial market. Until the researcher learned to use the standard industrial classification and SIC-related sources such as the *Census of Manufacturers*, the annual *Survey of Manufacturers*, *Sales Management*'s "Survey of Industrial Purchasing Power," state industrial directories, and other such data sources as trade associations and trade journal publications, the researcher would be hard pressed to come up with good secondary data. This is not necessarily a major problem, but it is a basic difference, and it often takes considerable time to learn the different sources of data available in the industrial market.

There are many other differences that could be mentioned here, but these appear to be the most significant. The point here is that although marketing research serves the same basic functions in both the consumer and the industrial markets, there are differences significant enough to affect performance if they are not recognized and adapted to.

Areas of Industrial Marketing Research

There are certain areas where the bulk of industrial marketing research efforts seem to take place. These can be summarized as follows: (1) market analysis, including the measurement of the size, potentiality, and feasibility of various industrial market segments; (2) product research, including all areas of product such as new product development and acceptance in the market-place, product alterations and deletions, service considerations, and so forth; (3) sales forecasting, including all aspects of data collection as related to the forecasting of industrial sales; (4) sales analysis, including the analysis of past sales results for the purpose of building a data base for more effective future marketing decisions; (5) advertising and promotion, including the measurement of advertising effectiveness in such media as trade journals, direct mail, catalogs, and trade shows; (6) customer analysis, particularly in regard to customer firms' buying practices, buying influences, and purchasing motives and attitudes; (7) competitor analysis, including all areas of competitor marketing behavior such as decisions made in product, promotion, pricing, and distribution; and (8) distribution, including research into both changing channels of distribution and into physical distribution changes to reduce the costs of distribution.

These appear to be the major areas of industrial marketing research as it is conducted by U.S. industrial firms. Obviously, the marketing manager in any particular company may have almost anything researched, but the above areas are the ones most commonly found. A study of 348 industrial marketing research directors disclosed that about 21 percent conducted market analysis studies, about 18 percent conducted product research, and about 9 percent conducted forecasting research.[10] These figures indicate that most industrial marketing research is conducted in a relatively few areas of concentration.

Profile of the Industrial Marketing Researcher

The average marketing researcher in the industrial market is well educated and technically competent. Studies have indicated an above average amount of education in this area with as high as 77 percent possessing more than a bachelor's degree, 31 percent having a master's degree, and 17 percent having a doctorate.[11] The average researcher is well experienced in the research area,

and, in most cases, the present job is not the only such job held, which indicates that he has worked elsewhere in the marketing research area. Most
research efforts are conducted for the company's sales department, primarily
in the area of marketing analysis, or for the product development department.
The researcher could, however, be involved in many types of field research
studies. In the job as marketing research manager, he reports to the marketing
manager and must be able to relate to field sales personnel, plant and production engineers, production personnel, purchasing agents, and other such
technically oriented individuals. What industrial companies seek in their marketing research managers is a good research background with a solid technical
background with heavy job responsibilities in the product and market analysis
areas. This can be seen in a help-wanted advertisement seeking a marketing
research executive by an industrial firm in central Massachusetts. That particular company was looking for a person to (1) establish and head a marketing research department, (2) find new markets for existing products, and (3)
identify new products for present markets. The person that they were seeking
had to possess a BS degree in engineering and a master's degree in business
administration and have a minimum of six to eight years of practical experience in the industrial market, particularly in instrumentation and the controls
field. What all this shows is that the industrial marketing researcher must have
qualifications quite different from those required of his consumer marketing
counterpart. If it is kept in mind that the marketing researcher reports to the
industrial marketing manager and that areas of research are often determined
by the manager, it can be seen that a good, technically competent marketing
researcher could offer invaluable aid to the decision making of the manager.
On the other hand, an industrial marketing researcher who does not possess
the required research and technical background could well ruin the marketing
manager with data that are not valid or representative.

Trends in Industrial Marketing Research

There has been a number of significant trends in industrial marketing
research that deserve mention inasmuch as they have increased the sophistication and effectiveness of research as it is being conducted in the U.S.
industrial market. These trends are as follows.

Increased Use of the Standard Industrial Classification System. Prior to
SIC, individual industrial marketing researchers classified customers and
prospects according to their particular respective needs. By the use of a standard numbering system such as the SIC, more meaningful comparisons can be
made. This is particularly true with the specialization offered by the five- and
seven-digit SIC numbers. As was developed in the third chapter of this text,
SIC opens up many sources of information otherwise not easily identified or

located. SIC and SIC-related sources are to the industrial marketing researcher what the census data are to consumer marketing counterparts.

Increased Emphasis on Large versus Small Customers. Another trend that has evolved relates to industrial marketing companies' differentiating their customers according to their relative size. There is nothing startling about this trend, but it indicates a recognition that purchase volumes are more important than straight geographic market segment analysis, which was the major emphasis for years. A good example of this trend can be seen in the previously discussed *Sales Management* "Survey of Industrial Purchasing Power," which provides data broken down by SIC and by plant size. This survey includes only plants with 20 or more employees because "those plants account for 95 percent of the consumption of any industrial product, even though they represent only one-third of all manufacturing plants in the U.S."[12] It is the recognition of this that has fostered the trend toward the emphasis on research based on sales volume and plant size as opposed to the traditional emphasis on geographic location.

Increased Use of Quantitative Methods. Probably the most dramatic of all industrial marketing research trends has been the increased use of quantitative methods. This has surpassed the contributions of classical statistics and is now, owing to the computer and its capabilities, well into the area of operations research or model building. Typical of what can now be found in industrial marketing research efforts are the use of regression analysis in sales forecasting; Bayesian statistics used in pricing, product, and channel decisions; probability models used to research bid pricing behavior; linear programming used in physical distribution and transportation problems; PERT and critical path analysis used in marketing planning and new product planning; as well as many other such techniques that have industrial marketing applications. Methods such as these have greatly broadened the traditional research function as it was performed in the industrial market, and their use has led to more effective decision making in some very complex areas.

Increased Use of the Behavioral Sciences. Another trend that has taken place involves the increased use of the contributions of the behavioral sciences to understand better the complex area of industrial buying. This trend has been caused by the recognition that industrial buyers and buying influences are people, and, as such, their behavior must be better understood. For years, industrial marketing researchers assumed their respondents to be totally rational in their buying, and thus they overlooked important emotional considerations. As was developed in the fourth chapter of this text, this is not a valid assumption, as a great deal of emotion is often involved in industrial purchasing. This trend is simply a recognition of this fact and an attempt to understand, explain, and predict buyer behavior better by using the contributions of psychology, social psychology, sociology, and cultural anthropology.

Increased Use of Mail and Phone Surveys. At one time, practically all industrial marketing research was conducted via personal interviews with the belief that only this method could uncover valid data. Personal interviews, however, are very expensive when compared to phone and mail interviews. A personal interview on the average may cost three to four times as much as a phone interview and eight to ten times as much as a mail interview. Of course, there are vast differences in the types of data that can be collected via each method, but in terms of cost savings, industrial marketing researchers have found that phone and mail interviews can bring about good results if properly implemented. This has brought about a trend toward a great many industrial marketing research projects now being conducted via phone or mail as opposed to personal interviews.

Increased Use of Outside Consultants. For many industrial companies, particularly those of small or medium size, the cost of maintaining a full-time in-house marketing research department is too much for the benefits that can be obtained. In other firms, marketing research is not considered a full-time responsibility. In both such instances, outside research consultants are often employed or retained on a limited duration basis. There are research firms that specialize in the industrial market, and they are generally able to do a better job for the industrial marketing firm than that firm could do for itself. A good example of this is Dun & Bradstreet's Marketing Services Division, which performs personal, phone, and mail interviews for industrial clients as well as other research-related data-gathering activities. The trend toward outside consultants is easy to understand because of the great cost involved in having a formal research department in the marketing firm's own organization. In addition, many companies simply do not need research full-time. When either of these situations occur, the obvious answer is to go outside to marketing research firms specializing in the industrial market, and this is what has been taking place.

CHAPTER SUMMARY

The purpose of this chapter has been to emphasize strongly the need for market information for incorporation into the industrial marketing manager's marketing plan and marketing strategy and subsequently into the substrategies. A marketing plan or marketing strategy without the benefit of input from the market is unrealistic and doomed to failure. Therefore, it is imperative that the marketing manager understand what types of market information or intelligence are required and know what sources could best provide such information. The differences between marketing intelligence and marketing research were developed, and the basis for an operational marketing information system (MIS) was discussed. The area of industrial marketing research was developed in terms of how it differs from consumer marketing research. The types of projects most common in industrial marketing research were discussed, and a profile of the industrial marketing researcher was developed. Finally, trends that have been taking place in industrial marketing research were reviewed.

The central theme of this chapter has been that the marketing information system (MIS) and marketing research both have wide application to the industrial market, but they both must be tied into the company's overall marketing plan and its marketing objectives if they are to be used with optimum effectiveness. To make industrial marketing decisions without benefit of industrial market input, however, is sheer folly and will ultimately have adverse effects on marketing strategies. Industrial marketing intelligence gathering is not a luxury—it is a competitive necessity, and the successful marketing manager is one who recognizes this and knows how to obtain the appropriate data required.

QUESTIONS FOR CHAPTER 6

1. What are the basic differences between industrial marketing research and industrial marketing intelligence?
2. What can the industrial marketing manager gain from the implementation of a marketing information system that he cannot gain from marketing research?
3. Industrial marketing intelligence can be defined as being either internal or external. What are the major differences between these two forms of marketing intelligence? What are the contributions of each to effective industrial marketing strategy formulation?
4. Why is it important that the industrial marketing manager tie the marketing information system into the marketing plan?
5. Do you believe that a consumer marketing researcher could perform effectively in the industrial market? If you believe he could, why do you believe so? If you believe he could not, why do you believe so?

7

PRODUCT STRATEGY IN INDUSTRIAL MARKETING

Overall marketing strategy is comprised of the four basic substrategies of product, channels, promotion, and price. Once market segments have been defined, located, and assessed and once appropriate marketing intelligence has been gathered, the industrial marketing manager must develop overall marketing strategy and construct a marketing plan for carrying out that strategy. Within this strategy and plan, decisions must be made regarding products and/or services to be offered, channels of distribution to be used, promotional efforts to be employed, and prices to be charged. The remaining chapters of this text are devoted to the areas of product, channels, promotion, and price and their implications for marketing decision making and marketing management.

INDUSTRIAL PRODUCT STRATEGY

Industrial product strategy actually involves such matters as the determination of a company's basic product policies, the establishment of specific product objectives that are consistent with previously defined marketing objectives, the determination of what particular products and/or services are to be manufactured and marketed, and the determination of what the specifications of those products and/or services will be. In other words, product strategy ranges all the way from the broad product policies down to specific grades, models, and sizes to be produced and specific services to be performed.

113

Inherent in industrial product strategy formulation is the area of product planning. The following is an excellent practical description of what is involved in product planning.

> Product planning is the continuous process of fully investigating the planning, timing, and pricing and the servicing required to add the new, discontinue the undesired, and maintain, modify, and improve the existing products, so as most profitably to meet marketing needs and justify the manufacture of these products by the company.[1]

This description implies a number of areas of responsibility for the marketing manager in product planning and product strategy in the industrial market. These areas are (1) establishing product policies, (2) setting product objectives, (3) searching out new product additions, (4) determining product specifications, (5) introducing new products, (6) modifying existing products, (7) dropping old products, (8) maintaining the proper product line, (9) packaging the products, and (10) providing the necessary technical assistance and pre- and postsale servicing required by the industrial customers.

Differences between Industrial and Consumer Product Strategies

Product strategy by definition is basically the same in both the consumer and industrial markets, although practices may differ considerably owing to the characteristics of the products and the customers involved. Table 7.1 illustrates some of the basic differences based on a survey of 334 industrial marketing companies and 139 consumer goods manufacturers. As can be seen, service plays a larger role in industrial product strategy than it does in consumer product strategy, and this is particularly so as regards service before the sale. It is also interesting to note that although technical research and development (R & D) plays about the same role in both markets, industrial marketing managers place much less emphasis on style research and development, which implies that many industrial marketing managers believe their buyers are more rationally than emotionally motivated in their purchasing.

Market research also seems to play a lesser role in the industrial market than it does in the consumer market. This latter is a phenomenon found quite commonly in the more technical industries such as are often found in the industrial market. The reasons for this are many, but generally products in such industries are developed by in-house engineering and R & D departments, which possess the technical sophistication necessary to develop such products, but which often do not believe the same level of sophistication exists in the customers for these same products. Therefore, little market research takes place.

Another difference, not shown in Table 7.1, is in the area of product packaging. Industrial product packaging is generally more of a protective

Table 7.1
RELATIVE IMPORTANCE OF THE ELEMENTS OF
PRODUCT STRATEGY

Product Effort Activity	Producers of:		
	Industrial Goods	Consumer Durables	Consumer Nondurables
Presale Service	23.7%	12.8%	12.1%
Postsale Service	17.7%	14.2%	9.2%
Technical R & D	34.5%	34.6%	38.6%
Market Research	15.7%	17.8%	27.5%
Style R & D	6.1%	18.8%	9.6%
Other	2.3%	1.9%	3.0%
Total	100.0%	100.0%	100.0%

Source: John G. Udell, *Successful Marketing Strategies* (Madison: Mimir Publishers, Inc., 1972), p. 48.
Note: Data are based on the average responses of 334 industrial, 52 consumer durable, and 87 consumer nondurable manufacturers.

nature than it is of a promotional nature, although the latter has become quite popular in OEM products of the off-the-shelf variety sold through industrial distributors. Other differences between product strategy in the two markets will arise at times in this chapter, with the point being that industrial marketing product strategy decisions differ from those found in the consumer market even though the basic principles are similar. As has been shown earlier in this text, product characteristics and the characteristics of industrial customers almost of necessity dictate a different approach to the products sold into the industrial market.

THE IMPORTANCE OF PRODUCT PLANNING

With few exceptions, sound product planning is essential to continued success in the industrial market. Viewed broadly in terms of product strategy, there are only three ways for a company to continue to exist and succeed: (1) the company can continue to increase sales of its existing products to both present and potential customers, (2) the company can introduce new products on a continuous and successful basis, and (3) the company can expand its product offerings via merging with or acquiring other companies and thus add new products in this manner.

Analysis of the above three options leads to one basic conclusion—unless the marketing manager continues to introduce a stream of successful new products over time, the long-range potential of the company is limited! To emphasize continued sales of present products as the basic product philosophy is foolhardy in the long run because of such factors as market saturation and the high rate of technical product obsolescence found in the industrial market. To emphasize mergers and acquisitions as the primary product philosophy also has shortcomings because of such factors as government restrictions, particularly in the antitrust area, reluctance of firms to be absorbed, image differences of merged companies, and various other reasons.

What all this means to the industrial marketing manager is that to be successful, he must recognize the need for new products in the marketing strategy. This does not mean, of course, that the manager would not continue to attempt to expand the customer base for his existing products, nor does it mean that he would not pursue merger or acquisition possibilities if they arose and were consistent with overall marketing and product objectives. What it does mean, however, is that the manager must somewhere in the product strategy and the marketing plan include emphasis on the development of new products. Not to do so may be tantamount to marketing disaster, and thus product planning is of critical importance to the industrial marketing manager. All of this discussion appears to be common sense, but in the actual industrial market, it is often overlooked, as marketing managers become obsessed with the marketing of their present products and they are not prepared to replace those products when their demand decreases or ceases to exist. This means that they are often caught unaware by competitive moves and as a result placed on the defensive in their strategy, which is not where any aggressive marketing manager wishes to be.

Although product planning is vital also for the consumer marketing manager, there are specific reasons for its importance in industrial marketing. Some of these reasons are as follows.

Increased Competition

Because of increased competition, both domestic and foreign, industrial buyers today have more choice in their purchasing. New materials, new processes, new technologies, new sources of supply, and the like place great strain on the industrial marketing manager as regards product strategy. Customers will not continue to buy existing products if better competitive choices come along. Thus, the manager must keep pace with competition, and this can be done through the use of matrix models in marketing strategy such as were described in chapter 5. The marketing manager using a matrix approach similar to that developed in that chapter could continuously monitor the progress of products in relation to competitive offerings. This is a very important consideration, for, depending upon the particular industry involved, anywhere from one-third to three-quarters of the sales of most industrial firms are accounted for by products that did not exist ten to 15 years ago. As can be understood, this places great responsibility on the industrial marketing manager and the product planning department to keep the company contemporary.

Derived Demand

Because of the derived demand aspect, the industrial marketing manager must pay very close attention to product planning. This is an era where ultimate consumer wants and needs are changing faster than they ever did before, and this has definite effects on the demand for industrial goods and services used to produce goods sold into the consumer market. This means that the industrial marketing manager cannot be complacent about the product line even if industrial customers are seemingly satisfied. Products must be planned to adapt to changing requirements in the ultimate consumer market that will, in turn, affect customers' requirements. In other words, as ultimate consumer wants and needs continue to change at a rapid pace, the emphasis is increased, in turn, on the importance of sound product planning by the industrial marketing manager supplying products to the manufacturers of the consumer goods being produced to meet those wants and needs.

Greater Sophistication in Industrial Purchasing

Another factor that is forcing closer attention to industrial product planning is the growing sophistication found in industrial purchasing professionals and other buying influences. As these people become more knowledgeable, more specialized, and more discerning in their purchasing, they become more picky in relation to competitive choices open to them. Industrial products are screened closely by buyers and buying influences on any number of different factors, as was previously discussed in detail. Product quality and performance are judged harshly by value analysis and other such sophisticated methods. This implies a distinct need for effective product planning to supply the buyers and buying influences with products that satisfy their particular requirements. It is not enough simply to produce products and/or services and then attempt to change the requirements sought by the buyers and their buying influences, as the latter will more likely switch to competitive alternatives rather than change their requirements. Thus, products must be planned with the growing sophistication of buyers in mind.

Laborsaving Requirements

For years now, American industry has been hit hard by rising labor costs, and in their purchasing manufacturers are constantly looking for labor savings in their equipment and materials. This means that purchases are viewed with this aspect in mind, and customers will switch suppliers for laborsaving reasons even if they are reasonably satisfied otherwise with their present products. For example, if a manufacturer presently were purchasing production line equipment that required three men to operate, it might very well switch to a competitor who could offer a similar piece of equipment that could be operated by two men or a single worker. This demand for labor saving by industrial customers has also placed great stress on the industrial marketing manager in product planning, particularly in firms selling to user customers.

THE COST OF INDUSTRIAL PRODUCT FAILURES

Another factor affecting the need for industrial product planning is the cost involved in producing and marketing industrial products, particularly capital goods. Although it is true that there are also high costs involved in producing consumer goods, the unit cost is usually less constraining. What this means, of course, is that the costs involved in product failures that can be attributed to poor product planning can be tremendous in the industrial market. A classic example of this was Convair's 880 and 990 jet airliners. The Convair Aerospace Division of General Dynamics lost more than $450 million on this product failure.[2] This is an exceptional case, but it makes the desired point—product planning is imperative in the industrial market because the cost of failure is often so high. Adding a product may mean a new plant, new equipment, new materials, new labor, and so on, all of which must be covered even if the product fails. Thus, the high cost of a product failure in the industrial market has placed great emphasis on product planning for the marketing manager.

Rate of Failure of Industrial Products

New industrial products are risky just as they are in the consumer market. Although it is difficult to define what constitutes a product failure, it is estimated that about 80 percent of all industrial products fail to meet company objectives and, therefore, are considered failures.[3] Adding to this fatality rate is the high cost of industrial product failures as was just discussed. These two factors collectively almost automatically impress upon the manager the need for careful and effective product planning.

Reasons such as these indicate clearly why product planning is so critical in industrial marketing product strategy. Without such planning, the company has no way to adapt to changes in the requirements of its marketplace, and it will ultimately end up with a line of obsolete and outdated products, which is hardly the blueprint for marketing success! The question now to be answered is this—how does the industrial marketing manager formulate effective product planning and strategy in overall marketing? The answer to this question may well lie in the manager's ability to implement and use effectively the concept of the product life cycle.

THE PRODUCT LIFE CYCLE

Just as in consumer marketing, probably the most widely recognized product planning concept is the product life cycle. So much has been written about product life cycles that a full development of the concept is not necessary in a text of this size. Basically, the concept holds that products and services have life cycles similar to the human life cycle. Products and services are born, grow up, mature, and die. Every product and every service have a life cycle and, in fact, have a different life cycle for each of their respective markets. This is just as true for industrial products as it is for consumer products, although it is sometimes argued that the further away from the ultimate consumer, the longer the product life cycle. For drugs, cosmetics, or grocery shelf items, the cycles may run from two to five years, whereas in producers' goods such as machine tools, the cycles may run from 15 to 25 years, and for basic industries such as coal, steel, or aluminum, life cycles may be as long as from 50 to 75 years.[4] But to assume figures such as these as rules would be a mistake because "industry's hardheaded purchasing agents are willing to buy a new product—or drop an old one—in short order if the reason is demonstrable."[5] Another way of saying this is that industry product life cycles such as 16 to 25 years for machine tools may be of considerable length, but the machine tools of individual manufacturers may have product life cycles of a much shorter duration. And, of course, the life cycles of particular models of those products can be very short for many of the reasons previously discussed. The point is that life cycles in the industrial market for particular models of particular products in particular markets can be just as short as they are in the consumer market, and the astute industrial marketing manager is well aware of this.

Product-planning Implications in the Life Cycle

Fig. 7.1 illustrates the typical conceptual product life cycle. The introductory stage is characterized by low sales volume as prospective buyers and buying influences are unaware or unfamiliar with the product. In this stage, the industrial marketing manager's primary task is to create awareness of the product. Net profits in this stage are usually low, if there are any, with most revenue being used to promote the new product. From a marketing management perspective, the important strategic variables would appear to the product and its promotion, although channels and pricing can and do play a sig-

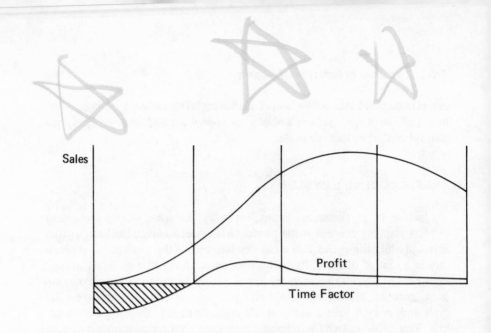

STAGE IN CYCLE	INTRODUCTION	RAPID GROWTH	MATURITY	DECLINE
Overall marketing strategy	To create awareness and acceptance	Establish an appreciable market share	Maintain market share in face of competition	Manage costs & maintain profit
Product Strategy	Develop & test market prototypes in customer plants	Plan replacement for the existing product demise	Introduce replacement product into the market	Drop the old product from product line
Product Design	Limited number of models to gain market acceptance	Differentiate product to match market requirements	Maintain competitive edge through differentiation	Provide only basic models for remaining customers
Promotion Strategy	Create awareness & provide foundation for sales efforts	Create a preference among customers and middlemen	Maintain preference among customers and middlemen	Use minimum effort to sustain decreasing demand
Channel Strategy	Get product to new customers for new market penetration	Control the channel for optimum market impact	Maintain control of the channel	Reduce distribution costs yet keep customers
Pricing Strategy	Match value of product to market needs	Adjust price as competition enters	Stabilize and avoid price fluctuations	Move stocks of built up inventories

Fig. 7.1. Conceptual model of the product life cycle.

nificant part. This is a crucial period for the product. Should it fail to gain acceptance in this stage, it will fail. Should it survive this stage, it will enter the growth stage. The manager's skill in testing, launching, and monitoring the progress of the new product is very important.

The growth stage is characterized by a rapid increase in demand for the product. The cumulative effects of the company's promotion and examples of industrial customers purchasing and using the product create a favorable image and stimulate more buyers and buying influences to consider the product. Often this increased demand encourages competition to enter the market, and the manager may have to consider the differentiation of the product. With specifications, this is not always easy to accomplish in the industrial market, but it can be done through improved product modifications and through selling and service features. With increased competition, such differentiation may be necessary to increase or maintain a market share. In this stage, there may also be strong competition for the services of industrial distributors and manufacturers' representatives if such middlemen are appropriate.

The maturity stage is characterized by the rate of sales increase beginning to decline. The early part of this stage finds relatively stable sales and declining unit costs of promotion. Thus, profits are often relatively high in this period. New customers at this point may be more deliberate and more price-conscious than new customers in the previous two stages. With sales volume stabilizing, less competitive suppliers may begin to pull out of the market. In the latter part of this stage, when sales volumes may show almost no increase, the market may be saturated. Without an expanding market to absorb productive capabilities and possibly to absorb build up inventories, some suppliers may begin to cut prices to protect their market shares and to maintain profitable operations. Companies using a direct sales channel may switch to independent middlemen in an attempt to continue servicing existing customers and reduce costs at the same time.

The decline stage is characterized by continuously declining sales as the product loses its appeal to past customers and few, if any, new customers are entering the market. Many competing suppliers have pulled out of the market in search of better opportunities elsewhere. Those who are left are seeking methods of retrenching their marketing efforts in an attempt to extend the product's life cycle. If the company has continued to use direct sales to this point, it may seriously be considering the use of manufacturers' reps or distributors if either is appropriate, or it may be making arrangements to franchise out service requirements to independents. Ultimately, the product will be selectively and slowly withdrawn as demand recedes. In this stage, the manager's task is basically that of managing expenditures to optimize the return for each dollar spent on the product. Finally, the product is withdrawn completely from the market as the company has better opportunities elsewhere.

There are a number of important marketing implications in the product life cycle and some of these are shown in Fig. 7.1. A strong argument can be made that knowledge of stage in the life cycle is a prime requisite for all marketing strategy decisions, particularly as those decisions relate to the sub-strategies of product, promotion, channels, and price. As stated, Fig. 7.1 illustrates many of those implications.

In this section, however, focus will be primarily on the product-planning implications in the product life cycle. Some of the major product-planning implications are as follows: (1) all products and services have life cycles—the marketing manager must recognize this and understand further that product life cycles will differ for each product in each market according to the product and individual market development rates; (2) the marketing manager must know where each product is on its respective life cycle for each appropriate market segment; (3) the manager should recognize that new replacement products should be planned in the rapid growth stage of the life cycle of the product eventually to be replaced; (4) the manager should recognize that the replacement product, planned in the rapid growth stage, should be introduced in the maturity stage—this will permit the manager's company to replace its own products in the marketplace rather than give such opportunities to competitors; (5) the manager should recognize that product modification, if feasible, should also be planned in the growth stage of the product to be modified rather than left to chance later in the cycle; (6) the marketing manager should recognize that there is a time to drop products in the sales decline stage—this means that there is a time when further actions such as product modification, promotional and pricing changes, and so forth, cannot save the product, but will, in fact, only incur additional unnecessary expenses—in other words, the astute manager will recognize that there comes a time in a product's declining years when it is terminal—it cannot be rescued, nor can its life cycle be lengthened; and (7) the manager should also understand the relationship of profit to sales in the life cycle.

As Fig. 7.1 illustrates, profits are not uniform throughout the life cycle, and the product planner may have more flexibility in those stages where profits are higher. In addition, the degree of risk taken with products might well differ according to where the product is in its life cycle and the relative profitability at that point. And the manager should realize that because profitability is not uniform throughout the life cycle, the profitability of the company's overall product line may depend upon how many products are in what stages of their respective life cycles. Finally, the marketing manager should recognize that profit life cycles are usually much shorter than product life cycles and that the former may be much more important in effective marketing decisions than the latter.

There are many other product-planning implications in the life cycle, but time and space will not permit discussion of all of them. The point of this discussion, however, should be clear. To make effective product decisions, as well as effective overall marketing decisions, the industrial marketing manager must make use of the product life cycle concept. If the manager does not know where products are on their respective life cycles, it is very difficult to make realistic decisions regarding product additions, deletions, and modifications.

Applying the Product Life Cycle to Industrial Marketing

Applying the concept of the product life cycle to industrial marketing can be relatively simple if a matrix planning model is used such as was discussed in detail in chapter 5. If we refer back to Table 5.4 in chapter 5, it can be seen that the segment analysis illustrated actually plots industry life cycles as well as individual company product life cycles by analyzing past, present, and potential sales figures. In addition, the segment analysis of the matrix plots such figures for each and every product in each and every market segment. If such a matrix planning model were used, the industrial marketing manager would know at all times where each of the company's products and/ or services stood in their respective life cycles for each market. This is so because each cell analysis is basically nothing more than past, present, and potential sales data, which are essentially the same data that constitute the product life cycle.

In addition, the cell analyses provide industry life cycles as well as company product life cycles because they force the manager to review past, present, and potential industry sales of each product as well as those of company products. Thus, by using the matrix model approach, the manager would know at all times where the company's product was and where the industry was on their respective life cycles. Once this is known, comparisons would be relatively simple, and product decisions could be more meaningful than if industry figures were ignored or unknown. Because of fewer customers and more precise product specifications, the use of the product life cycle in the industrial market in matrix modeling would appear to be easier than in the consumer market.

There is, however, little evidence to conclude that industrial marketing managers make good use of the life cycle concept. According to *Industrial Marketing* magazine, industrial product managers "ideally" should keep close watch on the product life cycle, not only on sales volume, but also on net profit. But the magazine contends that industrial product managers, "as is," often do not keep track of the product life cycle.[6] Another study of senior marketing executives showed that none used the life cycle concept in any strategic manner at all, and very few even used it in any tactical manner.[7] This behavior appears to exist despite all the factors shortening the life cycles of industrial products. As life cycles shorten, new product development understandably becomes more important. Yet "it is painfully evident . . . that the graveyards of business are full of people who thought their present product line was good enough."[8]

A FORMAT FOR NEW INDUSTRIAL PRODUCTS

The product life cycle provides an excellent product strategy tool once products are introduced into the marketplace and are accepted by industrial customers. But the life cycle is of little help in deciding which products to market. How does the industrial marketing manager decide what specific products and/or services to add to the product line? With an 80 percent fatality rate, it is apparent that the company cannot simply add all products that are suggested to it. Some form of screening process must be employed. In addition, in the industrial market, it appears there is never a shortage of product suggestions from such as salesmen in the field, engineering personnel, production people, purchasing agents, top management, and others within the company.

Fig. 7.2 illustrates what took place at International Minerals and Chemical Corporation when 540 new product ideas resulted in one commercial success. Note should be taken that a screening process reduced the number of new product ideas from a total of 540 suggested down to nine that were good enough to be considered in laboratory evaluation tests. Then, from these nine, one commercial success was obtained. What takes place in this screening process is extremely important as many industrial companies have found out. It takes time, money, and effort when product ideas are chased with little or no hope of commercial success. Thus, some format is required for an objective and orderly assessment of new product ideas, as no company wants to throw out good product ideas, nor does it want to spend inordinate amounts of money, time, and effort on product ideas that never materialize into commercial successes. The following format is typical of what might be used to screen products in the industrial market. The marketing manager should (1) establish objectives that products are to achieve, (2) assess the market potential for each product considered, (3) determine the company's capabilities of producing and marketing each product considered, and (4) determine the effect each product considered will have on the rest of the company. Because these are extremely important considerations for product success, it is worthwhile to look at them in some detail.

Establish Product Objectives

The most basic step in setting up a new product-screening process is to establish specific objectives for such products—objectives that are realistic, objective, capable of measurement, and consistent with overall corporate

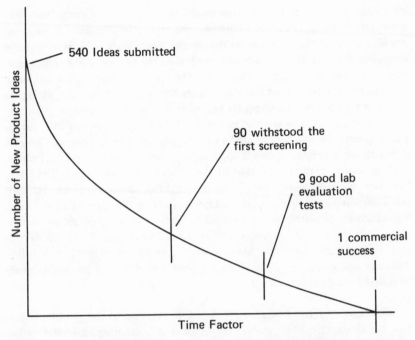

Fig. 7.2. Product idea mortality rate is high. (Source: E. Karns and H. T. McGee, "Product Planning Aids Industry," *Iron Age,* November 24, 1960, 93. Reprinted by permission from *Iron Age.* Copyrighted 1960, Chilton Company.)

goals and objectives and overall marketing objectives. To have product objectives that are inconsistent with overall corporate or marketing objectives makes no marketing sense whatsoever! It must also be understood that companies often do not have single product objectives, but rather pursue a number of them simultaneously. Once specific product objectives are established, potential product ideas are then assessed in terms of those objectives, and any ideas inconsistent with those objectives are immediately screened. This type of screening is probably what accounted for the reduction of 540 new product ideas submitted at International Minerals and Chemical Corporation down to 90 as shown in Fig. 7.2. There are many ways to define product objectives in the industrial market, and the following are typical of policy-type objectives found.

In Terms of Customer Functions to Be Served. Many industrial marketing managers define their product objectives in terms of their customers' requirements and will accept or reject product ideas on this basis. Continental Can, for example, has defined its product objectives in terms of providing packaging needs of customers. With this basic objective, the company has made some interesting product decisions. At one time, Continental Can rejected the idea of acquiring an airline via the conglomerate route because of its basic inconsistency with the product objective, even though an airline might have been a profitable venture at that time. On another occasion, the company adopted the production of hot dog casings because it viewed such casings as a form of packaging. Defining its product objectives in terms of customer needs, the company was able to expand its product offerings into metal, paper, plastic, or anything related to packaging needs of customers. Contrast this with what would happen if the company had defined its product objectives in terms of the production of steel cans used in packaging. The latter approach is much more limited and shortsighted, as industrial buyers may not care whether they purchase containers made in the form of cans, boxes, waxed paper, or plastic as long as product performance and prices are acceptable. Thus, by defining a product objective in terms of customer needs, the marketing manager can offer the company more flexibility in its product line offerings and at the same time have a higher probability of producing products that have customer acceptance in the marketplace.

In Terms of Basic Materials Produced. In contrast to the product objective based on customer needs, many industrial marketing managers define their product objectives in terms of supplying basic materials. A cement manufacturer, for example, may define its product objective in terms of cement, its basic material. Any product ideas not defined in terms of cement would be rejected. Although this approach is internally consistent in terms of company capabilities, it can be externally damaging in terms of competitive offerings or substitute products of another basic material. A good example of this is the substitute of asphalt for cement in paving. When contractors shift from purchasing cement to purchasing asphalt, the cement company that has defined its product objective in terms of the basic material of cement will lose sales because its product objective is too narrow. What this means is that a product objective of producing cement is quite different from a product objective of producing paving needs! Nevertheless, many industrial marketing managers do define their product objectives in terms of basic materials because they have always done so and because this form of product objective is easier for them to understand and implement. It is an approach, however, that does not consider the customers' needs to the extent that they should be considered in effective marketing.

In Terms of Technology. It is also quite common to find industrial firms defining product objectives in terms of their technological expertise. What this means is that the company will accept new product ideas consistent with its technological expertise, and any product ideas not consistent with that expertise will be rejected. An electronics manufacturer, for example, might accept product ideas that are based on an understood technology and reject other ideas if they do not utilize the same technology. Sometimes this is done regardless of market segments, and the technology is the only common thread in the company's entire product line, as when General Electric's product line ranged all the way from household toasters to computers. In that case, electricity formed the common technological bond between all its products. A product objective based on common technology is very common in highly technical industrial firms, and it makes good marketing sense in many instances because it restricts companies to areas of their technical competence. It is also possible, of course, to integrate the technical competence with customer needs, so that customer orientation is achieved at the same time. On the other hand, if technology is used as the sole product objective, it can lead the company into the production of products within its area of technical competence, but whose marketability is questionable.

In Terms of Profitability. In addition to any of the previous objectives, it is very common to find industrial marketing managers establishing product objectives in terms of specific profit figures. For example, the set of objectives of a steel company for its new products was (1) sales that would exceed $1 million annually within three years, (2) incremental profits of 7 percent after taxes, and (3) incremental net return on investment of 20 percent.[9] Such profitability objectives are typical and will be developed in more detail in the chapter on pricing. At this point, all that is required is an understanding that profitability objectives are common and, of course, can be used in screening out products. Any product ideas that do not appear to have the required profit potential will be rejected.

These are but a few of the types of product objectives employed by industrial marketing managers. The point is that product objectives should be established in terms of market demands, company capabilities, middlemen requirements, governmental or legal restrictions, and return on investment. Once objectives are established, the intelligent marketing manager will screen new product ideas against such objectives and reject at this point those ideas that are inconsistent. Without such an approach, the manager will be spending a great deal of time, effort, and money chasing ideas that have no merit at all from a marketing perspective.

Assess the Market

If a product idea is found to be consistent with the company's overall marketing objectives and its product objectives, then it should be screened further by the marketing manager in terms of its market potential. One approach to doing this is for the marketing manager to employ a checklist method to assess the market potential for the product in question. In such a checklist, the manager might look into detail into such areas as the following: (1) How big is the total market for the product?; (2) What sales volume levels can be expected, and in what time frames?; (3) Who will use the product?; (4) What buying influences will be involved with marketing the product?; (5) What are the purchasing habits of the purchasing people and the other buying influences?; (6) From whom do customer firms now purchase such products?; (7) How much do the customer firms now pay for such products?; (8) How often will the product be purchased?; (9) In what quantities will it be purchased?; (10) What is the expected life cycle of the product—how soon will it become obsolete?; (11) Is the market for the product growing or shrinking?; (12) How soon will design changes be required?; (13) Lastly, what service or technical assistance will be required?

Checklist questions such as these permit the marketing manager to screen further the product idea in terms of its market potential. This is a "go–no go" step! If the manager finds the answers to these questions are of a positive nature (the potential is good, the buyers would buy from his company, and so on), then the product idea proceeds for further screening. If, however, the answers are of a negative nature, the product idea should be scrapped. It should be recognized that these questions are consistent with the materials presented in chapters 4 and 5 of this text. If the marketing manager has followed a format similar to that which has been developed in this text, many of these questions would have been answered previously in the marketing strategy and marketing planning phases. The point being made here is that before any new product idea proceeds into the costly areas of research and development, engineering, and production, its market potential should be fully appraised by the industrial marketing manager.

Determine Company Capabilities

If the product idea is found to be consistent with corporate, overall marketing, and product objectives and if market potential is found to exist, the marketing manager should then proceed to analyze the company's ability to produce and market the product. This is really the acknowledgment that although the market potential exists, it may not exist for the marketing manager's own company. Again, a checklist approach might be employed to determine the company's ability to manufacture and market the particular product in its predetermined market segments. The following are typical of the types of questions that should be included in the checklist: (1) What technical resources and capabilities will be required to produce and market the product? (2) Does the company possess these resources and capabilities to the degree required, and should they be committed to this project? (3) Can the product be produced with existing manufacturing and warehouse facilities, or will new facilities be required? (4) Can the company's existing channels of distribution be used to reach potential customers, or will new channels have to be implemented? (5) Are existing customers also potential customers for the new product, or will the company be dealing with entirely new customers? (6) Does the company have the capital to produce and market the product, and will the return on investment be high enough to justify the use of this capital? (7) Are the company's salesmen technically competent to sell the new product? (8) Can the company produce a product that will be superior to competitive products now in the marketplace? (9) Does the company possess the service capabilities to provide the level of service and technical assistance that will be required? (10) Lastly, can the company produce the product in the quantities that will be required?

Checklist questions such as these are intended to force the industrial marketing manager to view realistically the company's capabilities to produce and market the product at a profit. Again, this is a "go-no go" phase! If it is discovered, through objective and realistic answers to such questions, that the company does have the capabilities to produce and market the product and that the return on investment is high enough, then the product idea proceeds to the next screening phase. If, however, it is found that the firm does not have the capabilities or that the return on investment is not high enough to meet company objectives, the product idea should be discarded and other opportunities assessed similarly. Again, it is important to realize that if the company uses a marketing information system similar to that developed in the previous chapter and if the manager performed an effective situational analysis in the marketing plan, answering such questions as posed here could be relatively simple. At any rate, questions such as these should be answered prior to actual production rather than after production has started. The point is that if the company does not possess the required capabilities, it is better to find this out before the product is commercially produced rather than afterwards. Those product ideas passing this phase of the format will then proceed to a final assessment in terms of their contribution to the total company. Those ideas not passing this phase should be rejected.

Determine the Product's Contribution to the Company

Even if the product idea successfully passes through the first three phases of this format, it may be that the company still should not produce and market the product because of its effect on other products produced by the firm or on other areas of the company. To illustrate, what is to be gained if the company adds a new product that is consistent with product objectives, has market potential, and can be economically produced, if that product has adverse effects on other good products in the company's product line?

This can happen, and, therefore, it is important that the product idea be subjected to one last round of questions such as the following: (1) Will the company's distributors or manufacturers' reps accept the product in preference to competitive offerings?; (2) Does the product fill a gap in an otherwise incomplete product line?; (3) Does the product enhance the marketability of all the products in the company's product line, or does it detract from other products?; (4) How will the new product affect the image of the company's present products?; (5) Will the new product give the company's salesmen a more complete product system to sell?; (6) Will the new product have any effect on present company reciprocal agreements—will it compete with the products of present customers?; (7) Will the new product compete with existing products and cause existing customers to split purchases between the company's own products?; (8) Will the company's salesmen be able to sell the new product without sacrificing sales of other products presently in the company's product line?; (9) Will the new product utilize any excess plant capacity and thus contribute in that manner?; (10) Will the new product help the company over seasonal fluctuations in the existing product line?; (11) Lastly, will the new product contribute because a large existing customer wants it and will switch all his present purchases if the company does not supply the product?

Checklist questions such as these are also of crucial importance and force the industrial marketing manager to view the new product idea from still another perspective—its effect on the overall firm. This is also a "go–no go" step! If the answers to such questions are of a negative nature, the product idea should be scrapped, as it would have an adverse effect on the total company. On the other hand, positive responses to the questions would imply a product idea thoroughly screened in terms of its marketing merit. The product idea would then proceed to research and development, engineering, and production for prototyping, testing, and perhaps ultimate production and entry into the market. At that point, the product would enter the introduction stage of its life cycle.

From a marketing point of view, this type of new product screening makes good sense. The same questions will have to be answered sooner or later, and the logic of answering them prior to producing a product makes much better sense than letting them be answered in the marketplace after production. This sort of screening process accounts for International Minerals & Chemical Corporation's whittling 540 new product ideas down to one commercial success, as is illustrated in Fig. 7.2.

Despite the logic of such a format, evidence exists to indicate that products in the industrial market are often marketed without benefit of such planning. The Convair 880 and 990 example cited earlier in this chapter is somewhat typical. Convair first built a beautifully engineered, medium-sized, medium-range airliner and then hunted for a market for the plane. To their regret, the Convair 880 came in second best to the bigger jets (Boeing's 707 and Douglas's DC-8), and, at the same time, it was too large to be a brisk seller as a replacement for much smaller, two-engine aircraft.[10] In short, the plane had no market and never should have been produced. As a result of the disregard of a planning format such as has been developed in this chapter, a product failed at a cost to its manufacturer of $450 million. In this case, the marketplace answered the questions after the plane was produced—questions that should have been and could have been answered prior to production.

In a way, the Convair example is typical of what goes on in the industrial market with many manufacturers of technically sophisticated products. Such companies sincerely believe that if they produce products of the finest technical quality, sales will be assured, as such products will ultimately seek out their own markets. These products are generated internally by technical people with little or no market delineation or assessment. This does not have to be the case! Contrasted with Convair's 880, Douglas went into the market first, collected its data, and then built the DC-10.[11] At the time, it was an excellent example of product planning based on market requirements in a highly technical industry. Analysis of industrial product failures, however, shows that such product planning does not always take place.

ANALYSIS OF INDUSTRIAL PRODUCT FAILURES

It is always worthwhile to attempt to learn from failure, and this certainly applies to industrial products. It is not easy, however, to define a product failure in the industrial market. As was stated earlier in this chapter, one estimate is that about 80 percent of all industrial products fail to meet company objectives and thus are considered failures by their firms.[12] This rate appears to be rather high, but this may be due to that particular definition of a product failure—one that does not achieve its objectives. Table 7.2 illustrates rates of commercial successes of products in selected industrial marketing areas. Note should be taken that the rate of commercial success of new product ideas is low, actually being less than 2 percent on the average. But as the screening process evolves, the rate of success continues to increase. Of those products considered good enough to move in the project development area, about 14 percent succeed. And, of all new industrial products actually introduced, about 62 percent actually become commercially successful as judged by their companies. Still, this implies that on the average about 38 percent of those products introduced into the marketplace fail, and the failure rate is as high as 41 percent in chemicals, nonelectrical machinery, and raw materials. This table indicates that product failures are a problem

Table 7.2

RATE OF COMMERCIAL SUCCESS OF INDUSTRIAL PRODUCTS

	Success Percentages		
	New Product Ideas	Projects Development Product	New Products Introduced
All Industry Groups	1.7%	14.5%	62.5%
Chemical	2.0%	18.0%	59.0%
Consumer Packaged Goods	2.0%	11.0%	63.0%
Electrical Machinery	1.0%	13.0%	63.0%
Metal Fabricators	2.0%	21.0%	59.0%
Raw Material Processors	5.0%	14.0%	59.0%

Source: Reprinted by permission of the publisher from Management Research Department, *Management of New Products* (Chicago: Booz, Allen & Hamilton, Inc., 1968).

in the industrial market and thus it is important that the reasons for such failures be analyzed. If the reasons for industrial product failure can be determined, then the marketing manager can guard against their taking place with the company's products.

Much has been written on product failures, and it is easy to find reasons why products in general fail. Perhaps the best summary of product failures appeared in *The Conference Board Record*. According to this source, there are eight basic reasons why products fail.[13] These are (1) inadequate market analysis, (2) product defects, (3) higher costs than anticipated, (4) poor timing, (5) competition, (6) insufficient marketing effort, (7) inadequate sales effort, and (8) weakness in distribution. These reasons apply to all products, industrial as well as consumer, but they are not specific enough to be of much value to the industrial marketing manager. In more specific terms, industrial products appear to fail for the following reasons.

Failure to Define the Specific Market Segment or Segments for the Product

Often industrial companies launch new products with only a general idea of who will use or buy those products. At other times, industrial marketing managers have no market segments in mind before producing the products and then hunt for markets after the products have been produced. When markets are not found, the products fail. As has been mentioned, this is very common in highly technical industries.

Inadequate Understanding of the Buying Process in Prospective Customer Firms

If the industrial marketing manager is ignorant of how products are purchased by prospective customers, those products will fail because the manager is unable to get them into those firms that will use them. Simply stated, the reason many industrial products fail is because their manufacturers do not realize how their customers actually buy such products.

Lack of Knowledge of Buying Influences in Prospective Customer Firms

As was developed in chapter 4 of this text, buying influences affect directly or indirectly those products that are purchased or not purchased. If the marketing manager does not know the buying influences or is unable to reach them, company products will fail because they do not penetrate the marketplace.

Lack of Knowledge of Required Marketing Effort

Many industrial marketing managers fail to realize how much effort will be required in marketing a new product or service until they are well into the marketing process and then realize they do not have the marketing capabilities to perform the effort required.

Lack of Awareness of Existing Customer-supplier Relationships

Many industrial products end up as failures because their marketing managers are unaware of or do not realize existing relationships between their prospective customers and the present suppliers of those prospective customers.[14] In such instances, the marketing managers do not realize from whom the prospective customer firms presently purchase and why they purchase from those particular suppliers. An industrial marketing manager attempting to sell a new customer on the basis of lower price will fail if unaware that something like reciprocity is the real reason for present customer-supplier relationships. What this means, of course, is that the customer's real reasons for purchasing are unknown, with the result that products fail because they are unable to penetrate the marketplace.

Underestimation of New Investment Requirements in Customer Firms

Products fail in the industrial market because many marketing managers fail to appreciate new investment requirements faced by prospective customers if those customers purchase the manager's product.[15] This applies to both OEM and user customers, and an example may help to explain it better.

A producer of a capital good such as a drill press may think of the cost to its customer as being only the price of the drill press. Yet to use that particular drill press, the purchasing firm may have to train workers in its operation or make modifications in its production line to permit the new machine to be integrated into the production process or take some other such action that involves cost. When the industrial marketing manager fails to realize all of the appropriate costs, that manager will not communicate with the customer firm, and the products may fail because of not fully understanding that customer's particular total required investment related to the purchase of the drill press.

Failure to Understand the New Product's Technical Requirements in Customer Firms

Products fail in the industrial market because many marketing managers also fail to understand a new product's requirements on a customer's technical and applications skills.[16] This is somewhat similar to the previous reason and takes place when the manager fails to realize that an adoption of a particular product will require the customer firm to hire new personnel or retrain existing personnel or take some other such action because that customer firm presently does not possess the required technical sophistication required to install and operate the product.

Overemphasis on Technical and Production Requirements

Many industrial products are designed to meet the specifications of the company's own research and development, engineering, or production personnel rather than the demands of the marketplace. As previously stated, this is quite common in industries where products are technically sophisticated and where in-house technical people believe that they know, because of their own technical expertise, what buyers are seeking. Thus, these people decide what products and services will be produced. Although this approach often results in products of high technical quality, it often also results in products that have little relationship to specific market needs and, therefore, contributes to product failures.

Time Lag between Research and Production

The time lag between field data collection and production also contributes to product failures in the industrial market even where industrial marketing managers have made honest attempts to go to the marketplace for product specifications and then built their products to those specifications. During the time between data collection and actual production, however, buyer specifications may have changed, or competitors have introduced new products to fulfill the specifications, or some other such action has taken place that renders the new product unmarketable.

It should be noted that many of these causes of industrial product failure could be minimized and even avoided if the industrial marketing manager would make use of appropriate marketing intelligence and a screening process for new products. Far too many industrial marketing managers appear to accept product failures as a way of life, assume them to be unavoidable, and simply accept them as an uncontrollable factor. This does not have to be the case if the causes of failure are recognized and action taken to avoid these causes. As can be seen, many of the reasons cited stem from not knowing the customer well enough or the market well enough to produce products that satisfy market requirements. If the marketing manager screened new product ideas in the manner developed in this chapter, many new product failures could be avoided.

THE PRODUCT MANAGER IN THE INDUSTRIAL MARKET

One final area of industrial product strategy is worthy of mention. Throughout this chapter reference has been made to the marketing manager as the decision maker in various product area decisions. In many industrial marketing companies, this is the way it is—marketing aspects of product strategy are the direct responsibility of the marketing manager. In other firms, however, specialists are utilized to manage the product area of the overall marketing mix. These specialists are normally referred to as product managers.

Product managers have evolved over time in the industrial market because many marketing managers have found the product area to be so critical and so complex that specialists were required to handle the area adequately. It has even been argued that in the marketplace companies do not really compete—it is their products that compete! This reasoning has led to the recognition that because products may well be the determinant of success or failure, the product area is no place for a generalist, with the result that specialists, the product managers, have come into prominence. Generally, the product manager has the responsibility of coordinating company marketing and sales efforts for particular products or product lines. In this responsibility, this person reports to the marketing manager, as does the advertising manager, the sales manager, the marketing research manager, and other such marketing officers. According to studies that have been conducted, the product manager, in making decisions, interacts with buyers, distributors, the sales force, engineers, advertising agencies, product development teams, and marketing research teams. The product manager's responsibilities may actually include development and screening of product ideas, planning of new products, development of a marketing plan for the product or products, working with sales managers and salesmen on sales strategies, working with advertising managers and advertising agencies on appropriate promotional programs, working with sales promotion people on packaging, working with distribution managers to bring about effective physical distribution of the product, pricing the product, and providing necessary service and technical assistance.

In short, the product manager takes the product from the idea stage to the operational stage in the customer's plant complete with service, technical assistance, and performance feedback—"from conception through profitable performance in the marketplace."[17] In summary, the product manager is a marketing tactician much as is the advertising manager, the sales manager, the distribution manager, the sales promotion manager, and the marketing research manager. One major difference, however, is that a company may have any number of product managers, depending upon the composition of its product line.

In spite of the great number of responsibilities carried by the product manager, this manager generally lacks corresponding authority. He has the normal responsibilities required of managers, but very often has little or no authority to carry out those responsibilities and is typically in a staff rather than a line position.[18] What this implies is that authority rests with the marketing manager and, therefore, whether an industrial firm uses a product manager or not, the basic product principles discussed in this chapter apply to the industrial marketing manager.

CHAPTER SUMMARY

Product strategy is generally considered the first substrategy in the overall marketing strategy formulation of the industrial marketing manager. This is so because without the product, the other substrategies of promotion, price, and distribution are almost impossible to select. Industrial product strategy was defined, and the basic differences between industrial and consumer product strategies were developed. The importance of industrial product planning was discussed, and the product life cycle was analyzed in relation to the types of decisions made in industrial product strategy. A format for screening new industrial product ideas was developed, and causes of industrial product failures were analyzed. Finally, the role of the product manager in industrial product strategy was discussed.

QUESTIONS FOR CHAPTER 7

1. The ultimate criterion in adding a new product to an industrial firm's existing product line should be that product's contribution to overall com-

pany profits. Do you agree or disagree with this statement? If you agree, why do you agree? If you disagree, why do you disagree?

2. How does the concept of derived demand affect the product offerings of an industrial marketing company? Explain your answer.
3. How do multiple buying influences in industrial customer firms make the task of industrial product strategy formulation more difficult?
4. What is the role of the product manager in industrial marketing?
5. Industrial products fail in the marketplace for essentially the same reasons that consumer products fail. Do you agree or disagree with this statement? If you agree, why do you agree? If you disagree, why do you disagree?

8

CHANNEL STRATEGY IN
INDUSTRIAL MARKETING

Once customer firms have been defined and located, a marketing plan formulated on the basis of sound marketing intelligence, and a product strategy developed, the next logical area to be addressed is that of getting the product physically to the customers. This is the area of channel strategy in the industrial market—setting up and maintaining those channels of distribution most effective in getting the company's product mix to the intended market segments in the most economical manner. The actual formulation of such a channel strategy to accomplish this basic task can be called channel management.

In the industrial market, channels can be "direct," which means that the marketing organization sells directly to its industrial customers. No middlemen are involved in the direct channel.

Industrial channels of distribution can also be "indirect," meaning that the marketing company utilizes independent middlemen, most usually industrial distributors or manufacturers' representatives or both, to reach its intended customer firms.

Both direct and indirect channels are widely used in the industrial market, and the circumstances leading to the use of each will be developed in detail in this chapter. Whether channels are direct, indirect, or a combination of the two methods is immaterial as long as the marketing manager can be assured that the chosen channels are covering each customer group and that they are covering each geographic area that must be covered and that they are properly presenting each of the product lines to the appropriate customer firms. When all three of these considerations are met, the manager has formulated an effective channel strategy.

139

INDUSTRIAL CHANNEL STRATEGY

Industrial channel strategy involves the determination of specific channel objectives, the choice of what kinds of channel arrangements are to be used, the decision to use or not to use middlemen, the determination of the types and number of such middlemen if they are to be used, the setting up of procedures and arrangements for working with such middlemen, the making of decisions regarding the physical distribution of goods and services through the selected channels, and the control and evaluation of the adopted channels. This implies a number of areas of responsibility in channels for the industrial marketing manager. These areas are as follows: (1) setting channel objectives; (2) evaluating channel alternatives; (3) choosing the channel or channels to be utilized; (4) determining the types and number of middlemen, if any, to be used; (5) establishing policies and procedures for serving those selected middlemen—policies and procedures that clearly define the responsibilities and rights of both the manufacturer and the middlemen; (6) creating contractual arrangements with those middlemen selected; (7) implementing or making operational the channel or channels selected; (8) moving goods physically through the channel or channels selected; (9) controlling the channel or channels to see if they are operating smoothly and attaining the defined objectives; (10) modifying the selected channel or channels as the occasion requires; and (11) redefining objectives, if necessary, as the occasion requires.

Differences between Industrial and Consumer Channel Strategies

By definition, channel strategy is channel strategy whether it be in the industrial or the consumer market—the basic areas of responsibility are essentially the same in principle. But the implementation of those principles can be quite different. There are basic differences between the two markets that affect decision making in the channel area of industrial marketing. These major differences can be summarized as follows.

Shorter Channels of Distribution. The industrial market is characterized by shorter channels owing primarily to buyer expectations or preferences and to product characteristics. Industrial purchasing agents buying high-priced, complex products do not want to deal with middlemen, preferring to buy from company representatives who have direct access to company headquarters and who can get immediate answers to their problems. In addition, it is often very difficult to find middlemen who possess the required technical and service capabilities to sell sophisticated products and/or services to the industrial buyers. On the basis of the dollar volume of industrial sales, it is estimated that about three-quarters of all industrial products are sold directly, with no independent middlemen involved. Another way of saying this is that the higher the unit value of the product or service being marketed, the higher the probability of a direct channel. When middlemen are used by industrial marketing managers, there are rarely more than two or three layers as contrasted with the consumer market, where brokers may sell to wholesalers, who then sell to jobbers, who, in turn, may sell to subjobbers, and so on.

Different Types of Middlemen. Where middlemen are found in the industrial market, they differ from those found in the consumer market. There are really no true retailers or wholesalers in the industrial market, although it is true that many industrial-type products such as power saws, drills, and so forth, are sold through such middlemen for ultimate sale into the consumer market. In these cases, however, industrial marketing actually is not taking place. Although a number of middlemen can be found, there are only two types of middlemen of real consequence in the industrial market—the industrial distributor and the manufacturer's representative, also called the manufacturer's agent or the manufacturer's rep or simply the MR. Both of these middlemen were described briefly in chapter 1, but they will be analyzed in depth in this chapter. In terms of the dollar value of industrial sales, these two middlemen account for the remaining one-quarter of industrial goods, with a slightly higher percentage being estimated for the distributor than for the MR.

Less Choice of Channels. The industrial marketing manager has less choice of channel options than does his consumer marketing counterpart. With reference to Fig. 8.1, a study of 156 industrial manufacturers in 220 product lines disclosed that six basic channels account for 100 percent of industrial sales. As Fig. 8.1 illustrates, these six basic channels are variations of three options—the direct channel, the industrial distributor, and the manufacturer's representative. It is also important to realize that the industrial marketing manager is not normally able to choose any of the six channels interchangeably. As will be shown, they all provide different functions, with the result that the choice is normally between two and three options. For example, it is normally not possible to substitute a distributor for a manufacturer's rep, which means that the marketing manager does not have the choice of these two middlemen, but rather is restricted to the use of one of them depending on the functions the manager wishes to have performed. In some instances, the manager has no choice at all in channel selection—customers have always purchased through one particular channel and are very reluctant to buy through any other. Sometimes there are accepted industry channels that should not be tampered with. And the marketing manager cannot always presume selected middlemen will, in fact, want to represent that manager's company or carry that company's products.

Higher Sales and Service Expectations of Middlemen. Because of customer expectations and the complexity of industrial products, there is much more emphasis on selling, service, and technical assistance in industrial channels than in consumer channels. Although it is true that middlemen in the consumer durable market also perform the functions of selling and service, they normally do not do so to the degree that industrial distributors and manufacturer's reps may have to do in the industrial market, where personal selling, pre- and postsales servicing, and technical assistance in setting up operations are prerequisites for effective marketing. As will be shown later in this chapter, manufacturers' reps are basically independent salesmen selling on behalf of their manufacturing principals, and distributors are also often chosen on the basis of the capabilities of their field sales forces.

Some other differences between channels in the industrial and consumer markets can be seen in Table 8.1, which is based on a survey of 298 industrial manufacturers, 52 consumer durable goods manufacturers, and 87 consumer nondurable producers. Note that the determination of channels and selection of middlemen are of much less importance to industrial marketing managers than to consumer marketing managers. This reflects the points made earlier regarding shorter channels and less choice of middlemen. The choice of the proper channel is less complex in the industrial market than it is in the consumer market. Notice should also be taken of the fact that industrial marketing managers appear to feel that development of and assistance to channel components are less important than do their consumer marketing counterparts. This can probably be attributed to the high level of expertise and capability found in many industrial middlemen. Finally, the table shows that the industrial marketing managers believe field warehousing and field inventory control to be more important than do consumer marketing managers. This is due to the production requirements of industrial customers. In the consumer market, if a retailer runs out of toothpaste, the customer may suffer an inconvenience, but it is highly unlikely that such a shortage would cause any major consternation. In the industrial market, however, if a distributor or a branch house runs out of OEM component parts, that stock-out could shut down the production line of an industrial customer, with disastrous marketing effects on the supplier, as most buyers will not tolerate late deliveries of such products. In some cases in the industrial market, customer firms unload incoming shipments right into the production line to avoid second and third handling of the same products. When this happens, field warehousing and field inventory control become a very critical part of the manager's channel strategy.

Table 8.1
RELATIVE IMPORTANCE OF THE ELEMENTS OF DISTRIBUTION

Distribution Activity	Producers of:		
	Industrial Goods	Consumer Durables	Consumer Nondurables
Transportation	23.8%	12.2%	26.8%
Warehousing and Inventory Control	28.3%	22.7%	23.6%
Determination of Channels	10.5%	14.7%	13.6%
Selection of Establishments in Channels	13.3%	21.7%	14.6%
Assistance to and Development of the Channel	19.1%	27.0%	21.4%
Other	5.1%	1.7%	0.0%
Total	100.0%	100.0%	100.0%

Source: John G. Udell, *Successful Marketing Strategies* (Madison: Mimir Publishers, Inc., 1972), p. 50.
Note: Data are based on the average point allocations of 298 industrial goods producers, 52 consumer durable goods manufacturers, and 87 consumer nondurable goods manufacturers.

This entire discussion implies there are major differences in the channel area between industrial and consumer marketing even though the same basic principles may be applicable to both. Because of this, a complete analysis of industrial channel strategy is in order.

FORMULATING INDUSTRIAL CHANNEL STRATEGY

As has been developed in this text, channel strategy is but one part of overall marketing strategy, and, as such, it must be formulated within the context of the company's marketing plan. Constructing industrial channels requires specific market segmentation and also a sound knowledge of the product or service and its requirements. Unless these two things are known, it is virtually impossible to construct realistic and effective channels of distribution. To attempt to build a channel of distribution without knowing whom it is supposed to reach makes no marketing sense whatsoever! Similarly, trying to pick channel components without knowing the product or its requirements is equally foolish. Thus, the logic in this text of developing SIC-defined market segments and determining product specifications to fill the needs in those segments seems to be in order. It is now necessary to match those products and market segments with an appropriate channel of distribution. To accomplish this, the marketing manager must undertake the following tasks: (1) channel objectives must be established, (2) channel alternatives must be assessed, (3) the appropriate channel or channels must be selected, (4) arrangements must be set up with the selected channel components, and (5) the selected channel or channels must be made operational and then controlled. Because these are important steps in effective channel management, they will be explained in some detail.

Establish Channel Objectives

Once segments have been defined and located and once product strategy has been formulated, the establishment of channel objectives should be undertaken. As was developed in the case of product objectives, channel objectives must be consistent with overall corporate and marketing objectives in the company's marketing plan. Some typical objectives used by industrial marketing managers in setting up their channels of distribution are as follows.

Low Cost of Operation. Everything else being equal, industrial marketing managers strive to reduce costs in their channels with the logic being that lower costs allow for higher profitability and lower prices with which to compete in the marketplace. As will be developed in detail in a later chapter, the highest cost channel in the industrial market is the direct channel, with the company's own salesmen calling on the customers. In recent years, many industrial marketing managers have switched to distributors and manufacturers' reps when such middlemen can be found who can supply the required sales effort to replace the company's own salesmen. This permits the manager to maintain the required level of sales effort and at the same time lower his distribution costs and achieve the objective of low cost channel operations. This is a very common industrial channel objective, although, in adopting such an objective, the manager usually relinquishes some control of his channel.

Control. It is also quite common to find industrial marketing managers desiring a high degree of control over their channels of distribution. This may come about because the manager feels the company's policies and strategies are best for its products and does not want individual channel components deciding otherwise. In other words, the manufacturer wishes to exercise considerable control of the channel of distribution! This objective often leads to direct channels, which may be the most expensive, but which are also the easiest to control. If middlemen are used by a manager with this channel objective, those middlemen had better be chosen on the basis of their willingness to be controlled by the manufacturer. Only as a last resort would the marketing manager in this case employ a recalcitrant middleman in the channel regardless of the latter's sales and service capabilities. If control is the basic objective of the marketing manager, it is imperative to use either a direct channel or one with middlemen that can be controlled. If this is not done, chances of achieving the objective will be reduced. On the other hand, it must be realized that this objective requires a company that is financially able to support it. Probably most industrial marketing managers would like to control their channels of distribution, but for many of them it is a financial impossibility.

Sales Effort. As has been stated on a number of occasions in this text, personal selling plays a great role in the industrial market. It also plays a great role in industrial channels, and many marketing managers have a high degree of sales effort as a basic channel objective. This has a number of effects on channels found in the industrial market. Some companies will sell directly because they are unable to find middlemen who possess the required sales ability. This often happens with very sophisticated technical products. In such cases, direct channels are not used by choice, but by necessity. In other instances where middlemen can be used, distributors and manufacturer's reps are selected for inclusion into a channel on the basis of their proved sales capabilities.

Service and Technical Assistance. As has also been developed, service and technical assistance are big factors in the industrial market, and this extends into the channel of distribution. For example, a marketing manager may use a direct channel and provide service facilities because of the inability to find middlemen with the capability or the desire to provide such service. On the other hand, the manager may choose middlemen, particularly industrial distributors, on the basis of their proved service facilities and personnel. In other instances, a marketing manager with this objective may be prohibited from using manufacturer's representatives in the channel because of the reluctance of the latter to provide such service or technical assistance.

Market Feedback. Some industrial marketing managers expect market feedback from their channels of distribution and make this a specific channel objective. When a company has such an objective, it may well lead to channel components being selected on the basis of their willingness to provide such feedback. For example, it would be unrealistic to expect manufacturers' reps or company salesmen compensated on a straight commission basis to take time out to search out market information when they are being compensated on the basis of the sales they make.

Company Image. The image of the company is often very important to the industrial marketing manager, and creation and maintenance of that image often extends into channels of distribution. Customers form impressions of a manufacturer and its products through their dealings with that manufacturer or its middlemen. What this means is that manufacturers with such an objective must find middlemen whose images are consistent with theirs. This may mean that distributors and/or manufacturers' reps are chosen on that basis. And it can even be that a direct channel might be used because sufficient middlemen with the proper image cannot be located or enlisted by the manufacturer.

These are but a few examples of the types of channel objectives found in the industrial market. This does not mean to imply that marketing managers have but one channel objective, although that could happen. Rather, it means that managers have a number of channel objectives that directly affect their choice of channels. To illustrate, two manufacturers of similar electronic components may behave quite differently because of their respective channel objectives. One firm has the objectives of control, sales effort, and feedback, which could very well lead to the implementation of a direct company salesman channel if the objectives are to be achieved. The other company has the objectives of low cost and sales effort, which could lead that manufacturer into the use of industrial distributors in the channel. Therefore, the establishment of channel objectives is imperative if realistic channel management is to take place.

Assess Channel Alternatives

Once channel objectives have been established, it is the task of the industrial marketing manager to study various channel alternatives that could be employed to attain these objectives. Can the channel objectives best be achieved through the use of a direct channel using the company's own field salesmen and service representatives? Or can those objectives best be achieved through a network of distributors or manufacturer's reps selling to the customers? With reference again to Fig. 8.1, it is clear that the marketing manager should analyze each of the six basic industrial channels to decide which of them—or possible variations—would best fit particular objectives, be compatible with products, and at the same time satisfy the purchasing requirements of customers in the marketplace. The manager may find that there is not a single answer here, but rather that multiple channels are needed where the company produces a number of product lines and sells them into a number of different market segments. At any rate, the manager should attempt to find a number of alternative channel possibilities that might be employed to realize channel objectives. Then, the manager must choose among those to find the best.

Choose the Appropriate Channel or Channels

After channel objectives have been established and after alternatives consistent with those objectives have been listed and analyzed, the manager must choose the channel or channels to be used. This choice is normally made on the basis of such factors as (1) buying practices in the defined market segments, (2) competitors' channels of distribution, (3) the unit value of the product, (4) the size or bulk of the product, (5) costs of channel alternatives, (6) technical sophistication of the product, (7) the level of service and technical assistance required by target market customers, (8) the sales effort required to sell the product effectively, (9) field warehousing required, (10) field inventory requirements, (11) special handling required by the product or the customer, and (12) breadth and depth of the market segments involved.

Factors such as these are used to screen alternatives, and, on their bases, generalizations such as the following can be made. Industrial goods of high unit value are normally sold directly, whereas those of low to average transaction value are normally sold through distributors. Manufacturers' reps are often used by companies that are financially strained and require personal selling, but cannot afford their own sales personnel. It is the task of the industrial marketing manager to choose the best channels of distribution for company products and customers based on characteristics such as were developed in the preceding paragraph as long as those characteristics are consistent with predetermined channel objectives.

Set Up Arrangements with Selected Channel Components

Once the appropriate channel or channels have been selected, the job of the manager is to set up operational arrangements with the selected channel components. If the direct channel is decided upon, channel management decisions, with the exception of physical distribution, are over, and sales management takes over. What this means is that if the manager decides the best channel is the company's own salesmen, then it is up to the company's sales manager to set up territories, establish sales quotas, hire salesmen, and so forth. With the exception of physical distribution, there are really no channel areas of responsibility left. Because of this aspect, no further discussion of direct channels will take place in this chapter, but will be covered in chapter

9, which will be devoted exclusively to industrial sales management and personal selling.

If, however, indirect channels are required, the channel management area becomes more complex. Specific types of middlemen must be selected and approached regarding their taking on the company's products. As stated previously, the only middlemen of consequence in the industrial market are distributors and manufacturers' reps; so the decision of what type of middlemen to use is not that difficult. The actual recruiting, however, of desired individual middlemen is quite difficult in many instances, particularly where new products are involved. It is often thought that the manufacturer, almost by virtue of being the manufacturer, has the upper hand when it comes to middlemen and that therefore the middlemen come to the manufacturers for their products. In the actual industrial market, such is often not the case! Quality distributors and manufacturers' reps must be sought out, contacted, and persuaded to carry the manufacturer's products. Often, this involves a tough selling job when middlemen are highly qualified and other manufacturers also want them to carry their products. The industrial marketing manager is forced to sell such middlemen on the merit of being associated with the company as opposed to being associated with competitors.

Setting up such channel arrangements basically becomes a legal problem where responsibilities and rights of both manufacturer and middleman are spelled out in a formal contract. These contracts cover such specific points as the following for distributors and for manufacturers' representatives.

Industrial Distributors. Arrangements between a manufacturer and an industrial distributor would cover such points as (1) sales territories or scope of coverage permitted the middleman; (2) F.O.B. points; (3) cash discounts, for example, 2/10: n/30; (4) trade discounts; (5) quantity discounts; (6) rebates; (7) consigned goods; (8) provisions for returned goods; (9) warranties and guarantees; (10) cooperative advertising arrangements; (11) conditions for termination of the contract between manufacturer and middleman; (12) selling aids and supplies to be furnished the middleman by the manufacturer; (13) required inventory levels expected of the distributor; (14) handling of inquiries and quotations; (15) rights of both parties upon the termination of the contract between manufacturer and distributor; and (16) service and technical assistance required of both the manufacturer and distributor.

The Manufacturer's Representatives. Arrangements between a manufacturer and a manufacturer's representative would cover such points as (1) sales territories assigned to the rep, (2) commission rates, (3) payment of commissions, (4) restrictions on handling competitive products, (5) termination of the arrangement—formal notice of termination, (6) provisions for arbitration in adjusting disputes, (7) conditions under which the rep can bind the manufacturer as principal, (8) selling aids and supplies to be furnished the rep by the manufacturer, (9) conditions of cooperative advertising, (10) handling of invoices and collections, (11) handling of inquiries and quotations, (12) rights of both the manufacturer and the rep upon the termination of the contract between them, and (13) consignment conditions.

Contract conditions differ between distributors and manufacturers' reps because distributors take legal title to the products and they also stock a field inventory. The reps, as agents, do not take title, nor do they normally take possession of the products in the field, although stocking reps can be found in some industries. As was discussed previously, these stocking reps are a hybrid between the distributor and the manufacturer's rep.

Setting up such specifics as were previously outlined is a very important consideration in setting up and implementing industrial channels. Prior to any goods ever being shipped, all these points should be agreed upon in writing in a contract signed by both parties. It is very often misunderstandings about seemingly minute points such as provisions for returned goods and the like that destroy effective channels of distribution. The industrial marketing manager must realize this beforehand and make certain middlemen are fully cognizant of all aspects of the arrangements. Only when this happens should products move through the channel.

Implement and Control the Channel or Channels

After arrangements are made with selected middlemen, the channel should be made operational. The marketing manager should then monitor the channels for their effectiveness via the marketing information system in terms of the channels and overall marketing objectives and requirements. This implies keeping current on channels and modifying channel arrangements and/or channel objectives as the occasion requires. It is important to understand that unless channel objectives are explicit, there is no way to monitor effectiveness, as there is nothing to compare performance with.

In summary, the following quotation describes the area of channel management in the industrial market.

Once the marketing department is established, it should determine what industry or industries, by SIC, will use the products. . . . If these are "direct" sales items, either full-time company salesmen will be required or manufacturer's representatives, or both. The selection, hiring, and training is an important and time consuming job. . . . If these are distributor sales items, the distributor must be selected and trained.[1]

ANALYSIS OF INDUSTRIAL MIDDLEMEN

By this time, it should be apparent that to make intelligent channel de-cisions in the industrial market, the marketing manager must have a thorough knowledge and understanding of both the industrial distributor and the man-ufacturer's representative. If this knowledge and understanding are not pres-ent, optimum use of either middleman can hardly take place. Therefore, an in-depth analysis of both the industrial distributor and the manufacturer's representative is in order.

The Industrial Distributor

An industrial distributor is an independently owned and locally managed operation that buys, stocks, and sells the production tools, operating equip-ment, and maintenance supplies used by all forms of industry. The distribu-tor differs from the wholesaler in that it services and sells the industrial mar-ket as opposed to the consumer market.

The size of industrial distribution deserves mention. According to *Indus-trial Distribution* magazine, 1973 sales by industrial distributors in the United States amounted to $20.8 billion. Table 8.2 shows the growth of sales by in-dustrial distributors during the period from 1957 to 1973. As can be seen in the table, the sales of industrial distributors have more than doubled in the past ten years ($7.8 billion in 1963 to $20.8 billion in 1973). Between 1972 and 1973 alone, distributor sales increased 27 percent despite the energy crisis, shortage of materials ranging all the way from structural steel to ax handles, lead times in ordering extending as much as 68 percent, and rising interest rates.[2]

These sales were accounted for by over 11,000 distributor units through-out the United States. According to *Industrial Distribution*'s "1973 Census of Industrial Distributors," 11,350 distributor units accounted for 80 percent of all distributors in the United States and Canada, which would amount to about 14,000 in total in the two countries. To qualify for this census, a dis-tributor must sell at least one of 98 standard industrial products to industry, stock what it sells, and employ at least one outside salesman.[3] *Industrial Dis-tribution* magazine is probably the best single source of information for the marketing manager in regard to industrial distributors.

There are three basic types of industrial distributors, which are as fol-lows.[4]

The Specialist. The specialist is the distributor who specializes in such lines as bearings, cutting tools, fasteners, machine tools, and so forth. The specialist distributor accounted for 62.6 percent of all the distributors in-cluded in *Industrial Distribution*'s 1973 census.

Table 8.2

ANNUAL DISTRIBUTOR SALES OF INDUSTRIAL
EQUIPMENT & SUPPLIES
(IN $ BILLIONS)

Year	Sales
1957	$ 6.3
1959	7.2
1961	6.9
1963	7.8
1965	9.6
1968	13.1
1971	14.1
1973	20.8

Source: Reprinted by permission from "Sales Top $20 Billion in '73—12% Gain Expected in Tough '74," *Industrial Distribution* 64 (March 1974), 24.

The General Line House. Contrasted with the specialist, the general line house is almost like an industrial supermarket, stocking a wide variety of goods and having no particular area of specialization. In the 1973 census, this type accounted for 16.2 percent of all distributors reporting.

The Combination House. The combination house is a type of distributor handling other such goods as plumbing supplies, hardware, and so forth, in addition to carrying industrial supplies. Basically, this type is a combination wholesaler and distributor operating in both the industrial and consumer markets. In the 1973 census, distributors of this type accounted for 21.2 percent of all those reporting.

There has been a definite trend toward specialization in the past decade. In 1964 only 23.0 percent were specialists as contrasted with 62.6 percent in this classification in 1973. On the other hand, general line houses accounted for 41.0 percent of *Industrial Distribution*'s census in 1964, but dropped to 16.2 percent in 1973, whereas the combination houses dropped from 36.0 percent in 1964 to 21.2 percent in 1973.[5] This trend toward distributor specialization has important implications for the industrial marketing manager, as it means that more and more distributors are available for consideration in the channels of producers of technically sophisticated products who previously had to use direct channels to obtain the level of technical expertise required by the marketplace. A continued trend toward even more specialization could well involve additional shifts from company salesmen to the use of distributors and their sales personnel.

Industrial Sales through Distributors. It is difficult to determine precisely how widely used industrial distributors are in the industrial market. In some industries they are used extensively, whereas in other industries they are rarely used, if at all. It is roughly estimated that on the basis of the dollar value of sales, about 15 to 20 percent go through industrial distributors. In terms of unit sales, about three-quarters of all industrial sales pass through distributors, as was illustrated in Fig. 8.1. It must be realized that in terms of unit sales, a nut or a washer counts the same as a blast furnace—it is one unit! Distributors are widely used by manufacturers of industrial products whose transaction values are relatively low. Table 8.3 shows the usage of distributors in eight primary industries in the industrial market. Usage of distributors ranges all the way from 35 percent in lumber to 5 percent in primary metals.

Table 8.3

DISTRIBUTION OF MANUFACTURERS' SALES THROUGH DISTRIBUTORS BY SELECTED INDUSTRIES

		Percent Sold through Distributors	
SIC Code	Industry	1958	1967
24	Lumber	33	35
28	Drugs & Chemicals	11	14
30	Rubber & Plastics	17	15
33	Primary Metals	3	5
34	Fabricated Metals	18	17
35	Machinery	18	12
36	Electrical Equipment	16	11
38	Instruments	15	12

Source: U.S. Department of Commerce, *U.S. Industrial Outlook 1972 with Projections to 1980* (Washington, D.C.: U.S. Government Printing Office, April 1972), p. 352.

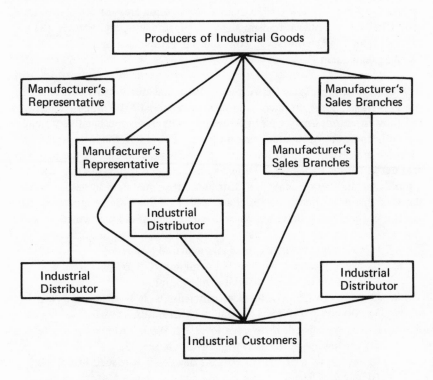

Channel of Distribution	Percent of Unit Sales
Producer–Distributor–Customer	48.7%
Producer–MR–Distributor–Customer	16.8%
Producer–Customer	12.7%
Producer–Sales Branch–Customer	9.6%
Producer–Sales Branch–Distributor–Customer	8.6%
Producer–MR–Customer	3.6%
	100.0%

Fig. 8.1. Channels in the industrial market. (Reprinted by permission from William H. Diamond, *Distribution Channels for Industrial Goods*, Columbus: Bureau of Business Research, College of Commerce and Administration, 1963.)

These general figures give an idea of the usage of distributors in the industrial market, and they show the variation that exists among industries. According to *Industrial Distribution*'s 1973 census, the five top areas of distributor specialization are (1) power transmission; (2) pipes, valves, and fittings; (3) industrial rubber; (4) contractor construction equipment; and (5) materials handling equipment.[6]

Profile of the Industrial Distributor. Industrial distributors come in all-size operations. Some are huge, and their sales exceed $100 million annually, and their inventories may exceed $3 million. Others are local and very small, and still others are of medium size. In terms of numbers, the majority of distributors appear to fall into the medium-sized classification. On the basis of data derived from *Industrial Distribution* magazine, it is possible to construct a profile of the average industrial distributor that may help in better understanding this middleman and his characteristics.[7] The average industrial distributor in the United States has characteristics such as the following:

1. It is an independently owned and managed business.
2. Its average annual sales are $2.4 million if it is specialized and $2.3 million if it is a general line distributor.
3. It processes 25,000 invoices annually if it is specialized and 36,000 invoices if it is a general line distributor.
4. If it is specialized, its average invoice is $96.00, whereas if it is of the general line type, its average invoice is $64.72.
5. Its inventory averages 15 percent of sales if it is specialized and 16 percent of sales if it is a general line distributor.
6. If it is specialized, 24 percent of its sales are made to OEMs, whereas 14 percent of its sales are to this type of customer if it is general line.
7. It employs a total of 31 people in its organization if it is specialized and 25 people if it is of the general line classification.
8. If it is a specialist, it averages six outside salesmen and four inside salesmen, whereas if it is a general line type, it averages five outside salesmen and four inside salesmen.
9. Approximately 25 percent of all distributors have branch operations, although about one-half of these have but one branch. On the other hand, about 9 percent of all distributors have between five and nine branch operations, and 1 percent of all distributors operates ten or more branches.
10. Approximately 30 percent of all distributors started their business since 1960, and almost two-thirds of them have been established since the end of World War II.

If a summary is made from this profile, it can be seen that the industrial distributor is a locally owned and operated middleman that provides field warehousing, sales, and service capabilities into the industrial market. As such, this middleman can be a very effective channel component for the marketing manager.

How the Distributor Serves the Marketing Manager. Although it is interesting to view the industrial distributor demographically as was done in the profile, the real value of doing this is for the purpose of understanding this type of middleman well enough to know how it could be of service to the industrial marketing manager. What is to be gained from using distributors in an industrial channel of distribution that could not be achieved via the branch house and company salesmen? The following are some of the ways in which the distributor can be used to advantage by the industrial marketing manager: (1) the distributor can provide necessary sales effort, (2) the distributor can provide local market coverage, (3) the distributor can provide warehousing for the manufacturer, (4) the distributor can perform a credit function for the manufacturer, (5) the distributor is often a good source of local market information, and (6) the distributor can lower the cost of distribution for the manufacturer. Because these are all important reasons for using distributors, it is important that their implications be fully understood by the marketing manager.

If it is assumed that the average distributor has five outside salesmen and that each salesman averages six calls per day, this amounts to 30 sales calls per distributor per day at virtually no cost to the manufacturer. The cost to the marketing manager of making the same 30 sales calls with company salesmen would be about $2,000 on the basis of the McGraw-Hill Research Department's 1973 figure of $66.68 for the cost of an industrial sales call.[8] This figure of $2,000 is for one distributor for one working day. In one work year of 260 days, this would amount to $520,000. Multiply this by a network of 50 or 100 or 250 distributors across the country, and the full savings in sales costs may be appreciated. The key to all this, however, lies in the selling effectiveness of the distributor sales personnel. If the latter are as good as the manufacturer's own salesmen, the savings are real. If the distributor's salesmen are not as competent as the manufacturer's salesmen, it is another matter entirely. Nevertheless, the point is clear—a good distributor could greatly reduce the sales effort required of the marketing manager if distributor salesmen could be used to sell the company's particular products.

Because the distributor is locally owned and operated, its personnel often knows the buyers and buying influences on a more personal basis than might the company's own salesmen coming into the community from outside. This is an intangible, yet real, asset in that many buyers prefer to purchase from local companies and from individuals they know and trust. In addition, local distributors can provide quick delivery and service on a local phone call. Thus, if the market of an industrial company demands some form of local representation, the marketing manager can make good use of the industrial distributor.

Inasmuch as distributors do stock goods in the field, using them can reduce warehousing required by the marketing manager. The distributor takes title to the goods it stocks and, therefore, can free the manufacturer of the cost of maintaining such inventories in the field. In addition, the distributor maintains its own buildings, materials handling equipment, and personnel all at virtually no cost to the manufacturer. The alternative, of course, is for the manufacturer to provide the same facilities and inventory via its own branch house with all the accompanying costs. And because distributors carry many lines, their warehousing allows their customers to buy many products from one source, which is something not possible with the manufacturer's own branch house. The industrial marketing manager desiring field warehousing and inventory may find the distributor a worthwhile component in the company's channels of distribution.

Distributors can also reduce the credit requirements of the industrial goods manufacturer. Because the distributor takes title, it extends credit to its customers, thus relieving the manufacturer of this requirement. Assume, for example, the case of a manufacturer of transistors selling its products to OEM manufacturers of electrical machinery and equipment. Such an industrial manufacturer could easily sell such horizontal products to 10,000 customer firms, and if these customers were sold directly, the manufacturer would have to bear the costs and efforts of credit and collection for each of them. If, however, those same 10,000 customers could be reached by a network of 100 or 200 distributors, the credit function could be greatly reduced for the marketing manager in the manufacturing firm.

Because distributors are local, they are often in a position to possess local market knowledge that would be very difficult for a national or regional manufacturing company to obtain elsewhere. And as distributors are very often technically oriented, they are good sources of technical data. To the marketing manager desiring such assistance, the right local distributors could offer considerable benefit.

In many areas of the industrial market, the industrial customer pays less when it buys from a distributor than it would pay if it bought direct from the manufacturer. A good example of this can be found in the case of distributors in the steel service industry. In a publication entitled *We Could Save You a Few Thousand Bucks,* which was published by the Steel Service Center Institute, Ducommun Metals & Supply Company, the West's largest industrial distributor, stresses to potential customers what they could save by buying from Ducommun rather than by buying direct. Ducommun cites savings of 37.7 percent for the customer through shifting the costs of possession to the distributor.[9] Based on $1 million of inventory, the 37.7 percent savings is computed as follows: (1) 6.8 percent reduction for the customer in housing costs of the inventory, (2) 9.1 percent savings in cost of capital of the $1 million inventory, (3) 8.5 percent savings in scrap costs to the customer because the distributor cuts steel to the requirements of the customer and eliminates scrap costs incurred by the customer when it buys standard sizes and cuts itself to its own specifications, (4) 2.5 percent savings in equipment costs to the customer since it does not need it because the distributor is performing the inventory function, and (5) 10.8 percent savings in personnel or manpower costs owing to reduced labor requirements. This amounts to a 37.7 percent savings in total cost to the customer of the $1 million in inventory. Based on this $1 million figure, savings of 37.7 percent or $377,000 could be realized by the customer shifting the above costs to the distributor. This is a strong argument for the customer benefits to be derived from using distributors and, of course, has meaning to the industrial marketing manager in the manufacturing company who wishes to get products to customers at the lowest possible price.

Limitations to Using Industrial Distributors. The preceding section implies so many benefits from using the distributor that an industrial channel of distribution without this middleman seems illogical. Yet for many marketing managers in the industrial market, distributors may make little sense. They may be impossible to control and, in some cases, may actually dominate the channel. They may not possess the technical sales or service capabilities to handle sophisticated products. Often they will handle competing products and will not emphasize the marketing manager's products in particular. Their product lines could have adverse effects on the products of some manufacturers. Like many consumer market middlemen, distributors look for turnover and margin, and they may not accept products that take considerable time to sell or that demand a great deal of particular attention. Moreover, because their warehousing costs them money, distributors may be very reluctant to handle industrial products of large bulk. Finally, the use of a distributor may make little sense if customers prefer to purchase directly from the manufacturer.

In short, distributors make good sense for low transaction value, off-the-shelf industrial products sold into a widely dispersed horizontal market. They make good sense in other instances also, but they must be screened closely against channel objectives. As Table 8.2 illustrated, the increase of distributor sales from $7.8 billion in 1963 to $20.8 billion in 1973 would indicate that they are making more and more sense to industrial marketing managers and that their contributions exceed their limitations for many manufacturers.

Locating Industrial Distributors. For the industrial marketing manager considering the use of distributors in the company's channels of distribution, data on distributors are relatively easy to find. Distributors can be defined by SIC, as with SIC 5084 (distributors of industrial machinery and equipment) and with SIC 5085 (distributors of industrial supplies). Once the marketing manager defines required distributors by SIC, individual firms can be located in the same manner prescribed back in chapter 3 of this text. Another good source of information on individual distributors is the *Directory of Industrial Distributors,* which can be purchased from *Industrial Distribution* magazine. Finally, information regarding industrial distributors may be obtained from associations such as the National Industrial Distributors Association, the Southern Industrial Distributors Association, and the National Association of Wholesalers-Distributors.

The Manufacturer's Representative

The other middleman most often found in the industrial market is the manufacturer's representative, commonly called the manufacturer's rep, or simply the MR. In some markets, they are known as manufacturing agents, engineering representatives, and even brokers, although the latter term is technically incorrect. In this section, the term *MR* shall be used to describe this middleman.

The MR is an independent middleman who works as an agent for manufacturing principals on a contractual basis. Although women MRs may at times be found, the great preponderance of MRs in the industrial market are men. Unlike the distributor, the MR does not take title, and usually he does not even take possession of the goods involved. Basically, the MR is an independent salesman! He usually sells within assigned territories, and he is compensated on a straight commission for those sales. He may represent any number of manufacturers in that territory or closely related territories, whose products are normally complementary rather than competitive. With his line of complementary products from various manufacturers, the MR is often able to supply a complete product line to his customers. Under normal conditions, he possesses limited authority with regard to prices and terms of sale. Simply stated, the MR is an independent salesman and is used by manufacturers in the industrial market in lieu of their own company salesmen. The basic function of the MR is to sell his principal's products in the assigned sales territory.

In all likelihood, the average MR probably began in business by working as a salesman for a manufacturer or a distributor or another manufacturer's rep, although MRs have come from such areas as purchasing, production, and engineering. After working in the field and building customer contacts for a period of time and believing those contacts to be loyal, he quit his job and started his own sales business, continuing to sell to his customers. MRs are often thought of as the elite of industrial salesmen, and they are often just that! It takes an excellent salesman to live on a straight commission form of compensation. If he does not sell, he does not eat! There is little calling for the MR who is a poor salesman—they simply do not survive in the industrial market.

The impression being created here is that MRs are one-man operations. This is not necessarily the case, although many MR operations are accounted for by single individuals using their homes as offices. On the other end, however, are multiman, multioffice operations that are incorporated and employ large numbers of people.

It should also be understood that some MRs do carry inventory for their principals and they ship from that inventory. They are known as stocking representatives, and they are a relatively small percentage of all MRs in the industrial market. Strictly speaking, a stocking rep is more of a combination distributor and MR than a true manufacturer's representative.

MRs do not work only in the industrial market. They can be found also in various areas of the consumer market, often being lumped together with brokers. It is in the industrial market, however, where their greatest marketing impact seems to be.

Industrial Sales Through MRs. Estimating how much of industrial sales pass through the MR is difficult to determine, but some general figures may help to provide insight. If Fig. 8.1 is referred to again, it can be seen that, based on unit sales, about 20 percent of industrial sales involve the MR, with 16.8 percent accounted for by MRs selling to distributors, but only 3.6 percent by MRs selling direct to the user or OEM industrial customer. In the electronics industry, it is estimated that reps account for about 12 percent of the total sales of that industry.[10] Table 8.4 illustrates the percentage of total sales through MRs of selected industrial products by SIC number and provides insight into sales by MRs in comparison with the other industrial channel components. This table does not include industrial goods sold directly without any middlemen or branch operations whatsoever, and thus actual percentages accounted for by MRs would be even smaller than those shown in the table. This table does indicate, however, that there are great variations in the usage of MRs, all the way from 4.9 percent in SIC 5082 (construction, mining machinery and equipment) to 21.7 percent in SIC 5065 (electronic parts & equipment). All told, MRs are probably the least utilized in total of all possible industrial channel components.

Table 8.4
SALES THROUGH INDUSTRIAL CHANNELS OF
SELECTED INDUSTRIAL PRODUCTS

SIC	Products	Percent through Manufacturer's Sales Branches	Percent through Distributors	Percent through Manufacturer's Reps
5063	Electrical apparatus, equipment, supplies	22.6	64.1	13.3
5065	Electronic parts & equipment	10.3	68.0	21.7
5081	Commercial machines & equipment	32.0	61.7	6.3
5082	Construction, mining machinery, equipment	6.9	88.2	4.9
5084	Industrial machinery & equipment	17.1	66.3	16.6
5085	Industrial supplies	13.7	75.3	11.0
5086	Professional equipment & supplies	14.6	80.5	4.9

Source: Adapted from U.S. Department of Commerce, *1967 Census of Business. Wholesale Trade* (Washington, D.C.: U.S. Government Printing Office, 1967), pp. 1–7.

Profile of the Manufacturer's Representative. Manufacturers' reps come in all forms and differ according to the size of their operations, territories covered, depth and breadth of product lines carried, number of principals represented, commission rates, and their technical and sales capabilities. In spite of all these differences, it is possible to construct a profile of the average MR, which may be helpful in better understanding this middleman and his characteristics. The average MR in the United States has characteristics similar to the following:

1. He runs an independently owned and operated business.
2. The business organization is generally small in size, averaging about six to ten employees, and it is more than likely to be incorporated.
3. Commissions average 5.9 percent, but can range from 1 percent in

Table 8.5

COMMISSION RATES RECEIVED BY MANUFACTURERS'
REPRESENTATIVES IN SELECTED INDUSTRIAL
PRODUCT CLASSIFICATIONS

MR's Product Classification	Number of Reps Interviewed	Average Commission Rate	Highest Commission Rate	Lowest Commission Rate
Construction Machinery, Equipment	61	10.0%	35%	3%
Electronics	270	8.8%	50%	1%
Farm Supplies	29	9.0%	20%	2%
Industrial Chemicals	78	13.5%	50%	1%
Industrial Machinery, Equipment, Supplies	566	14.2%	52%	1%
Iron, Steel Products	180	6.4%	36%	1%
Nonferrous Metals	125	6.3%	20%	1%
Plastics	52	6.3%	50%	2%
Plumbing, Heating Equipment & Supplies	190	10.6%	50%	1%
Professional Equipment, Supplies	17	10.0%	25%	4%

Source: Reprinted by permission of the publisher from *A & R Commission Rate Survey* (Los Angeles: Manufacturers' Agents National Association).

the food industry to 35 percent for the sale of instruments and machinery.[11] For a more complete breakdown on commissions paid to MRs, see Table 8.5. In most MR operations, the sales commission is the primary source of company income.

4. The average MR provides no warehousing and carries no stock. He does not ship from inventory, nor does he take title to the products involved. In most instances, goods are drop-shipped from the manufacturing principals to the customer.

5. The average MR does not assume credit, nor does he have the authority to set prices in the marketplace.

6. He represents an average of 12.4 manufacturing principals, whose products are compatible and complementary and that provide the MR with a complete product line for his customers. He has represented these 12.4 principals for an average of 12.5 years.[12]

7. His major expenses are selling expenses, which account for over one-half of his total operating expenses.

8. He covers assigned territories that are often very large in area (even up to five or six states), with the result that he is most likely to concentrate his efforts on large customers for large orders.

9. His sales volume can range anywhere from under $50,000 per year to over $2 million per year depending upon his size and his sales capabilities.

These characteristics show that there is a great difference between the industrial distributor and the manufacturer's representative. The characteristics also point out quite clearly that these two middlemen are not good substitutes for one another in most cases. The distributor may be viewed by the marketing manager as a substitute for the sales force and the branch house operations, whereas the MR is basically a substitute for the company salesman. Therefore, it is imperative that the industrial marketing manager understand well the differences between these two middlemen and know what each can contribute to an effective channel of distribution.

How the MR Serves the Marketing Manager. The real value again in looking at the MR in detail is to learn enough about this middleman to know when he could be of service to the industrial marketing manager. What is to be gained by using MRs in the industrial channel of distribution? What do they offer the marketing manager over company salesmen? The following are some of the ways in which the MR can be used to advantage by the industrial marketing manager: (1) the MR has established contacts in the marketplace and can provide immediate entry into markets; (2) the MR by virtue of his representing many manufacturing principals can offer a broader product line than can the company salesman and often the other products in his line can contribute to the sales of the marketing manager's products; (3) the MR can reduce the costs of selling when the marketing manager faces a seasonal demand for products; (4) the MR can be used to advantage in areas that cannot support full-time company salesmen and yet where the marketing manager desires representation; (5) because MRs are paid by commission only when they sell, they can be used to advantage by managers whose companies are financially constrained, but yet require personal selling; and (6) the MR is often technically trained and can provide the manager such technical expertise at reasonable cost. Because these are important considerations in choosing MRs in industrial channels, it is worthwhile to look at each of them in a little more detail.

Because MRs have established contacts in the marketplace, they can provide immediate entry for new companies entering a market or for established firms entering new markets. By using an MR, the manager can gain almost immediate entry to these contacts. The alternative is for the marketing manager to put in company salesmen and allow them the time and money required to establish the contacts. This sometimes takes years to accomplish effectively, with the result that MRs are often used if immediate entry is a prime objective.

As has been stated, MRs are able to market complete product lines by representing a number of different manufacturing principals. This often gives the MR an advantage over company salesmen because the latter can only carry their own company's products. With many industrial purchasing agents, being able to buy a complete line of products from a single source of supply is a powerful influencing factor regarding what is actually purchased and from whom. To understand better what the product line of the MR is like, please refer to Table 8.6, which shows some of the principals represented and their respective products handled by a manufacturer's rep who specialized in the southern California aerospace and electronics industries. Because this particular MR represented 20 principals and carried their products on a collective basis, it is evident that his product offerings were broader than what could be offered by the salesmen of any one particular company. If the MR's product line is a good one, the products will complement one another and actually contribute to the sale of one another at times. This is an advantage the marketing manager cannot normally obtain through the use of that manager's own salesmen.

If the industrial marketing manager faces a seasonal demand for products, the use of MRs could be advantageous because sales overhead could be reduced in the slack periods. This is something that could not be accomplished with company salesmen, who would have to be carried through both peaks and troughs in the seasonal demand. Because commissions are paid only upon

Table 8.6

EXAMPLE OF THE PRODUCT LINE OF A
MANUFACTURER'S REPRESENTATIVE

Principals Represented	Products Carried from Principal
Concoa Corporation 5137 N. Elton Street Baldwin Park, California 91076	Rack and Panel Connectors, Crimp Style Removable Contacts
Circuit Structures Lab 3200 North San Fernando Blvd. Burbank, California 91504	Plastic P.C. Card Guides, Adj. Card Frames Transmounts, Transistor Insulation Pads
D-Cemco, Inc. 3200 North Fernando Blvd. Burbank, California 91504	Electronic Hardware, Handles, Terminal Boards, Terminals, Standoffs, Spacers, Cable Mate
J S H Electronics Company 8549 Higuera Street Culver City, California 92030	Semiconductors, Vacuum Tubes, Readout Tubes, JAN Tubes
Micro Precision Corporation 55 9th Street Brooklyn, New York 11215	Instrument Housings, Case Assy's, Bezels, Tube Forms, Decks, Deck Assemblies, Plates, Machined Parts
Orbit Instrument Corporation 131 Eileen Way Syosset, L.I., New York 11791	Servo Instrumentation, X-Y Ball Trackers, Joy Sticks, Indicators, Counters, Camera-Mount Assemblies
Pressure Systems, Inc. 2017 Camfield Avenue Los Angeles, California 90022	Advanced Titanium Metal Fabrication, Precision Pressure Vessels, Rocket Motor Cases
Stake Fastener Company 1710 North Potrero Avenue South El Monte, California 91733	Pan-L-Screws, Pan Head Screw with Colored Head and Captive Washer
Standard Insert Company 12270 Montague Street Pacoima, California 91331	Inserts for Metal and Plastic, Bushings, Spacers
Transformer Engineers 1039 East Valley Boulevard San Gabriel, California 91776	Transformers, Mil-S and Commercial—Power Supplies

Source: Reprinted by permission from Hildebrand Associates, Manufacturer's Representative, 6132 Tarragona Drive, San Diego, California 92115.

Note: This is a sample of Hildebrand Associates' total 20 principals and 75 product line classifications.

sales, there would be no fixed sales expenses during the slack periods. Paying the company salesmen via straight commission to accomplish this same thing probably would not work because the salesman would not be able to sell enough during the slack periods to survive. But the MR could do it because he could be selling other products in his line during the slack periods. Thus, the MR could perform in markets that could not economically support full-time company salesmen owing to slack sales periods.

Many times, industrial products can be sold into markets that are not by themselves economically capable of supporting full-time company salesmen. Yet, in such cases, the marketing manager may wish to have products represented, and at the same time those products require personal selling efforts. The MR permits the manufacturer to cover such markets without incurring the high costs of personal sales accompanying the use of company salesmen.

If the industrial marketing manager is operating under the constraint of limited finances and yet requires personal selling in marketing the company's products, the MR can often be used to advantage. Because the MRs are paid by commission only when they sell and when the account pays, they allow a financially strapped company the required personal selling at a cost it can afford.

For many industrial companies, particularly small ones, it is very difficult and expensive to attract technically trained field salesmen, and yet such salesmen may be required to sell the products involved. For such companies, the MR may be a way to obtain technical and selling competence at reasonable cost. Many MRs are very highly trained and oriented technically, and they are a good source of technical sales ability for the marketing manager.

Limitations to Using MRs. In spite of contributions such as were just discussed, there are serious limitations to using MRs in the industrial channel of distribution. These limitations must be understood by the industrial marketing manager. MRs can be very difficult to control, and their broad product lines often make it impossible for any one principal to direct their efforts to the manager's advantage. If a product requires a great deal of specialized care, the MR may be unwilling to take the time to provide such care. Because of their straight commission form of compensation, it is often very difficult to get them to furnish market feedback, provide necessary service, and perform other such functions that take them away from selling and thus reduce their immediate earning revenue. Generally, the MR prefers to concentrate on large customers and large orders, so if an industrial company has many small firms in its market target, it may be impossible to use MRs to reach those customers. Moreover, because the MR normally provides little, if any, field inventory, this middleman is of little help when local service or parts are required. In addition, great differences exist in the selling and technical competence of individual manufacturers' reps. They must be screened very carefully in terms of the marketing manager's channel objectives. To engage an MR in place of a company salesman because of reduced selling costs makes little sense if sales produced are disproportionate to the savings in cost. Simply stated, a good rep may be a better choice than an equally good company salesman, but a poor MR is worthless! And, finally, the use of MRs in the industrial channel makes little marketing sense if the buyers and buying influences in the target market will not buy from them, but prefer to purchase directly from the manufacturer.

In choosing manufacturers' reps, industrial marketing managers normally look for three factors.[13] The first and usually the most important is selling and technical competence. The second is the ability of the individual MR to operate his business in a reputable, profitable, and lasting manner. The third is the possession by the rep of such desirable characteristics as honesty, openness, conscientiousness, reliability, and integrity. Of course, these factors apply only when the use of the MR is consistent with corporate, overall marketing and channel objectives and is also compatible with the company's product characteristics and customer buying patterns.

Locating Manufacturers' Representatives. For the industrial marketing manager considering the use of MRs in the channel of distribution, there are a number of sources. Again it is possible to define required middlemen by SIC and locate specific reps in the same manner as was described earlier in this chapter for locating distributors. Other good sources of information on manufacturers' representatives can be found in the *Manufacturers' Agents' Guide,* published by the Manufacturers' Agents Publishing Company, and in the *National Directory of Sales Representatives,* published by the Manufacturers' Agents National Association. Information may also be obtained from such associations as the Manufacturers' Agents National Association, the Electronics Representatives Association, and others. From data sources such as these, the industrial marketing manager can find information on specific rep organizations in terms of product lines carried, principals represented, territories covered, markets specialized in, and so forth. With such sources, the marketing manager seeking to use MRs in the channel can obtain a great deal of information regarding specific MRs at minimum cost and effort.

PHYSICAL DISTRIBUTION IN THE INDUSTRIAL MARKET

Regardless of the channel or channels selected, the industrial marketing manager must also manage the physical distribution of the company's products through selected channels. Physical distribution refers to that area of marketing management responsible for getting the goods physically to the customer in the right amount and at the right time. There are six major areas of physical distribution management, which are as follows:

Transportation

Transportation involves the decisions of the actual mode or modes of transportation to be used in shipping the goods to customers and/or middlemen. For the marketing manager, choices include shipping by air freight, rail, motor carrier, water, and, in some instances, pipeline. In deciding among modes of transportation, the manager should consider such factors as the speed, dependability, capability, and availability of each mode as well as its operating costs.

Field Warehousing

Field warehousing involves the physical location of warehouses in the field to best supply goods and sometimes service to customers and/or middlemen. Choices here include the use of private or public warehouses or, in some instances, warehouses of distributors, when the latter are used in the channel. Two major considerations here are where to locate the field warehouse and how many such warehouses to include in the physical distribution system.

Field Inventory Control

Inventory must be properly maintained in the field warehouses to supply the needs of customers and/or middlemen. Both over- and understocked inventory levels are costly, and the manager's task here is to maintain optimum levels. In deciding such levels, the manager should consider such factors as the average month-end unit levels, turnover rates by individual warehouse, average value of the inventory, and inventory carrying costs.

Materials Handling

Materials handling involves the actual physical handling of inventory in the warehouses or elsewhere in the total physical distribution system. Included in this area are such as the use of forklifts, handlifts, conveyors, cranes, hoists, industrial tractors, motorized handtrucks, and the like to move and store inventory physically. Included also are the personnel required to perform the materials handling function.

Protective Packaging

Goods to be shipped and stored must be packaged in a manner that will protect them both in shipment and in the warehouse. This is the protective packaging function of physical distribution. In this regard, the manager should consider such factors as filling and container costs, repackaging costs,

Interstate Commerce Commission requirements, possibilities of standardization, and changing customer requirements that affect packaging.

Order Processing

Along with the transportation, field warehousing, field inventory control, materials handling, and protective packaging functions, the manager must establish an order-processing system to service those functions. This system will normally take into consideration order processing, communications, and other related data-processing activities required to permit the entire physical distribution arrangement to function properly.

Most industrial companies view these six areas not as individual functions, but rather as a total integrated system of physical distribution. Thus, distribution decisions are often trade-offs such as transportation costs versus the costs of field warehousing or transportation costs versus field inventory costs, and so on, and this is what is referred to as the total cost concept in physical distribution. This approach to physical distribution has led to industrial companies shipping via air freight, even though its cost is higher, because its mode is faster and the speed cuts down on required field inventories, thus reducing total distribution costs.

Physical distribution is a cost to the industrial marketing manager, and, as such, it has definite effects on channel selections, particularly if low cost is a primary channel objective. For example, distribution costs as a percentage of sales in the industrial market range from 9.8 percent in machinery to 16.1 percent in wood products to 23.1 percent in chemicals, petroleum, and rubber to 26.5 in primary and fabricated metals.[14] Another study indicated an all-industry average of physical distribution as 21.8 percent of sales, of which 13.9 percent is accounted for by transportation, warehousing, and inventory control.[15] It must be realized that when the industrial marketing manager uses the direct channel or the manufacturer's representative, that manager's company must underwrite these physical distribution costs. On the other hand, if the manager can use distributors in the channel, many of these costs can be shifted to or shared with the distributor. Thus, it is imperative that industrial channels of distribution be chosen with adequate input regarding the physical distribution characteristics involved. Physical distribution is often a forgotten part of marketing management in both the consumer and industrial markets, but its costs can be a significant factor, and it cannot be overlooked by the astute marketing manager. To emphasize this point, some comparisons between distribution costs as a percentage of sales and selling expenses (the cost of compensation of salesmen, sales management, travel, lodging, meals, and entertainment, advertising, and promotion) as a percentage of sales are worthwhile. Figures on selling expenses as a percentage of sales were compiled from the Executive Compensation Service of the American Management Association.[16] Based on these figures and on the distribution costs as a percentage of sales previously discussed, some interesting comparisons can be made. For example, in the chemical industry, distribution costs as a percentage of sales were 23.1 percent, whereas selling expenses as a percentage of sales were 5.4 percent. Similarly, distribution costs as a percentage of sales in fabricated metals were 26.5 percent, whereas selling expenses as a percentage of sales in fabricated metals were 4.8 percent. In machinery, distribution costs were 9.8 percent of sales, whereas selling expenses were 5.5 percent of sales. These comparisons help make the point that physical distribution is an important aspect of industrial marketing management, and it must not receive short shrift in the overall marketing and channel strategy of the industrial marketing manager.

CHAPTER SUMMARY

Channel strategy can be a critical part of industrial marketing management because of the great emphasis on personal selling in the industrial market. A format for developing industrial channel strategy was developed, and differences between industrial and consumer channels were discussed. Analyses were undertaken of the two most common industrial middlemen, the industrial distributor and the manufacturer's representative. Characteristics of each were developed, and the contributions and limitations of each type were analyzed from the point of view of the industrial marketing manager. Finally, a discussion of physical distribution and its importance in industrial marketing management was undertaken.

QUESTIONS FOR CHAPTER 8

1. Why is physical distribution such a vital part of industrial channel strategy and overall industrial marketing strategy? Explain your answer.
2. It is generally acknowledged that the product and its characteristics primarily determine the channel of distribution that is to be used in the industrial market. Do you agree or disagree with this statement? If you agree, why do you agree? If you disagree, why do you disagree?
3. The choice for an industrial marketing manager between independent middlemen and the company's own sales force usually boils down to the total costs of coverage desired. Do you agree or disagree with this statement? If you agree, why do you agree? If you disagree, why do you disagree?

4. If you were the manufacturer of relatively standardized, low-priced industrial products that were to be marketed into a horizontal market, what channel arrangements do you believe would be most appropriate for both you and your customers? Explain your reasons.

5. What do you believe to be the most important differences between an industrial distributor and a manufacturer's representative? How do these differences affect the choice of each as an industrial channel component?

9

PROMOTIONAL STRATEGY IN INDUSTRIAL MARKETING — PERSONAL SELLING

After markets have been defined and located, a marketing plan formulated to reach those markets, product strategy developed, and channels of distribution chosen, it is necessary to promote those products to the specified market segments. This is the promotional area of marketing management and a very important aspect of the marketing of industrial goods and services. In today's market, it is not sufficient to produce technically perfect products and then wait for customers to come in. The merits of these products must be communicated to industrial purchasing agents and other buying influences in prospective firms. This is the role of promotion in overall marketing strategy—communicating with the market to stimulate demand for the company's goods and services.

The methods of communication used are normally considered to comprise the promotional mix. The three major components of the promotional mix are generally considered to be (1) personal selling, (2) advertising, and (3) sales promotion. Personal selling is just what the term describes—direct personal contact with present and prospective customers for the purpose of selling those customers needed goods and/or services. Advertising, sometimes referred to as mass or nonpersonal selling, is communication with present or prospective customers via the use of such media as television, radio, print, direct mail, and outdoor advertising. The third component, sales promotion, is a catchall category and refers to all promotional efforts other than advertising and personal selling. Included in this category of promotion are such as point of purchase (POP) materials, samples, premiums, trade shows and expositions, catalogs, contests, trading stamps, publicity and public relations, and other such promotional devices.

It is probably safe to say that a good promotional mix usually has some combination of personal selling, advertising, and sales promotion, but this is not a rule! Some companies have been very successful without personal selling, and other firms have succeeded without much emphasis on advertising. Still others have succeeded with no sales promotional activities at all. Marketing managers have differing opinions about the effectiveness of each component, and market considerations affect the valid use of each. What components are in a promotional mix is not important as long as the overall mix communicates effectively with the target audience of buyers and buying influences, convinces them to purchase or take some other desired action, and competes favorably in the marketplace with the promotional mixes of competitors. And, of course, the components of any particular company's promotional mix should not compete with each other, but should rather complement one another. If the company's promotional mix does not accomplish these things, then the firm's promotional strategy will be ineffective. The actual decisions going into the formulation and implementation of this mix can be termed the promotional strategy. As with the other substrategies, to be effective, promotional strategy must be compatible with the company's objectives and its marketing plan and, at the same time, be integrated into its product, channel, and pricing substrategies.

INDUSTRIAL PROMOTIONAL STRATEGY

In industrial promotion, there are sales managers, advertising managers, and sometimes sales promotion managers who head their own departments and report to the marketing manager in their own respective specialized areas. It is then the task of the marketing manager to integrate personal selling, advertising, and sales promotion into one total promotional package that is then further integrated into the total marketing strategy with product, channel, and pricing decisions. In view of this division of promotional efforts, no format for overall industrial promotional strategy will be developed. Instead, formats will be developed individually for sales, for advertising, and for sales promotion. This chapter will cover the personal selling area of promotion, whereas the following chapter will cover the areas of advertising and sales promotion in the industrial market.

Difference between Industrial and Consumer Promotional Strategies

It is in the area of promotion that industrial and consumer marketing practices differ sharply even though the basic tasks may be the same. To understand these differences—and all of industrial promotion, for that matter—it is first helpful to understand the tasks involved in promotion in the industrial market. According to McGraw-Hill's Research Department, there are six basic steps or tasks to be accomplished in promotion.[1] These are (1) making contact, (2) arousing interest, (3) creating preference, (4) making specific proposals, (5) closing the order, and (6) keeping customers sold. This implies that the combined functions of personal selling, advertising, and sales promotion are to make initial contact with a prospective customer; arouse interest; create a preference for the firm's product or service over those offered by competitors; answer specific questions; close the order; and, once sold, take care of that customer so that there is little reason to look elsewhere. Accomplishment of these tasks would indicate an effective promotional strategy, whereas the inability to do so would indicate a lack of effectiveness if the marketing manager had a competitive product and a clear understanding of market targets to be reached.

Keeping the McGraw-Hill tasks in mind, refer to Table 9.1. Some great differences can be observed between the relative importance of promotional mix components as seen by consumer and industrial marketing executives. Personal selling plays a much greater role in the industrial market, again with emphasis on the importance of personal contact with industrial buyers and buying influences. Mass media are used far less in the industrial market, and so are promotional branding and promotional packaging. And although the use of print media plays a significant role in industrial promotion, as it does in the consumer area, it is different, media normally being of the trade publication variety. What Table 9.1 actually shows is that industrial and consumer marketing managers differ in their assessments of which promotional components work best in achieving the McGraw-Hill Research Department's six basic tasks. For example, in the consumer market, it is very possible that via mass advertising and effective promotional packaging, a consumer goods manufacturer could bring the ultimate consumer through the six tasks or steps. For the manufacturer of sophisticated electronic products being sold to engineers, such a promotional approach would lead to marketing disaster. Stated briefly, consumer marketing promotional strategies differ from those found in the industrial market primarily because buyer expectations are different and product characteristics differ.

There are also other differences of importance. As stated, media differ in the two markets. Most of industrial advertising is in trade journals and direct mail media. In addition, industrial advertising themes or messages are generally less emotional than those found in the consumer market. They are generally more factual and economic benefit-oriented, with emphasis often on derived demand. Sales promotion also differs, with the bulk of industrial sales promotion being in trade shows, catalogs, directories, and specialty advertising items.

These are a few of the general differences, but they are sufficient to make

Table 9.1
RELATIVE IMPORTANCE OF THE ELEMENTS OF
MARKETING COMMUNICATIONS

Sales Effort Activity	Producers of:		
	Industrial Goods	Consumer Durables	Consumer Nondurables
Sales Management & Personal Selling	69.2%	47.6%	38.1%
Broadcast Media Advertising	0.9%	10.7%	20.9%
Printed Media Advertising	12.5%	16.1%	14.8%
Special Promotional Activities	9.6%	15.5%	15.5%
Branding & Promotional Packaging	4.5%	9.5%	9.8%
Other	3.3%	0.6%	0.9%
Total	100.0%	100.0%	100.0%

Source: John G. Udell, *Successful Marketing Strategies* (Madison: Mimir Publishers, Inc., 1972), p. 47.
Note: Data are based on the average point allocations of 336 industrial goods producers, 52 consumer durable goods manufacturers, and 88 consumer nondurable goods manufacturers.

the desired point. There are enough differences between industrial and consumer promotional strategies to merit an in-depth analysis of each of the components of personal selling, advertising, and sales promotion. In these analyses, more specific differences between industrial and consumer promotional strategies will be developed as they relate to personal selling, advertising, and sales promotion.

PERSONAL SELLING IN THE INDUSTRIAL MARKET

In the majority of cases, personal selling is an important component in the marketing strategies of industrial marketing managers. This is borne out by the large number of direct channels in the industrial market. As was discussed in the preceding chapter on channel strategy, it is estimated that about three-quarters of all industrial goods, based on their dollar volume, are marketed without benefit of independent middlemen. This, in turn, implies the use of company salesmen. Moreover, as has also been shown, even manufacturers' reps and distributors are chosen because of their sales capabilities. Reference again to Table 9.1 emphasizes the great importance placed on personal selling by industrial marketing managers.

Personal selling has great application to the marketing of industrial goods and services because conditions in the industrial market fit almost perfectly those cited in the classic marketing textbooks as ideal for this form of promotion. To illustrate, the customers are relatively few in number, and they can be specifically defined and located. The products are often complex and expensive, and large dollar volume sales are common. Buyers and buying influences require and demand very technical, on-the-spot answers to complex questions before they will purchase, and post- and presale service and technical assistance are common requirements. Conditions such as these account for the great emphasis on this personal selling form of promotion in the industrial market. Although exceptions can be found, it is rare that industrial goods and services are marketed without benefit of personal selling somewhere along the way either by company salesmen, by distributors' sales personnel, or by manufacturers' reps performing the selling function. If the topic of personal selling in the industrial market is to be discussed adequately a division must be made between the personal selling function as performed by the industrial field salesman and the management of this sales function as performed by the sales manager.

The Industrial Salesman

The industrial salesman can be defined as a technically oriented individual, whose primary responsibility is to sell industrial goods and services to buyers and buying influences in industry, government, and the institutions. These salesmen can be classified into the following groups: (1) the sales engineer, (2) the executive salesman, (3) the industrial supplies salesman, (4) the inside salesman, and (5) the missionary salesman. A description of each of these types follows.

The Sales Engineer. The sales engineer is a type of industrial salesman who may or may not possess an engineering degree, but who often does have such a degree in electrical or mechanical engineering. This salesman is highly technically trained and calls upon technically oriented personnel such as purchasing agents, plant engineers, production engineers, production supervisors, and so forth. Products sold are normally of a complex technical nature and require technical competence to sell. The sales engineer may be selling to OEMs or users or to distributors in cases where the latter resell such equipment to the

OEMs and users. Simply stated, this type of industrial salesman is an engineer who sells!

The Executive Salesman. The executive salesman is a type of industrial salesman who also possesses a high degree of technical competence, but of a type different from that possessed by the sales engineer. The executive salesman is a loose term to describe all those salesmen selling products and services to business executives. Typical of this type are salesmen selling computer software programs, consulting services, company insurance programs, advertising, and so on, to such executives as purchasing directors, comptrollers, personnel managers, production managers, data-processing managers, advertising managers, and other such corporate officers. The products sold by this type of salesmen are not normally used in the production of goods and services, but are, of course, required in the operation of the customer's company.

The Industrial Supplies Salesman. The term *industrial supplies salesman* is used to describe those salesmen selling into the industrial market who are not specifically sales engineers or executive salesmen, but yet who operate in the field. The term defines those industrial salesman who sell for manufacturers or distributors relatively standardized industrial products such as component parts, raw materials, processed materials, and other such goods. Though technically oriented and trained, they do not require the engineering background of the sales engineer, although they must have knowledge of production machinery, processes, and the like. Generally, this type of salesman sells to to OEMs rather than user customers, and although industrial salesmen do call on buying influences, they probably deal much more with purchasing agents than do sales engineers and executive salesmen.

The Inside Salesman. The three types of salesmen previously discussed all operate in the marketplace as field salesmen. A relatively new concept in the industrial market is the inside salesman. The inside salesman is basically a phone salesman. Such persons do not work in the field as do the others. They are called inside salesmen because they sell via phone from within the manufacturer's or distributor's facilities. Inside salesmen are most often used where customers are already established and personal sales calls are not required. More often than not, the customer calls the marketing company as opposed to the opposite. Such salesmen are used for repetitive accounts because they are much less expensive than field salesmen. They often have assigned territories and are responsible for accounts within those territories. Inside salesmen have been found very useful by distributors, and it is estimated that such inside salesmen account for about 90 percent of the business conducted by steel distributors.[2] These salesmen are also technically oriented and must be capable of handling customer problems over the phone. In most cases, they are not a substitute for field salesmen, but rather are used to complement the field sales activities of the latter.

The Missionary Salesman. Another type of salesman found in the industrial market is the so-called missionary salesman, who works with industrial customers and middlemen in a consulting or advisory capacity as opposed to selling per se. Sometimes called a factory representative or factory rep, this type is more involved with indirect sales that might accrue from helping a customer with technical assistance, aiding a distributor with inventory control, training distributor salesmen, training customer employees in the operation of machinery and equipment, and other such similar functions. Basically, this type of salesman does not sell, but can be instrumental in future sales. The factory rep, too, must possess the technical competence necessary to communicate with knowledgeable buyers and buying influences and distributors.

As can be seen by these classifications, there is no such thing as "the industrial salesman." There are a number of types, and their functions and responsibilities differ. It could probably be argued that every company's salesmen are different even if the products and the markets served by those companies are basically the same. Nevertheless, there are some basic areas common to all salesmen in the industrial market. To be effective in the industrial market, any industrial salesman would have to possess the following forms of knowledge: (1) an understanding of the customer's business operations, (2) an understanding of the product involved, (3) an understanding of the buying influences involved in buying the product in each customer firm, (4) an understanding of these buying influences as individuals, and (5) a knowledge of competition. Inasmuch as these are very important considerations, it is worthwhile to look at each of them in some detail.

Knowledge of the Customer's Business Operation. To sell industrial customers, the salesman must have a sound knowledge of the business operations of the company's customers. It is imperative to know who they are, how big they are, how much they buy, whom they buy from, how often they buy, and how the company's products fit into the customer's production requirements. Tied into this knowledge is the requirement that the salesman be well acquainted with the behavior of the industry of which the customer is a member.

Knowledge of the Product. The industrial salesman must know the product being sold, not only in a technical sense, but also in the manner that the product can be applied by the customer in the latter's business operation. The salesman must know the products well enough to relate them to problems faced by the customers.

Knowledge of Buying Influences. Unless an industrial salesman knows who the buying influences are in each customer firm for each product in the company's line, these products cannot be sold. If the salesman is unaware of, or cannot get to see, the key buying influences, there will be no personal communication with them, and it is doubtful that those buying influences will recommend or buy the salesman's products.

Knowledge of Buying Influences as Individuals. The industrial salesman must not only know who the key buying influences are in each customer firm, but it is also necessary to understand what motivates each of them. As was developed in detail in chapter 4, people, not companies, buy industrial goods and services. Thus, it is incumbent upon the industrial field salesman to understand buying influences not only in terms of their formal responsibilities, but also in terms of their personal characteristics. This implies an understanding of their interests, attitudes, opinions, feelings, preferences, prejudices, and so on. Without such knowledge, effective communication necessary for industrial selling is difficult to attain.

Knowledge of Competition. The industrial salesman must know competition. More specifically, it is necessary to know who the competitors are as well as their products, their prices, their service capabilities, their ability to deliver when promised, their advertising and sales promotion techniques, approaches used by their salesmen, and the like. The salesman cannot underestimate his competitors and cannot be ignorant of them and still stand up to the penetrating questions posed by industrial buyers and buying influences. A good industrial salesman knows the competitors well enough to assess their strengths and weaknesses and his own strengths and weaknesses in comparison. In this way, the salesman can capitalize on his strengths and attempt to stay away from and correct his weaknesses.

Because of requirements such as these, it is very difficult to find effective industrial salesmen. It is estimated that about 75 percent of industrial sales are accounted for by about 25 percent of all industrial salesmen.[3] This implies that only about one-quarter of all industrial salesmen actually are able to master the stringent requirements for selling in this market. The inability to find topflight industrial salesmen because of the almost impossible requirements of the job has brought about some recent trends in industrial field selling.

Trends in Industrial Selling

Certain trends have occurred in industrial selling in the past few years owing mostly to the inability of companies to find individual salesmen who possess all the required characteristics. One such trend has been toward more team selling by industrial companies. Team selling normally takes place in situations where customer firms employ committee buying, which is basically a form of team buying. Assume for example that an industrial customer wishes to buy punching and shearing machines for its production line. Because of the large investment involved, the firm may appoint a committee to make the decision as to whose equipment is to be purchased. This committee could be comprised of such people as the production supervisor, the purchasing agent, production foremen, the comptroller, a plant engineer, and a quality control expert. All of these may be considering the same manufacturer's equipment, but at the same time they may all be looking for something different in that equipment.

What then is the task of the industrial salesman trying to sell all of these buying influences in their own specific areas of expertise? The job is almost impossible for one man to perform. What often happens in such cases is that the salesman is able to call upon his own company for help; and such personnel as an engineer, a financial specialist, a vice-president of marketing, and so on, come into the field and team-sell the equipment with the salesman. Together, it is the team that is able to answer specific questions relating to engineering, financing, installation, production capabilities, service, and other such factors that the salesman alone might have been incapable of answering.

Another trend that has been observed is the resident salesman. This concept has been used in highly technical markets where large customers are found and where technical assistance and training are extremely important to those customers. What happens here is that the salesman is actually assigned to a customer firm and works in-house exclusively in an advising-consulting capacity with that customer for a specified period of time. Once the customer is prepared to operate on his own, the salesman is transferred to another such customer and performs the same similar functions. This resident salesman has found considerable usage in the chemical industry, where customer firms continually seek help in the processing of purchased chemicals.

Still another trend found recently in industrial selling is the use of creative and maintenance sales teams. This concept works in the following way. The creative member of the team has the responsibility for finding new customer accounts, calling on them, and initially selling them. Once this member of the team sells a new customer, he goes to look for more new prospects, and the maintenance member of the team takes over the account. Sometimes industrial companies will use inside salesmen to perform the maintenance task. This is a form of specialization in field industrial salesmen—one member of the team is specialized in opening new customer accounts—the other member of the team is specialized in taking care of such accounts after they are opened. They work in tandem, and it is possible that neither member of the team could perform both prospecting and maintaining as well as the two members are able to do collectively.

One other trend that seems to be making an impression is the increased role of women in industrial sales. A few short years ago, this would have been unheard of, and all kinds of excuses would have been given by marketing managers to show that women could not sell industrial products. But over time many so-called girl Fridays have developed into very effective inside salesmen and from there have moved into outside field sales positions. This movement has been quite pronounced with industrial distributors. In 1969 a survey found that 12 percent of distributor firms used women in inside sales, and another 2 percent employed them in outside sales capacities. This same survey also found that 35 percent of the distributors surveyed would consider women for outside sales, and 61 percent would consider them for inside sales positions.[4] Because the survey has never been updated, there are no current data on this topic. Very likely, if the survey were conducted again, the findings would be even more impressive. What has happened and what is continuing to happen is that industrial sales managers have found that women can sell industrial goods and services and that they can learn the technical aspects required. When this takes place, women make very effective industrial sales personnel.

All these trends are really part of what is taking place because industry purchasing practices are becoming so sophisticated. As this takes place, industrial selling must match the level of sophistication. The salesman of the seventies must be a business consultant and an advisor to customers. The salesman of today must be systems-oriented and skilled in the areas of finance, human behavior, and communications in order to identify customer needs and relay them back to management.[5] The stage version of the salesman, the glib, boisterous glad-hander who rides on a shoestring and a spicy story, is gone. The glad-hander has been replaced by an industrial salesman who is more of a technician who advises his company on new products and counsels customers on how to use them.[6]

Profile of the Industrial Salesman

Probably the best single source of information on industrial salesmen is the McGraw-Hill Research Department's survey conducted of 1,089 industrial salesmen.[7] Based on that survey, the following characteristics can be defined.

1. The average industrial salesman works nine hours and 22 minutes daily for 243 days a year, or 2,276 hours per year.

2. Of this nine hour, 22-minute day, the average industrial salesman spends only three hours and 52 minutes or 41 percent of his time in actual face-to-face selling, while spending 34 percent of his time traveling and waiting; 20 percent on reports, paper work, and attending sales meetings; and 5 percent on service calls.
3. The average industrial salesman calls on 214 companies per year, of which 111 are active present accounts and 103 are prospective customers; and there are four buying influences per customer, amounting to 856 required sales calls.
4. With 214 companies and four buying influences per firm, the average industrial salesman makes 2,041 28-minute sales calls per year.
5. The average industrial salesman sees each of his assigned buying influences about 2.4 times each year, which means that he can spend but 66 minutes each year with each of his buying influences.

In addition to these characteristics, the Executive Compensation Service of the American Management Association has compiled data on the compensation of industrial salesmen that can be added to the previous characteristics in better understanding the industrial salesman.[8] The following summarize the American Management Association data.

1. Industrial salesmen are most often compensated by the following methods—28.1 percent by straight salary, 25.6 percent by salary plus commission, and 22.0 percent by salary plus individual bonus.
2. Their annual compensation runs from $9,310 for a sales trainee on a straight salary to $19,992 for a sales supervisor paid on a salary plus incentive basis. Experienced salesmen averaged $12,105 on a straight salary and $13,432 on a salary plus incentive basis, whereas senior industrial salesmen average $15,862 on a straight salary to $17,695 on a salary plus incentive basis.

All of the above are average figures, but they do give insight into industrial salesmen and the roles they play in the marketing of industrial goods and services.

SALES MANAGEMENT IN THE INDUSTRIAL MARKET

The use of salesmen in the promotional mix requires the management of those salesmen. This is the function of sales management in the industrial market—the management of the outside sales force. The executive in charge of this area is the sales manager, who is normally responsible to the marketing manager. A highly complex area, sales management includes such tasks as the following: (1) developing a sales plan consistent with the company's overall marketing plan; (2) setting of sales objectives; (3) setting up sales budgets and forecasts; (4) organizing the sales force by product lines, customer groups, regions, and so on; (5) organizing of the in-house company sales department to work with the salesmen in the field, including sales analysts, inside salesmen, clerks, and the like; (6) appointing regional and/or district sales managers if required; (7) writing of the job description for field salesmen; (8) recruiting and hiring salesmen; (9) training salesmen; (10) defining sales territories and setting sales quotas; (11) assigning salesmen to those territories; (12) evaluating salesmen's performances; (13) compensating salesmen; (14) transferring salesmen to other territories and/or to new positions; (15) promoting salesmen; (16) motivating salesmen to increase their sales; and (17) terminating salesmen who cannot produce.

These tasks indicate that sales management is a rather specific area and is not to be confused with marketing management. Where the marketing manager is responsible for the entire marketing program of the company, the sales manager is responsible for but one part of that program—the personal sales aspects! Viewed in another manner, the sales manager reports to the marketing manager, as do the product managers, advertising managers, marketing research managers, sales promotion managers, and other such functional marketing officers.

The Importance of Sales Management

As has been stated numerous times throughout this text, personal contact is of great importance in industrial marketing. This, of course, implies a great emphasis on personal selling, which, in turn, places equally great emphasis on the sales management function. The tasks of the sales manager were covered in the preceding section, and they are all-important for effective marketing. In this text, however, neither time nor space permit an in-depth analysis of each of the listed tasks. Therefore, discussion shall center around those considered to be the most critical in effective industrial sales management. The factors that will be covered are (1) costs of recruiting and training an industrial salesman, (2) the problem of salesman turnover, and (3) the rising costs of personal sales calls in the industrial market. The implications of these three factors for more effective sales management shall then be discussed.

Costs of Recruiting and Training an Industrial Salesman. The direct channel of the company salesman to the industrial customer is a very expensive one. One of the reasons for this is the high cost of recruiting an industrial salesman and training him until effective in the field. There are a number of estimates of this cost, and they vary according to the industry involved and product and buyer characteristics. In 1964, for example, a survey conducted by the Sales Manpower Foundation revealed that it cost an average of $10,593 to search out, select, train, and supervise one industrial salesman until productive. This was an average figure extracted from data, with extremes from "less than $1,000 to $30,000 to $50,000."[9] Although this is an old survey, it is useful for comparison with later surveys. Another study found the cost of locating and training an industrial salesman, exclusive of salaries, to be about $6,400 per man.[10] Still another estimate in 1974 is that it costs anywhere from $5,000 to $20,000—and sometimes as much as $30,000—to find and train one industrial salesman and another $15,000 to $20,000 to maintain him on the road for one year.[11] Rex Chainbelt, Inc., estimates that it spends $5,000 to $20,000 to train a salesman and $30,000 to $35,000 a year to keep him on the road.[12] Although these figures do not agree closely, they all point toward one thing—it is expensive to search out, select, hire, and train industrial salesmen. To understand fully the implications of these costs, imagine what it would cost to make a sales force of 50 or 100 or 500 salesmen productive in the field! As might be suspected, the costs involved in getting productive salesmen into the field account for much of the shift toward manufacturers' reps and distributors where trained salesmen are already available.

The figures cited here are out-of-pocket costs and do not reflect opportunity losses from salesmen in the field who, although trained, are not yet fully productive and lose sales because of this. In some industries, it takes years for a salesman to make contact with and gain support with all decision-making buying influences. And until the salesman is able to do this, sales will be lost by his company. All of these costs place a tremendous burden on the sales manager and stress the importance of effective selection of industrial salesmen.

Industrial Salesmen Turnover. Adding to the industrial sales manager's problems with the costs involved in recruiting and training salesmen is the turnover of such salesmen once trained. Again figures differ regarding the actual turnover rate, but most authorities agree that it is a problem area in industrial sales management. The previously mentioned survey conducted by the Sales Manpower Foundation determined that 49.7 percent of new sales trainees hired by industrial firms leave within a year's time, and 10.5 percent of experienced salesmen hired leave within a year.[13] Another study by the Sales Manpower Foundation revealed that 100,500 manufacturing firms employing 20 or more employees would lose 74,898 salesmen in a year's time either through their quitting or being fired.[14] Still another study conducted by the Sales Manpower Division of the Sales Executive Club of New York found 15 major manufacturing industries would lose 62,000 salesmen in a year's time either by their quitting or being fired primarily because of poor selection when hired.[15] A reasonable 1974 estimate is that from 40 to 70 percent of industrial salesmen turn over annually, depending upon the industry involved. What all these figures imply is that salesman turnover is a very definite problem that costs money and contributes greatly to the total cost of the direct channel, which, in turn, places great emphasis on more effective selection of industrial salesmen by sales managers.

The Cost of an Industrial Sales Call. Another factor placing great stress on the industrial sales manager is the rising costs of industrial sales calls. Table 9.2 illustrates the change in the cost of an average industrial sales call between 1952 and 1973 based on surveys conducted by McGraw-Hill's Research Department. A sales call is defined as "each time a salesman makes a face-to-face presentation to one or more buyers or prospects," whereas direct selling costs are defined as "salaries, commissions, bonuses, travel, and entertainment."[16] The figures in Table 9.2 show in no uncertain terms that the cost of a direct channel of company salesmen is rising at an astronomical rate, much higher than the rate of climb of the cost of living. For example, between 1963 and 1973, the cost of an industrial sales call rose by +113.6 percent, whereas the consumer price index rose by +45.1 percent, and the industrial commodities wholesale price index rose by +32.9 percent.

These figures indicate that the costs involved in personal selling in the industrial market are greater than the increases in the cost of living due to

Table 9.2
THE COST OF AN INDUSTRIAL SALES CALL

Year	Cost of an Industrial Sales Call for the Average Company
1952	$16.94
1955	17.29
1958	22.33
1961	30.35
1963	31.31
1965	35.55
1967	42.92
1969	49.30
1971	57.71
1973	66.88

Source: Reprinted by permission from McGraw-Hill Research Department, *Laboratory of Advertising Performance Report #8013.2* (New York: McGraw-Hill Publications Company, 1974).

inflation, and, in turn, this implies a very careful assessment of the continued use of company salesmen in a direct channel of distribution in a company's marketing strategy. Again these rising costs have had an effect on many industrial firms switching to manufacturer's reps and industrial distributors when feasible and undoubtedly help account for the tremendous growth in distributor sales such as was illustrated in Table 8.2 in the previous chapter.

There are considerable differences in the costs of industrial sales calls among industrial firms whose sales forces differ in size. Table 9.3 illustrates the differences in the average cost of an industrial sales call based on the number of salesmen in the company sales force. As can be seen, the cost to small companies is considerably more than the cost to larger companies, and this has very definite marketing management implications. For the small firm, the cost of maintaining its own sales force may be prohibitive, whereas a larger firm may well be able to cover such costs. This has probably led many marketing managers in small firms to adopt channels of distribution using manufacturer's reps and distributors to provide the personal contact required to market their products and, at the same time, reduce the costs involved in providing such personal contact.

There are also differences in the costs of industrial sales calls and the channels of distribution used. Table 9.4 shows these differences according to direct sales through middlemen. As can be seen, the direct channel is the most ex-

Table 9.3
COST OF AN INDUSTRIAL SALES CALL
BASED ON SIZE OF SALES FORCE

Number of Salesmen Employed	1971		1973	
	Number of Companies	Cost of Industrial Sales Call	Number of Companies	Cost of Industrial Sales Call
Under 10	168	$63.90	167	$80.55
10–25	125	60.69	112	64.85
26–50	73	46.18	71	58.16
Over 50	65	45.18	87	45.29
Not Answered on Number of Salesmen	18	71.19	13	93.84
Total	449	$57.71	450	$66.68

Source: Reprinted by permission from McGraw-Hill Research Department, *Laboratory of Advertising Performance Report #8013.2* (New York: McGraw-Hill Publications Company, 1974).

Table 9.4
COST OF AN INDUSTRIAL SALES CALL
BY METHOD OF DISTRIBUTION

	1967		1969	
Method	Number of Companies	Cost of Industrial Sales Call	Number of Companies	Cost of Industrial Sales Call
Direct to Industry	176	$54.64	166	$58.98
Through Distributors & Reps	134	39.62	112	46.65
Both	320	38.31	318	45.43
Not Answered	13	31.81	8	39.60
Total	643	$42.92	604	$49.30

Source: Reprinted by permission from McGraw-Hill Research Department, *Laboratory of Advertising Performance Report #8013* (New York: McGraw-Hill Publications Company, 1974).

pensive, although it must be realized that there are additional costs in the form of discounts or commissions to middlemen, which are not reflected in the table. Although these data are not as current as might be desired, they are representative of cost differences due to channels of distribution. Again the marketing management implication is that if personal contact is required, it may be worthwhile to consider reps and/or distributors in favor of company salesmen if cost is considered a major factor.

Finally, there are great differences in the costs of industrial sales calls, depending upon the individual products involved. Based on the findings of McGraw-Hill's Research Department, these costs range all the way from a cost of $8.00 per sales call for a manufacturer of drain pipe and $9.00 per sales call for a manufacturer of cold finished steel to $350.00 per sales call for a manufacturer of vibrating materials handling equipment and $650.00 per sales call for a chemical process equipment manufacturer.[17] What this means is that in some industries personal selling costs are reasonable and can be tolerated by the sales manager and the marketing manager. In other industries, however, the cost of personal selling is so high that a company-owned sales force may be an expense that cannot be borne, and other forms of promotion must be studied for possible adoption. The important thing to realize is that the cost of a personal sales call can differ according to the industry and the product involved.

Sales Management Implications

The three factors of cost of recruiting good salesmen, salesmen turnover, and the rising costs of industrial sales calls are constraints under which industrial sales managers and their marketing managers must operate. Yet ample evidence exists to conclude that such costs can be challenged—they do not have to be accepted. In fact, it can be argued that the costs of the direct company salesman channel are high because sales managers do not adequately control them. For instance, a study of 257 companies by the Sales Executive Club of New York showed that 54 percent of those companies had not conducted an organized study of their salesmen's use of time, 25 percent did not know the number of calls it was economical to make on an account, and 24 percent did not have set sales objectives for accounts.[18] In short, the study showed that many sales managers did not manage their salesmen and thus contributed unwittingly to the rising sales costs. The sales managers either did not seem to understand that time misspent in the field by their salesman cost their companies money, or they did not do anything about the problem.

Another factor pointing toward inept industrial sales management in the industrial market relates to the previously mentioned area of salesmen turnover. When salesmen are hired and either quit or are fired before becoming productive, the cost of industrial selling rises. Better than one-half of industrial saelsman turnover is accounted for by those who are released because they cannot produce in the market, and another 30 percent are released because they have bad habits or are unreliable, lazy, or insubordinate.[19] Certainly, it can be argued that most of these people never should have been hired in the first place, and this indicates poor selection by industrial sales managers. Add to this the contention that 75 to 80 percent of all industrial sales are accounted for by 20 to 25 percent of the industrial salesmen, and the poor selection accusation is reinforced.[20]

Data such as the above imply two areas where industrial sales managers need to improve: (1) better selection methods for recruiting salesmen and (2) better field time management of salesmen. A brief discussion of each is in order.

Selection of Industrial Salesmen. Finding applicants who will turn out to be successful salesmen is a real problem in the industrial market. As has been shown, the selling job calls for professionals who possess both the technical and sales capabilities in addition to other important personal characteristics. It is very difficult to find individuals who have the technical ability and the desire to sell at the same time. In addition, sales managers often do not know what characteristics are important in selling their products and what characteristics are not! Job descriptions are often so loosely written that they are of no help in screening applicants. Many sales managers are uncertain of the path to follow in building their sales forces. Because they cannot find candidates in sufficient number who possess both technical and selling capabilities, they face a dilemma. Should they hire technically oriented individuals such as engineers and teach them to sell? Or should they recruit people who want to sell and teach them the technical aspects of industrial field selling?

There is a lot of controversy among sales managers over which approach is best, and the uncertainty in the minds of many sales managers undoubtedly contributes to salesmen turnover. There appears to be a trend toward recruiting applicants with the desire to sell and then training them technically, the logic being that technical skills can be learned, but that selling ability is inborn. In the terms of some authorities in this area, there are characteristics that comprise a "sales personality," and selection of salesmen should focus primarily on those characteristics, as they are the ones that are much less able to be developed on the job.[21] In simple terms, the feeling is that if applicants are hired who want to sell, turnover will be reduced. The following indicates positive and negative factors that may be used to screen applicants more effectively and reduce the number prone to turnover.

Proponents of the "sales personality" concept hold that there are certain traits that characterize the person with an inborn desire and ability to sell. If these traits can be identified in a prospect, that can be viewed as being positive. Although there is no universal agreement as to what such traits must be, the following are typical of those that comprise the "sales personality." These traits are (1) energy, (2) aggressiveness, (3) creativity, (4) drive, (5) ability to communicate, (6) sensitivity, (7) tendency to plan, (8) realistic thinking, (9) initiative, and (10) self-discipline.[22] Applicants are then screened by a battery of tests in terms of these characteristics. These tests indicate the presence or lack of presence of the desired characteristics in the applicant. The more of these traits an individual has, the more likely it is that the person has the disposition to sell and thus is less likely to turnover.

On the negative side, such characteristics as the following are considered to detract from effective field selling and thus are to be avoided if possible. These factors are (1) a record of job-hopping, (2) recent business failure, (3) marital difficulties, (4) untidy appearance, (5) emotional instability, (6) excessive indebtedness, (7) too high previous earnings, (8) too low previous earnings, (9) unexplained gaps in the employment record, and (10) poor credit rating.[23] Applicants are screened in terms of these factors, and the more of these factors are found in an individual, the more prone he may be to turnover.

What is implied here is that candidates ranking high on the positive factors and low on the negative ones will want to sell and will have the emotional characteristics to sell effectively. Those applicants with reverse rankings are more likely to be the ones who will find selling unproductive, unfulfilling, discouraging, and generally distasteful. The latter are, of course, the kind that contribute to high turnover—the kind that were never psychologically adjusted to the selling task.

Factors such as these should only be used as guidelines and not as hard-and-fast, inflexible criteria. Nevertheless, there is logic in their use! If a candidate with high positive rankings can be taught such things as product knowledge, shop experience, how to locate the key buying influences, and so forth, it does seem logical to conclude that he or she could become a productive salesman and thus reduce costs affiliated with the turnover problem. Certainly, a 40 to 70 percent industrial salesman turnover rate suggests the need for selection criteria similar to what has been offered here.

Field Time Management of Salesmen. Another area of industrial sales management in need of attention is the time management of industrial salesmen. As stated earlier in this chapter, McGraw-Hill's Research Department claims that the average industrial salesman spends only 41 percent of his time actually selling, and this figure differs little among industries. Another 34 percent of his time is spent traveling and waiting for interviews, as has previously been discussed. Another study showed that industrial salesmen spend 25 to 30 percent of their time actually selling, but actually should be spending 40 to 50 percent of their time in this capacity.[24] "Rising sales call costs this year can be blamed in no small way on the fact that many sales managers manage salesmen almost as if time did not equal money."[25]

What this means in simple terms is that many sales managers are not managing their field salesmen effectively. They are allowing them to spend too much time traveling and waiting and not enough time actually selling. And at a time when the cost of an industrial sales call is rising out of proportion to the cost of living, this amounts to an intolerable situation for many industrial marketing companies. The point being made here is that the cost of an industrial sales call could be reduced if more sales calls could be achieved in the field. And more sales calls can only be achieved through salesmen spending more time in selling and less time in doing other things, particularly traveling and waiting in offices. The key to accomplishing this is to impress upon the salesmen the need for better time management on their part and then for the sales manager to show them how this might be accomplished. These are not easy tasks because industrial salesmen, just like most salesmen, are an independent group and not always easy to control.

One approach that has been used with some success is for the sales manager to impress upon the salesman how valuable the salesman's time is to himself. Most industrial salesmen are not impressed by figures such as the McGraw-Hill figures, which relate to the rising costs of an industrial sales call to their companies. Controlling these costs they believe is the problem of the sales manager, not the field salesmen! But they are impressed when it comes to the value of their own time. To illustrate, per the McGraw-Hill data previously presented, the average industrial salesman works 2,276 hours per year. Of this, 41 percent is spent in actual selling, which means that he has about 933 hours a year actually facing customers and selling. If desired annual income is $35,000, this means that selling time is worth $37.51 per hour to the salesman. Sitting in an office waiting for an hour or driving around needlessly for an hour costs the salesman $37.51. This has a sobering effect on field salesmen, and use of this argument can contribute to improve time management by field industrial salesmen. To use this technique, an individual sales manager would have to substitute company figures for the McGraw-Hill figures, but that is easily accomplished.

Another approach has been for sales managers to instruct field salesmen on ways to manage their time better via sales seminars, training programs, and other similar functions. The following tips were suggested by a Sales Executive Forum conducted by *Industrial Marketing* magazine for helping salesmen use their time in the field more effectively.[26] These tips are: (1) prearrange appointments by phone; (2) once appointments are made, keep them, and be punctual; (3) know the convenient calling hours of all customers, and get there during those hours; (4) make a schedule of calls in advance, and plan itineraries to travel systematically and not haphazardly to those calls; (5) organize travel so that a maximum number of calls can be made with a minimum amount of travel; (6) know who is going to be seen at each customer plant, and have something specific to accomplish on each call—lay off the casual visits; (7) learn to get as much information as possible from receptionists regarding waiting time, interest level, and so on; and (8) eliminate calls on marginal accounts that require inordinate time, travel, and effort.

Yet another approach that has been used is to use the computer's capabilities to help the salesman use field time more effectively. An example of this is a computer-based system used by Pennwalt Chemical Corporation in Philadelphia, Pennsylvania.[27] In this system, the salesman feeds the computer data on each of his accounts, such as the number of calls made in the current three-month period, the number of expected calls in the upcoming three-month period, average time per call, expected annual sales, minimum and maximum sales calls that could be made, expected sales for each account, and a sales adjustment factor based on the account's impact on profitability due to purchased products or commissions. With such data, the computer is then programmed to fit sales response curves through expected sales volumes of different call frequencies. It then prints optimum call policies designed to maximize sales, profits, or commissions. This approach allows the salesman to contribute to time management and at the same time, relieves the salesman of the time for calculating such data himself.

The fuel shortage in the winter of 1974 caused by the energy crunch forced many industrial sales managers and their marketing managers to look more closely at call frequencies and routing of their field salesmen. Waiting in line for an hour to buy five gallons of gas (maximum permitted by many service stations) cut deeply into salesman productivity and shook up many lethargic sales managers. Many managers pressured their salesmen to plan calls more effectively, drive less, use the phone more, and utilize more public transportation. These things may have always made good marketing sense, but it took a crisis to make many sales managers and field salesmen realize it.

The point being made here is that although direct selling by company sales personnel is an expensive channel of distribution that is getting more expensive every year, it is a necessary channel for many industrial marketing managers. This being the case, the industrial sales manager must look for ways to lower this cost, and two areas very opportune for such savings are the selection process of industrial salesmen and the more effective management of salesmen time in the field.

FORMULATING INDUSTRIAL SELLING STRATEGY

If it is assumed that personal selling is an appropriate component in an industrial marketing manager's promotional mix, a selling strategy must be developed that is consistent with corporate and marketing objectives, the company's overall marketing strategy and marketing plan, and with the substrategies of product, price, and channel. With these considerations in mind, a sales strategy would be developed based upon the following criteria:

1. Define specifically in terms of SIC those customer firms on whom the sales force will be expected to call.
2. Determine where these customer plants are located by county and by the size of the company. This can be accomplished relatively easily by using the *Sales Management* "Survey of Industrial Purchasing Power" or some of the other sources cited in chapter 3 of this text.
3. Determine the size of the markets in terms of potential sales of the companies defined in the previous two steps. It should be recognized that if the format of this text were followed, the first three steps would already have been performed in the company's overall marketing strategy and marketing plan.
4. Establish sales territories based on market potentials determined in the previous three steps and also on geographic limitations.
5. Establish sales quotas and profit objectives for each of the defined

territories based on the sales potential and competitive constraints involved in each territory.

6. Determine how the defined territories will be covered; how many regional and/or district sales managers, if any, shall be used and where they will be headquartered.

7. Determine specifically what buying influences must be reached by the salesmen if they are to sell effectively, and determine what their influencing motives are. For example, what are purchasing agents in the chemical industry looking for as opposed to plant engineers and other such key buying influences? Again, if the basic format of this text were followed, the sales manager would already know the answers to these questions from the overall marketing plan and strategy.

8. On the basis of the products to be sold and the buyer characteristics involved, develop a job description for the field salesman specifically outlining his duties, responsibilities, requirements, and other such factors.

9. Formulate a compensation plan based on salary, commission, bonuses, and other such considerations that is compatible with the products being sold, the customer's expectations, the breadth and depth of the market, the time required to close the sale, and other such factors. The plan formulated must be one that is capable of attracting good salesmen, retaining good salesmen, providing incentive to the salesmen, and meeting company objectives.

10. Recruit, select, hire, and train salesmen and assign them to the defined territories.

11. Motivate the salesmen, evaluating their performance in the light of the job description and the sales objective, transferring them when necessary, promoting them when appropriate, and replacing them when necessary.

12. Modify all of the previous 11 steps as the occasion requires.

This format is admittedly superficial, but time and space do not permit an extensive and exhaustive analysis of the industrial sales manager's job. Notice should again be taken that at least the first five steps in this format would already have been performed for the sales manager by the marketing manager if the latter followed something like the marketing plan outlined in this text. This again shows that personal selling, as with products and channels, is not an entity in and of itself. To be effective, personal selling must be integrated into the entire marketing plan and marketing strategy.

CHAPTER SUMMARY

Promotional strategy is of major importance to the industrial marketing manager because, in many instances, product specifications make competitive products very similar, and price stabilization objectives of industrial competitors bring about nonprice competition. This means that the real areas of competition take place in promotion, particularly in personal sales. Differences between industrial and consumer promotional strategies were analyzed with particular attention to personal selling. Types of industrial salesmen were described, and requirements for effective field selling were discussed. Trends in industrial sales were viewed, and a profile of the industrial salesman was developed. The area of industrial sales management was then described with particular attention paid to the rising costs of personal selling in the industrial market. Some methods for reducing those costs were developed in the areas of better selection of industrial salesmen and better management of their time in the field. Finally, a format for developing an industrial selling strategy and integrating it into the overall marketing strategy was illustrated.

QUESTIONS FOR CHAPTER 9

1. Fortunately for the industrial marketing manager, the so-called sales personality may be taught to any potential salesman. Do you agree or disagree with this statement? If you agree, why do you agree? If you disagree, why do you disagree?
2. Personal selling plays a very important role in industrial marketing, as there is often little distinction among competing products regarding price and quality. Do you agree or disagree with this statement? If you agree, why do you agree? If you disagree, why do you disagree?
3. How may the use of inside salesmen help the industrial marketing manager offset the rising costs of personal selling in the industrial market? Explain your answer.
4. A rough estimate is that about 75 percent of industrial sales are accounted for by about 25 percent of all industrial salesmen. What do you see as the major marketing management implications in this statement?
5. What do you believe is the relationship between better time management of company field salesmen and increased sales productivity? Explain your answer.

10

PROMOTIONAL STRATEGY IN INDUSTRIAL MARKETING – ADVERTISING AND SALES PROMOTION

As was related in the previous chapter, the formulation of an effective promotional strategy normally requires an integration of personal selling, advertising, and sales promotion. The importance of personal selling as a component in industrial promotion strategy has been developed, but does not in the least play down the importance of advertising and sales promotion in industrial marketing. They each play their own part in contributing to an effective overall promotional strategy.

ADVERTISING IN THE INDUSTRIAL MARKET

In a general sense, advertising is advertising whether it be in the consumer market or the industrial market. It is basically a communication process that, like all communication processes, aims to reach and influence people with its message. The type of influence might be educational, persuasive, or cognitive. Viewed in this context, the general objective of advertising is to bring about some kind of change in a target market—a change in awareness, the level of knowledge, attitude, or whatever. This kind of desired change is positive, but advertising is also used to maintain levels of awareness or levels of knowledge, and so on. In this sense, advertising's objective is the avoidance of a negative change.

Advertising is characterized by its nonpersonal mass appeal. In a way, it is the other end of the communication spectrum from personal selling, which is usually aimed at the individual. As such, these two promotional components should not compete, but should, in fact, work in tandem and collectively provide a more effective promotional mix overall. In the industrial market, this is very true! Advertising is a much cheaper form of communication than personal selling and, as such, can perform tasks much more economically than can company salesmen. On the other hand, as has been shown, industrial marketing frequently requires personal contact if sales are to be consummated. Industrial buyers rarely buy goods and services initially through advertising alone. This means that advertising can perform some of the previously discussed McGraw-Hill Research Department's promotion tasks better than can the salesman, but the latter can perform other tasks more effectively than can advertising. This almost naturally leads to a blending of the two components, although many industrial marketing managers probably fail to realize it. It is, for example, still quite common to find sales managers and advertising managers quarreling over budget, assignments, tasks, relative value of each other, and so forth, to the detriment of the total company. The industrial sales manager who fails to realize that advertising can make salesmen more effective does the company a great injustice and possible harm, just as does the advertising manager who believes advertising is so influential that it can do all things. The marketing manager's job is to make the two work together in a blend that gets optimum productivity out of each. This is emphasized in the following quotation.

A new breed of industrial marketers is winning ball games by using advertising to relieve the salesman of as much of his communication job as it can. . . . The secret of efficient and profitable communication is to use cheap multiple communications to do as much of the job as they can do, and to use expensive individual communication only to the extent you must. The result is lower communication cost per sale or higher sales per dollar of communication costs.[1]

Advertising's Roles in Industrial Marketing

Industrial advertising's roles differ from the roles played by advertising in the consumer market. Consumer marketing managers are often able to use advertising alone to bring a prospective customer all the way from awareness to the closing of the sale and even use advertising to keep that customer sold. In most cases, industrial advertisements cannot do this. Product complexities and buyer expectations require personal contact. This alters advertising's role in the industrial market. The following are some of the major roles played by advertising in the industrial market.

To Create a Favorable Climate for Personal Sales. One of the major roles played by advertising in industrial marketing is to lay a foundation prior to the salesman's call. The best way to illustrate this is with a picture. The McGraw-Hill "Man-in-Chair" advertisement that follows is considered an industrial marketing classic. The moral of the ad is straightforward and simple. No industrial salesman should have to take time out of a sales call to answer questions such as the purchasing agent in the ad is asking. These questions should have been answered by advertising prior to the salesman's arrival. Advertising is perfectly capable of providing information of a general nature on the company and its products, and it should be doing so. Recalling that the cost of an industrial sales call was $66.68 in 1973, it does not make good marketing sense to use the highest cost communication medium to answer questions that could be answered by advertising. Cold calls by salesmen can only increase the cost of industrial selling to a company.

To Stimulate Derived Demand. Because of the volatility of derived demand in the industrial market, many industrial marketing managers use advertising to stimulate demand for the products of their customers, thus bolstering direct industrial demand. Examples can be found in beer and soft drinks where glass, steel, and aluminum manufacturers advertise into the consumer market to persuade ultimate consumers to purchase drinks in steel cans versus aluminum cans versus glass bottles, using such arguments as quick chill properties, recycling, and so forth. As was discussed earlier in this text, this type of advertising takes place because industrial marketing managers cannot just react to changes in derived demand. They must actively stimulate it, and advertising is a most logical medium.

To Project a Favorable Corporate Image. Owing to the furor and concern brought about by environmentalists and others in the ecology movement that has developed in recent years, many industrial companies have used advertising to project a favorable image to the public. This type of advertising is also related to derived demand, but more indirectly. To illustrate, when Xerox underwrote the prime time television series on Black America in the late 1960s, the company certainly never intended to induce more blacks to buy Xerox products. Rather, it was an attempt to portray a social conscience and create a favorable attitude that might not directly contribute to sales, but that would help defray negative feelings about the firm.

It is important for large industrial companies like Xerox to create a favorable corporate image for numerous reasons. For example, to be accused of not having a social conscience or not caring about contemporary social issues can have damaging repercussions with ultimate consumers and consumerism groups who are more concerned than ever with the overall quality

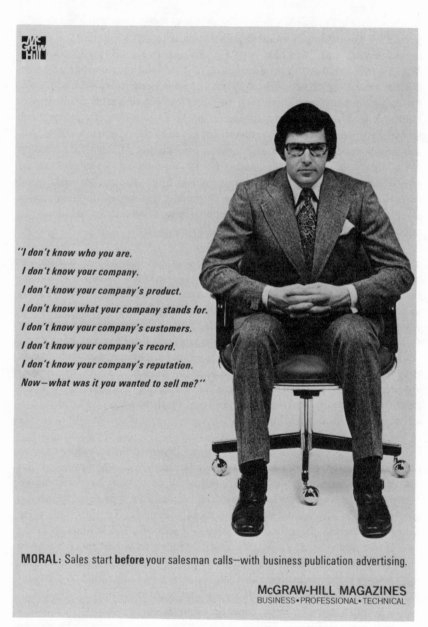

Fig. 10.1. McGraw-Hill's "Man-in-Chair" Advertisement. Photograph courtesy of McGraw-Hill Research Department.

of life in the United States. Large industrial companies simply cannot chance being labeled socially undesirable. Thus, they use advertising to help create an image favorable to themselves. In addition, buyers and buying influences in the industrial market do consider the images of competing suppliers in making purchasing decisions. This is especially true when such factors as price, service, technical service, delivery, and so on, are relatively equal in all suppliers. In short, there is too much to gain from a favorable image and too much to lose from an unfavorable image.

Other examples can be found in the lumber industry, the aluminum industry, the container industry, the glass industry, and numerous others. For some industrial companies, particularly the larger ones, this form of advertising has become quite common.

To Provide the Most Economical Promotional Mix. Advertising plays a major role in industrial marketing because it can reduce promotional costs, often without any detrimental effects. Typically, the proper combination of advertising and personal selling can be more effective than the use of either alone. An example may help make the desired point. In 1965, U.S. Steel was interested in advertising's ability to perform a role in the market as an indirect salesman. Through arrangements with one of its customers, the Harnischfeger Corporation of Milwaukee, U.S. Steel studied the roles of its salesmen and advertising in marketing to Harnischfeger. The company found out that its salesmen (U.S. Steel's salesmen) could not reach all of the appropriate Harnischfeger buying influences, nor could they call often enough. Thus, U.S. Steel concluded that advertising seemed likely to carry the bulk of the contact work. From its study, U.S. Steel estimated at least 850 completed advertising calls through business publications advertising at a total cost of $350.00, or about 15 cents per call.[2] At that time (1965), McGraw-Hill Research Department's cost of an industrial sales call was $35.55, as was illustrated in Table 9.2 in the previous chapter. This is not to imply that advertising calls and personal sales calls are equal in effectiveness, but rather to illustrate that if advertising can be used in the awareness and interest stages, the overall cost of promotion can be lowered with no adverse effects.

To Reach Inaccessible Buying Influences. Often buying influences are inaccessible to company field salesmen. For various reasons, they refuse to see salesmen, and yet, as buying influences, they may still exert considerable influence on products being purchased by their companies from various suppliers. These people, however, may read trade publication journals and general business publications and thus might be reached by advertising. Industrial advertising often fulfills a role of reaching such buying influences.

To Reach Unknown Buying Influences. There are other times when field salesmen do not know all of their buying influences. This is often the case with new salesmen or new customers, but it can even be true with experienced salesmen where customer corporate reorganizations and the like have shuffled buying influences. Because the buying influences often read trade publications, it is possible to communicate with them through advertising. In the previously illustrated U.S. Steel-Harnischfeger example, advertising calls located prospects the salesmen did not know of.[3] It is even possible that ads can get these buying influences to identify themselves through requests for further information from the advertisements. Once identified, the salesman can follow up with the call.

These few points show that advertising can and does play an important part in effective industrial marketing, although many people seem unaware of this fact. To argue that advertising does not have application to the industrial marketing manager because of the technicality of the products and the rational buying motives of industrial buyers only shows an ignorance of the total communication process and the special capabilities of advertising.

Media in the Industrial Market

Almost all types of advertising media have been used at one time or another by industrial advertisers, but three types have found the widest application. These are (1) space advertising in trade journals, general business publications, and general magazines; (2) direct mail; and (3) industrial directories. Table 10.1 illustrates media usage in the industrial market from 1971 to 1974. As can be seen, the three media just mentioned account for approximately 85 percent of all industrial advertising budget media purchases. The percentages in Table 10.1 account for pure advertising expenditures and do not include spending for trade shows, catalogs, dealer and distributor materials, and publicity and public relations. All of these will be regarded as sales promotion rather than advertising and will be covered later in this chapter. Newspapers, radio, and television advertising forms are not very widely used even though they may be the most appropriate media for stimulating derived demand. Thus, the great bulk of industrial advertising is carried by three media, and a brief examination of each would be beneficial.

Space Advertising. Space advertising loosely defines all advertising placed in (1) general magazines such as *Newsweek, Time,* and *U. S. News & World Report*; (2) general business publications such as *Fortune, Business Week,* and *The Wall Street Journal*; and (3) trade journal publications such as *Purchasing Magazine, Chemical Week, Industrial Distribution,* and the *Journal of the American Oil Chemists Society.* What this means is that space advertising can range all the way from broad brush corporate advertisements in the general

Table 10.1
ADVERTISING MEDIA IN THE INDUSTRIAL MARKET

	Percentage of Ad Budget Spent on Media			
Media	1974	1973	1972	1971
Business Publications	65.8	63.1	59.5	60.5
Direct Mail	13.2	13.7	13.6	12.5
General Magazines	7.6	5.9	7.2	7.7
Industrial Directories	4.7	5.9	5.1	5.0
Newspapers	1.3	1.8	0.6	0.7
Television	0.4	1.2	1.8	0.5
Radio	0.4	0.6	0.4	0.2
All Other Kinds	6.6	7.8	11.8	12.9
Total	100.0	100.0	100.0	100.0

Source: Adapted from the twelfth, thirteenth, fourteenth, and fifteenth "Annual Censuses of Industrial Advertising Budgets." Data from appropriate issues of *Industrial Marketing*.

Note: 1974 figures are based on *Industrial Marketing* projections.

magazines read by many businessmen to very specific and highly technical product advertisements in very specialized trade journals read only by highly trained and technically competent specialists.

Properly selected, space advertising can reach all the buying influences with a message appropriate for each. For example, if the marketing manager knows that the buying influences will be company presidents, plant engineers, and the purchasing directors, that manager can find out what periodicals are read by such buying influences and then place ads in those journals. Research may find that the company presidents read the general business publications; the plant engineers read such journals as *Plant Engineering*; and the purchasing people read such journals as *Purchasing Magazine, Purchasing Week,* and so forth. Data exist to match publications readership to industries based on their SIC system, and thus, with proper selection, the marketing manager or advertising manager can pinpoint media. This is what accounts for the wide usage of space advertising in the industrial market. Properly chosen, it can be matched to buying influences with very little waste involved. But if the marketing manager does not specifically know what buying influences are involved, it is virtually impossible to make effective use of space advertising.

From an industrial marketing manager's point of view, the value of trade, general business, or general magazine publications depends upon the ability of the individual publication to reach the intended buying influences in defined customer firms. More specifically, before the manager would advertise in an individual publication, it would be necessary to know information such as the following: What is the publication's circulation? Who specifically reads it in terms of the position of the reader and the SIC number of the company? How well is it read? How good is its editorial content? How good are its articles? and How much are its advertising costs?

Information pertaining to these criteria can be found in studies conducted by and for the individual publications themselves and also from independent rating services. Some of the better-known rating services that provide data on industrial publications are (1) Standard Rate and Data Service's Business Publication Section (BPS), which lists over 2,500 publications in over 150 market classifications; (2) the Association of Industrial Advertisers; (3) the Audit Bureau of Circulation (ABC); (4) Business Publications Audit (BPA); (5) Controlled Circulation Audit (CCA); (6) Verified Audit Circulation Corporation; and (7) *Market Data Book*, which is published annually by *Industrial Marketing* magazine. These rating services can provide many of the answers sought by industrial marketing managers and advertising managers contemplating the placing of ads in industrial space media. Properly used, they take a lot of guesswork out of space media selection because many of these services are now able to define readership broken down by circulation in four-digit SIC numbers and by title and function of the readers.

In addition, the individual publications themselves can provide data to the manager to aid in making media decisions. Typical of the information that is provided is (1) evidence of editorial content, including Starch Noted Scores, which would show the percentage of readers remembering editorial content; awards for editorial excellence; qualifications of the editorial staff, and so on; (2) circulation data in terms of total recipients; four-digit SIC, plant size, and location; percentage of subscribers by name and title; industry concentrations of readers, and so on; (3) advertising readership, including Starch Average Noted Scores of page ads, which would show the percentage of readers reading 50 percent or more of the written material in the ad; percentage of readers buying directly from the ads or contacting sources for more data per independent audits; point differences in noted scores of ads from front to back of publication, and so on; (4) advertiser acceptance in terms of number and percentage of total advertisers using the publication; number and percentage using it exclusively, and so on; (5) reader preferences of the publication and competing publications by outside independent studies; and (6) cost figures relative to cost figures in competing publications.[4] Information such as this is available from almost all trade publications at no cost, and certainly any industrial marketing manager or advertising manager serious about space advertising should obtain such data prior to placing ads in space media. These are the types of data that are necessary to make intelligent decisions regarding media selection.

In selecting space media, the industrial marketing manager and advertising manager should be guided by three factors. These are (1) to reach as many people as possible in those companies in the defined target markets, (2) to reach as many of the known buying influences as possible within those customer firms, and (3) to accomplish both of these at the most reasonable cost. To accomplish these three things, the manager must implement a format such as the following:

1. Define the market or markets specifically in terms of at least four-digit SIC numbers. This is a basic necessity because many sources provide data based on SIC numbers.
2. Know the appropriate buying influences that are to be reached by name and position if possible, but at least by position.
3. Know what the individual buying influences are looking for in publications, and know why they read them. This is of critical import in building advertising themes or appeals, which will be covered later; but it is also important in media selection, as the objectives of some publications may be inconsistent with reader objectives.
4. Through data provided by the rating services and the publications, match publications with intended audiences by four-digit SIC numbers and positions of the buying influences. This permits the determination of those journals most appropriate for reaching intended buying influences.
5. Rank the publications for each buying influence by such factors as circulation, readership, cost, editorial content, value of articles, and the like.
6. Choose the publications providing the best penetration to each of the buying influences for dollars expended. This may mean but one journal with some buying influences and a number of journals for others. The real decision here must be in terms of market coverage for dollars expended. The point of diminishing return can come quite quickly when a number of publications are available. A study conducted in 1968 showed the following in this regard. In SIC 33 primary metals industry, the top five journals could reach 72 percent of the market at a 1968 cost of $5,191. The top ten journals could reach 75 percent of the market, but at a cost of $12,031. The top 15 journals also reached 75 percent of the market, but at a cost of $17,741. And the top 20 journals also reached 75 percent of the market, but at a cost of $21,216.[5] These figures are typical and show that advertising in all journals appropriate to four-digit SIC buying influences just does not make

good sense from an economic viewpoint. In choosing specific journals, the marketing manager and advertising manager must trade off increases in market penetration against cost in arriving at the optimum number of trade journals per buying influence. If they fail to do this, space advertising dollars are expended ineffectively. In the case just illustrated in SIC 33, to increase market penetration from 72 percent to 75 percent would have doubled the cost—a consideration the manager must weigh very carefully.

Space advertising in general magazines, general business publications, and trade journal publications is widely used in the industrial market because if it is properly used, it can pinpoint ads to buying influences with very little waste. The high percentage of usage of this medium in Table 10.1 bears this out.

Space advertising can also be advantageous in that it is a relatively low-cost form of promotion, certainly lower than the cost of personal selling. In addition, space advertising of the trade publication variety often has a great deal of credibility with industrial buyers and buying influences. Purchasing agents, plant engineers, production supervisors, and so forth, read trade journals in their respective fields, and they look to these journals for information and assistance with their problems. Space advertising also has the ability to reach buying influences who will not see salesmen. For example, a production supervisor may well refuse to spend time talking to salesmen calling upon the company, but he may diligently read production-oriented trade journals. Space advertising can also sometimes reach unknown buying influences in customer firms. This happens when the company salesman is unaware of that particular buying influence and never reaches him. Through advertising in the proper trade journal, the promotional message may be communicated to the buying influence. Data can also be found regarding what industries by SIC number are prime readers of what specific trade publications. With such data, space advertising can be matched with appropriate buying influences in SIC industries in the company's target market. Finally, space advertising in trade publications has some general advantages. These publications are normally edited for a specific group of readers with special interest in the content. The readers of such publications may often exert considerable buying influence in their companies, and the editors of such publications often provide advertisers with advertising and marketing assistance.

At the same time, the manager must realize that space advertising has definite disadvantages. One big disadvantage is that ads will compete in the same issue with competitor ads. The reader's attention will be divided among competitive ads! Quantity and quality of circulation are often troublesome. Some journals have large circulations, but are distributed free, which may mean that they are not well read by all subscribers. In addition, different publications, even in the same general area, are perceived differently in the marketplace. What appear to be basically similar trade journals often are seen as being quite different by buying influences in prospective customer companies, and ads placed in one journal may have a different market impact from that of ads placed in another. Most of the disadvantages of space advertising, however, are involved with choosing among alternative journals rather than with deciding whether or not to use space advertising. As Table 10.1 shows, 60 to 65 percent of industrial advertising budgets are spent in space advertising, indicating that the advantages of space advertising overshadow the disadvantages.

Direct Mail Advertising. As Table 10.1 illustrates, the second most used industrial advertising medium is direct mail. Direct mail is defined as any printed or processed form directed to selected individuals by controlled distribution.[6] There are three basic types of direct mail: (1) direct mail advertising, which is basically the same as other advertising except that it utilizes the direct mail medium—the ad copy may be identical to that used in space advertising; (2) direct mail sales promotion that tries to get the respondent to react in some manner, such as to obtain leads for salesmen, to open the door for salesmen, to get the respondent to identify himself by offering further information, and so on; and (3) direct mail selling where the sender actually tries to sell via mail with no personal selling involved. This latter type is not as common in the industrial market as the first two types, but it can be used effectively with established customers who know and trust the advertiser. In this discussion, no differences between the three types will be emphasized, and they will all be treated as direct mail advertising. Direct mail advertising shall mean any or all of the three types.

Direct mail can be an effective industrial advertising medium when prospective buying influences can be identified and located by name. It is an extremely selective and flexible medium. Almost any format or approach can be used with direct mail, which is not the case with other media. Industrial companies have used direct mail to send brochures, catalog sheets, letters, bulletins, folders, sales manuals, price lists, and even samples. No other advertising medium offers such flexibility. Direct mail can also be the most personal of all media. It can be sent to the prospect by name and position in his company, and information of a confidential nature can be communicated. Direct mail also can be timed more precisely than other media, as it is not restricted to publication dates of journals, and the date of delivery can be timed to mail deliveries. In a sense, there is less competition with direct mail—

there are no competitive advertisements nor any journal articles or editorials to distract the reader.

There are, however, definite disadvantages to using direct mail. If prospects cannot be pinpointed, direct mail can be wasteful and expensive. Moreover, direct mail advertising is often labeled as "junk mail" and treated accordingly by many industrial buyers and buying influences. Nevertheless, properly used, it can be an effective and economical industrial advertising medium used separately or in conjunction with space advertising.

Whether direct mail can be used effectively or not in the industrial market depends a great deal upon the adequacy of the industrial marketing manager's mailing list. A mailing list is simply a list of prospects to whom the ads will be directed. In the industrial market, the prospects should be the buying influences in customer firms for the company's products. If the ads can be mailed directly to the appropriate buying influences in their name, direct mail can be a very effective medium in terms of reaching the defined market.

To compile an effective industrial marketing mailing list, three factors are required: (1) prospect firms must be identified by SIC number and specifically located, (2) buying influences must be identified for the marketing manager's products involved, and (3) those buying influences must be identified by name. Most industrial marketing managers making use of the direct mail medium are able to do this—they have compiled over time customer and prospect mailing lists of key buying influences in companies in their target markets.

There are two ways to compile a mailing list. The first, though not necessarily the best, way is to build such a list from within the company. After market segments are defined and buying influences determined by position, the marketing manager makes a concentrated effort to find the names of those individuals filling those positions in each customer firm. This can be accomplished from input from salesmen in the field, distributors, reps, personal contacts, and other such sources. Names can also be obtained from trade show leads and requests for additional information coming from space media advertisements. Names can also be found through the use of state industrial directories and other private sources such as the directories described in detail back in chapter 3. The approach here is to build a mailing list without going outside the company to purchase it. This approach takes time, effort, and constant attention to upgrading it, but it is often used with effectiveness. It is not usually the quick way to build a mailing list, however, and if an industrial marketing manager wants such a list in a hurry, this approach is not normally considered appropriate.

The second method, which again is not necessarily the best, is to purchase the mailing list from outside the company. Mailing lists can be purchased from companies specializing in such lists. Examples of such firms are R. L.

Polk & Company, National Business Lists, Inc., and Dun & Bradstreet's Marketing Services Division. Polk's prospect list totals 116,889 executives in the top 22,000 companies in the United States, with an average of five officers for each firm.[7] National Business Lists' files contain more than 4,000,000 businesses, institutions, and professional firms all classified by four-digit SIC numbers.[8] As can be realized, using such outside sources to build a mailing list can be very quick and relatively cheap if markets are previously defined in specific terms. Such lists, however, may not be precise enough for some managers in terms of required customer types or buying influences. The purchased mailing lists may not contain the names of the required buying influences. Of course, both methods could be used in conjunction to build a single mailing list. For the marketing manager requiring such a list in a hurry, purchasing that list from an outside source is probably the best course of action provided the required buying influences are included. To purchase a list without such information, no matter how low the price, makes little marketing sense.

The mistake should not be made that direct mail is a substitute for space media advertising or that the use of one precludes the use of the other. Properly used, direct mail and space media advertising can complement one another. An example of this took place with a California industrial company that advertised in 20 business publications and accompanied its ads with reader action cards. The ads were general in that they related to the nature of the product rather than to that product's application to specific industries. The action cards produced 12,000 inquiries, which were then followed up with a direct mail campaign providing more specific industry data. The end result was to double company sales.[9]

With all its advantages, direct mail advertising is used by only 12 to 13 percent of industrial advertisers as Table 10.1 illustrates. It is questionable whether industrial marketing managers use direct mail to its fullest capacity. The following quotation bears out this contention.

> I think there are a great many opportunities which industrial marketers miss—of using direct mail as a relatively inexpensive medium to lock in the people who have registered some interest . . . in response to a message that they have read in other media.[10]

Industrial Directory Advertising. As Table 10.1 illustrates, the third medium of consequence in industrial advertising is in industrial directories, which are also called industrial buyers' guides. Advertising in directories accounts for about 5 to 6 percent of industrial advertising budgets. In a sense, this figure is misleading because some industrial marketing managers and their advertising managers use them extensively and swear by their effectiveness, implying that although their overall usage may be relatively low, they account for a big part of the advertising budgets of some industrial companies.

The idea of advertising in industrial directories seems inconsistent to many marketing managers and advertising managers. Basically, an industrial directory lists supply sources for various products that are intended for use as buying guides in industry. If a purchasing agent or plant engineer or whatever wishes to purchase a certain product, that person may refer to a directory to find out who could supply such a product. Thus, all appropriate suppliers are generally listed whether they advertise in the directory or not. To many industrial advertisers, this implies duplication if they advertise in the same directory in which they are listed. This is probably not a valid conclusion to draw, however, because the buyer at the time of using the directory may be looking for information that is not in the listing. If the sought information is in the advertisement, this could well be an influencing factor in the decision to pick a source of supply.

Research has shown that directories are used by buyers and buying influences. A 1949 study conducted by the National Industrial Advertisers Association posed the question, "How did you first learn of the company whose product you sought?" to industry plant and engineering people. The most often mentioned source was industrial directories, cited by about 23 percent of the respondents. In a later study conducted in 1969 by the Conover-Mast Purchasing Directory, the same question was asked of the same type of respondents. This latter study again found that industrial directories were the most often mentioned answer, being cited again by about 23 percent of those responding.[11] These figures show that directories may be a good medium for creating awareness and stimulating interest, the first two of McGraw-Hill's six-step promotion process.

There are many industrial directories in which an industrial company could advertise. As was discussed in chapter 3, each state has an industrial directory, and a number of private directories are also available. Probably the best-known and most comprehensive of all directories is the *Thomas Register*, an 11-volume directory that is published annually. Each year, some 40,000 industrial companies purchase new *Thomas Registers*, and it is estimated that older editions are still in use in over 200,000 plants. In addition, there is now a *Thomas Register Catalog File*, called *Thomcat*, which accompanies the register. *Thomcat* is a three-volume feature consisting of manufacturers' catalogs bound together in alphabetical order and cross-referenced within the product volumes of the register itself. Other well-known directories include the *Conover-Mast Purchasing Directory*, the *Poor's Register*, the *Million Dollar Directory*, and the *Middle Market Directory*, among others. Because these directories all contain advertising space, they make a most appropriate industrial advertising medium.

There are advantages and disadvantages to advertising in industrial directories. On the positive side, directories are good in that they are used as reference materials by buyers and buying influences. Thus, although a direct mail piece or a specific issue of a trade publication may be thrown out, industrial directories are kept for reference even after new issues of the directories are published. It is commonplace for previous editions to be passed on to others. Advertisements in directories are more permanent. Moreover, as the previously quoted Conover-Mast study showed, buyers do refer to directories when they make decisions. Directories are a highly credible medium—for many in the industrial market, the directory is the basic buying tool. In addition, ads in directories are often good complements for company catalogs, as will be shown later in this chapter in the section on catalogs.

On the negative side, it costs money to advertise in directories; and because the company is listed anyway, advertising could mean duplication. Because directories also include competitors, advertising readership is often fractionalized, which could be a disadvantage. In addition, directories are expensive, and many industrial companies do not purchase them for this reason. Ads placed in directories will not reach prospective companies not purchasing those directories. Finally, directory advertising is more of a shotgun approach than is advertising by direct mail or in trade journals. The former does not have the capability of matching ad message with the defined buying influence as do both direct mail and trade journal advertising.

The three media of space advertising, direct mail, and industrial directory advertising comprise the bulk of industrial advertising. Although newspapers, radio, and television are used at times, they are not considered of major importance in industrial advertising. Industrial advertisements must reach the buying influences, and if they do not, they are of little value to the marketing manager. In the minds of most industrial marketing managers and their advertising managers, space advertising in trade publications and direct mail offer the best chances of communicating with these buying influences.

Industrial Advertising Themes

In addition to selecting media, the industrial advertiser must decide upon the message or messages to be used in company advertisements. The basis for the message or theme has to be the buying influence that the ad is supposed to reach. As has been discussed, buying influences are interested in different things—their problems differ, and so do their responsibilities. Thus, they look for different things in their ads even though they are all being exposed to the same product or service. To illustrate, assume that a user customer is considering the purchasing of forging machines for use in its production process. The key buying influences are found to be the purchasing agent, the comptroller, the vice-president of production, and the production supervisor.

Although each is considering the purchase of the same product (the forging machines), each is looking for something different. The purchasing agent may be concerned with price, ability of the supplier to deliver on time, freight rates, F.O.B. points, reputation of the supplier, whom else the supplier now sells these products to, and so on. The comptroller may be interested in price, financing arrangements available, the payback period of the investment, the return-on-investment from the machines, and the like. The vice-president of production may be looking for information on technical assistance offered, service requirements, certainty of the supplier to deliver on time, ability of the new machines to be integrated into the present production process, employee training or retraining required, and so forth. The production supervisor may well be interested in such factors as ease of operation of the machines, number of men required to operate them, training or retraining required, and so on.

The point being made here is clear—all four buying influences, although looking at the same product, have different wants, needs, expectations, and desires. If the advertisements used by the marketing manager or advertising manager do not relate to the interests of the particular buying influence, there is no communication and, therefore, no real advertising. In this example, an ad aimed at the purchasing agent stressing training or retraining requirements may have little meaning if purchasing agents are seeking other information to make their decisions.

This again reinforces the point made continuously throughout this text— it is imperative that the buying influences be identified and located specifically for effective industrial marketing. In the case of advertising, to advertise effectively in the industrial market requires media that will reach the specified buying influences and ads placed in those media that will communicate information relevant to the interests of those same buying influences.

Corporate versus Product Advertising. An age-old controversy exists in the industrial market in relation to ad themes or messages. That controversy centers around whether ads should sell the corporate image or the company's products! Proponents of the corporate ads claim that to sell a company's products, it is first necessary to create a favorable corporate image. This image, they claim, contributes to sales because industrial purchasers are influenced in their buying by corporate image and reputations. Proponents of the product advertising approach argue just the opposite. They claim that industrial firms buy products for what those products can do for them, not because of who manufactured them! Their logic is that product advertising leads to product adoption and use that in time achieve the desired image for the company. Given the right buying influences and proper execution of the ad involved, both approaches work, and this accounts for the strong proponents of each and the controversy that exists. This is not to imply that an ad must be either product or corporate exclusively, as both can be involved at the same time. But overall advertising campaigns must usually emphasize either a product or a corporate orientation based on objectives in the overall marketing plan, and this is where the disagreement among industrial advertisers arises.

This area has been researched extensively. One study conducted by *Industrial Marketing* magazine found that about two-thirds of the executives interviewed spent less than 10 percent of their ad budgets in corporate advertising. On another related question, these same executives stated that although 55 percent of them planned to increase their total advertising budgets, only 29 percent planned more corporate advertising, as opposed to 61 percent planning more product advertising. On still another related question, 93 percent of the executives interviewed felt that product advertising provided the greatest return per dollar spent, as opposed to 7 percent feeling that corporate advertising provided the greatest return.[12] These data indicate a decided preference, at least in that study, toward product advertising. But there are a lot of industrial advertisers who disagree! The ecology movement that has developed in recent years has stimulated many large industrial companies to advertise their corporate social responsiveness.

Whether the advertising message be corporate or product-oriented is an interesting academic question, but it may be immaterial to the practicing marketing manager. If buyers and buying influences are seeking product knowledge, then product-oriented advertisements should be used. But if the buying influences are impressed by the corporate images of suppliers, then corporate ad themes should be employed. It all comes back to the point that advertising is a form of communication and, as such, must relate to the interests of those being reached. This again reemphasizes the need for careful determination of key buying influences and in-depth assessment of their particular wants and needs. The long-run purpose of advertising in the industrial market is to contribute to company sales; thus, advertising messages and themes must provide incentive for customers to increase their purchasing from the advertising firm.

SALES PROMOTION IN THE INDUSTRIAL MARKET

In many industrial firms, little difference is made between advertising and sales promotion. Often the two areas are handled as one—there is a single budget out of which allocations to both areas are made, and one manager is responsible for both areas. In other companies, advertising and sales promotion are separate departments, each having its own department head who reports directly to the marketing manager. In this section, sales promotion shall be defined to include those nonpersonal areas of promotion other than advertising. Table 10.2 illustrates those areas of sales promotion most common to the industrial market during the period from 1971 to 1974. As can be seen, four areas account for almost 100 percent of what industrial firms spend in their sales promotion budgets. A discussion of each of these four areas may help to provide more insight into the use of sales promotion in the industrial promotional mix.

Catalogs

As Table 10.2 shows, industrial firms consistently spend over one-half of their sales promotion budgets in catalogs. In terms of total advertising and sales promotion budgets, catalogs account for about 20 percent, and it is estimated that industrial firms in the United States spend in excess of $25 million per year in this particular area of promotion. Broadly defined, a catalog is "complete or comprehensive printed information about a product, designed for demonstration and/or reference work."[13] The catalog is unique in that it is a reference form of promotion. Buyers and buying influences in industry keep catalogs in their plants; and when purchasing opportunities come up, they refer to their catalogs for comparisons of specifications, prices, terms, and so on, to screen potential suppliers in this manner. The manufacturer of industrial products whose catalog is not available to the purchaser may not even be considered. Sometimes referred to as the "silent salesman," the catalog is a natural complement to the industrial sales call—it is there for reference

Table 10.2

SALES PROMOTION MEDIA IN THE INDUSTRIAL MARKET

	Percentage of Sales Promotion Budget Spent on Media			
Media	1974	1973	1972	1971
Catalogs	56.4	55.0	55.9	52.6
Trade Shows	21.8	22.5	21.8	23.7
Dealer & Distributor Materials	11.5	12.5	10.9	14.3
Publicity & Public Relations	10.3	10.0	11.4	9.4
Total	100.0	100.0	100.0	100.0

Source: Adapted from the twelfth, thirteenth, fourteenth, and fifteenth "Annual Censuses of Industrial Advertising Budgets." Data from appropriate issues of *Industrial Marketing.*

Note: 1974 figures are based on *Industrial Marketing* projections.

before the salesman arrives, and it can be referred to after the sales call is completed.

There is no single form of industrial catalog. The catalog for an infrequently purchased user product would be quite different from the catalog of an off-the-shelf standardized OEM product. Buyers' needs and product sophistication require different formats if effective communication is to be achieved. The OEM product might be sold right off the catalog page, whereas the manufacturer of the user product might use the catalog to precondition the prospect for the personal sales call that will follow.

Effective use of the catalog depends upon how well it is prepared, how well it is distributed, and the use the sales force makes of it. A poorly prepared or incomplete catalog soon loses credibility regardless of how well it is distributed to those who would use it. On the other hand, even the perfectly organized catalog is of little practical value if it never reaches those buying influences making the decision. Moreover, if the salesmen are not properly trained to use the catalog in the field, there can hardly be effective integration of personal selling and sales promotion in the overall promotional mix. In regard to preparing the catalog, the Thomas Publishing Company of New York, publishers of the previously discussed *Thomas Register* and *Thomcat*, have a suggested format for organizing the catalog, and this format is reproduced on the pages that follow. Adherence to such a format can aid greatly in effectively using the catalog as an industrial promotional tool.

ORGANIZATION OF THE CATALOG

1. Determine Which Products Will Be Included . . . Which Will Not . . . This is very important because a belated discovery that a product has been left out (or erroneously included) can wreak havoc in an otherwise soundly planned catalog.

2. If There Are a Number of Products, Can They Be Grouped Into "Families"? . . . If so, it helps in the intelligent organization of your catalog. It helps the prospective buyer find what he wants more readily, and may stimulate the purchase of accessory products.

3. Make Folders for Each Product or Group of Products . . . And gather all pertinent data on each. This will include previous catalogs, technical bulletins, engineering reports, sales literature, photos, illustrations, testimonials, competitive literature, and anything else helpful.

4. Review the Folders for Completeness . . . When you've gathered

all the data, review it for completeness. You'll immediately spot gaps . . . missing data, photos, etc.

5. Take Steps to Obtain What's Missing . . . This is an area where catalogers most often run into trouble. At this point, you have to determine who's holding you up . . . and how to get him off dead center.

6. Make a Rough Outline of the Contents . . . This outline is the skeletal framework of the finished job, and is most helpful in budgeting, scheduling delivery dates, and, of course, in layout. These are generally speaking the elements involved: (A) The Cover; (B) Table of Contents (Index); (C) General Company Background—history, policies, what makes the company unique, etc. (optional); and (D) Product Pages comprised of: (1) General description of user benefits the product provides. Testimonials can be helpful; (2) More detailed description of product features; (3) Performance data, specifications, engineering characteristics, and price if applicable; and (4) How to get more information—sales offices, dealers, etc.

7. Determine the Format to Use . . . What size (8½" × 11", pocket-sized) should your catalog be? How will it be bound? How many colors?

8. Make an Organizational Layout . . . Which is really a refinement of your rough outline, and a graphic interpretation of the contents. This will help you determine about how many pages will be required, and put you in position to turn over the job to a competent layout artist, just as soon as you can—

9. Plan and Write the Copy . . . Or have someone write it for you. If someone else does the writing make sure he realizes the fundamental purpose of the catalog is to inform . . . to provide helpful buying information in as complete and comprehensive a manner as possible. There is no place in catalog copy for writing that exhorts, entices, beguiles, or pounds the table. On the other hand, it can be persuasive—as well as informative.

10. Establish a Working Schedule for Completion of the Job . . . At this point, the catalog becomes an exercise in logistics. You set up a timetable for photography, retouching, finished art, printing, binding, and distribution.

Source: *How to Build and Distribute Your Next Catalog* (New York: Thomas Publishing Company). Reprinted by permission of Thomas Publishing Company, New York.

Distributing the catalog is a problem for the industrial marketing manager. Catalogs are a relatively high-priced promotional medium, and their cost appreciates rapidly when ineffectively distributed. Overdistribution increases out-of-pocket costs of production and distribution, whereas underdistribution brings about opportunity losses because the catalogs do not reach the key buying influences, who then specify competitive products. For the industrial marketing manager contemplating the use of catalogs in the promotional mix, specific delineation of customer firms by SIC and precise definition of key buying influences are necessities. As has been the theme throughout this text, these factors should be known prior to producing the catalog. If the required distribution is too broad and too expensive, then another medium should be considered.

There are four general methods for such distribution, which may be used collectively or individually, according to overall marketing and promotional objectives. These four methods are: (1) distribute them by mail to the buying influences; (2) use space ads and direct mail to get prospects to request catalogs—this often turns up unknown buying influences and can easily be used in conjunction with mail distribution; (3) have salesmen distribute them to the buying influences; and (4) distribute them in a pre-filed catalog that is a bound volume of catalogs of many manufacturers, such as the previously mentioned *Thomcat*. Generally, combinations of these four methods provide the most effective distribution. It would appear that for most industrial marketing managers, reliance upon a single method of distribution would have disadvantages easily overcome by multiple distribution.

The major point to remember with catalog promotion is that it is constantly in-house with the customer, and buying influences use catalogs as references much as they use industrial directories. If these buying influences do not have the manufacturer's catalog, sales can be lost without the marketing manager even realizing it. The major consideration with catalogs is not whether the manager can afford them, but rather whether he can afford not to use them! The fact that catalogs account for over one-half of industrial sales promotion budgets and over one-fifth of total industrial promotional budgets indicates that most industrial marketing managers feel they must have them to remain competitive.

Trade Shows

As Table 10.2 illustrates, trade shows are a common form of industrial sales promotion. This is about the oldest form of industrial promotion, and its origin can be traced back to medieval times, when artisans exhibited their wares at fairs. In a general sense, today's trade show is still an industrial fair, complete in many instances with all the characteristics of any fair. Trade shows have a basic characteristic different from all other forms of industrial promotion—they bring the customer to the company as opposed to the opposite, resulting in a concentration of customers that might not be achieved in any other manner. Often the trade shows in an industry bring the bulk of buyers and buying influences under one roof for the express purpose of shopping. Trade show promotion has concentrated power as does no other form of industrial promotion.

Analysis of trade show promotion, however, shows that there is not universal acceptance of trade shows as an industrial sales promotion medium. Industrial marketing managers who believe in them do so strongly and use them extensively. Those who do not believe in them appear to be just as strong in their convictions. Industrial marketing managers do not appear to be indifferent toward trade show promotion—they either like them or they do not! The result is that a relatively small number of industrial companies appear to account for most trade show promotion. A survey by *Meetings & Convention* magazine found that only 11.9 percent of corporations participate in trade shows, with the great majority of these firms participating in from one to four shows per year.[14] On the other hand, some managers put great emphasis on this form of promotion. For example, Minnesota Mining & Manufacturing Company goes to about 600 trade shows a year and to about 1,000 if dealer-support shows are included. To quote a spokesman at Minnesota Mining & Manufacturing, "The trade show is a major marketing tool."[15] Another good example is Union Carbide, which participates in about 200 trade shows per year.[16]

There is little doubt that trade shows are big business. It is difficult to obtain data on private trade shows held by individual companies, but data are available on trade shows sponsored by trade associations, many of which relate to the industrial market.[17] To illustrate, in 1971 there were 9,221 conventions and/or trade shows sponsored by associations at an average cost of $190,813. Of these, 45.3 percent had exhibit space areas purchased by individual firms. The average exhibit space was 23,305 square feet, with an average of 101 exhibitors per show. Of these shows, 87 percent reported attendance increases over the preceding five years, and 83 percent claimed their exhibit expenditures had either remained constant or had increased over the preceding five years. Other studies report similar trends. In spite of materials shortages, fuel shortages, recession, higher prices, and all the rest, the attendance at industrial trade shows has not dropped off.

The Value of Trade Show Promotion. Perhaps the best way to understand the role the trade show plays in industrial promotion is to look at some examples of how it is used. For example, Honeywell uses trade shows with the following objectives in mind: (1) meeting potential customers, (2) accumulating a mailing list, (3) introducing new products, (4) discovering new applications for existing products, (5) demonstrating nonportable equipment,

(6) hiring new personnel, and (7) establishing new representatives and dealers.[18] It is highly unlikely that any other single form of industrial promotion could be used to accomplish such objectives effectively and economically.

Another way to look at the value of trade show promotion is to compare trade show leads with leads obtained from other forms of promotion. Westinghouse found that some 7,000 sales leads were uncovered annually. Of the 7,000, 50 percent or 3,500 came from publicity, 35 percent or 2,450 came from advertising, and 15 percent or 1,050 came from trade shows. Actual sales converted from these leads, however, tell a different story! Of the 3,500 leads uncovered by publicity, 10 percent or 350 were converted to actual sales. Of the 2,450 uncovered by advertising, 50 percent or 1,225 were converted to sales. Of the 1,050 trade show leads, 80 percent or 840 were converted to sales.[19] These figures show that although trade shows uncovered the fewest number of sales leads, they were the best leads in terms of conversion to actual sales, which may be the real test for the effectiveness of a promotional medium. Probably the major reason for this is that good industrial trade shows draw few casual visitors, and thus sales leads come largely from buying influences who are truly interested. This may not be so true with advertising and publicity leads.

Still another way to view trade show promotion is in its cost and its effectiveness. It is an expensive medium, but it can be effective if properly used. To illustrate, Hewlett-Packard had a 2,200-square-foot exhibit in the 1973 National Computer Conference in New York. This exhibit reached 100 percent of its potential audience at the show at a cost of but $9.51 per visitor reached.[20] At that time, the average cost of an industrial sales call was $57.71 per the McGraw-Hill figures. These figures indicate that when personal contact is required, trade show promotion can be an effective substitute and/or complement in regard to personal salesmen, and the medium does have value in this aspect.

Selection of Trade Shows. For the industrial marketing manager, choosing trade shows to enter is much like choosing trade journals in which to advertise. There are many trade shows, even within specific industries, and to enter all of them would be both expensive and wasteful. This means the manager must determine some means of selecting those shows to enter. Until recently, it was quite difficult to obtain quantitative measurements of the effectiveness of different trade shows. It still is not easy to find such data, although auditing of trade shows has taken place by such organizations as the Audit Bureau of Circulation and the Trade Shows & Exhibits Committee of the Association of Industrial Advertisers. Most shows yet seem to lack such audits, however, as a study showed that only 17.4 percent of associations provide independent audits of their shows, and only another 3.7 percent had any intentions of offering such audits.[21] Naturally, it follows that the dearth of objective data on the effectiveness of individual trade shows makes selection difficult for the manager.

The key to selection depends upon what factors make a good trade show for a particular industrial marketing manager. Exhibits Surveys, an organization specializing in industrial trade show evaluations, specifies the following indicators as the best for measuring trade show activity and audience quality.[22] These factors are (1) buying plans—the percentage of the audience at a trade show planning to buy or recommend to buy one or more of the products seen at a show; (2) buying influences—that percentage of visitors at a show who have a final say or who can specify or recommend the purchase of the type of products produced by the exhibitor; (3) audience interest—that percentage at a show who stop to talk or get literature at a selected sample of the exhibitors at a show; (4) time spent at a show—the amount of time the average visitor spends at a show; and (5) traffic density—an average of the number of visitors per 100 square feet of exhibit space. According to Exhibits Surveys, a density factor of 4.0 is considered ideal—when it is smaller, traffic is too light—when it is higher, the show tends toward congestion.

What these factors mean to the industrial marketing manager is easy to see. When possible trade shows are reviewed in terms of these factors, those with the highest percentage of buying plans, the greatest number of buying influences, the highest audience interest factors, the most time spent at the show, and a density factor close to 4.0 are the most appropriate candidates. Data such as this must be purchased from such trade-show-evaluating organizations as Exhibits Surveys, but with such data the manager can get the most for every dollar spent on trade show promotion. Moreover, as has been stated, trade show promotion is expensive, with estimates of approximately $300 per running foot of exhibit, which would account for 40 to 50 percent of the total show budget, depending upon the distance from plant to show location.[23] With proper selection criteria and effective exhibits, trade show promotion can be a very productive sales promotion medium.

Dealer and Distributor Materials

Approximately 10 to 15 percent of industrial sales promotion budgets go toward dealer and distributor materials that manufacturers provide to their middlemen to help the latter promote effectively in their local markets. Typical of such materials are point-of-purchase (POP) displays for dealer showrooms, technical bulletins, dealer sales kits, specialty advertising items such as calendars and business gifts, direct mail stuffers, price lists, and other such similar pieces of promotion. For any manufacturer using distributors and/or manufacturer's reps in its channel of distribution, this form of promotion is virtually a necessity if any degree of control is to be exercised over local promotion at the middleman level.

Publicity and Public Relations

As Table 10.2 shows, publicity and public relations account for about one-tenth of industrial sales promotion budgets. There is often confusion regarding these two activities and their functions. Publicity is defined as "non-personal stimulation of demand for a product, service, or business unit by planting commercially significant news about it in a published medium or obtaining favorable presentation of it on radio, television, or stage that is not paid for by the sponsor."[24] Properly used, publicity can be a good supplement to advertising—it can be used as a tool to help build a favorable corporate image and, as such, can contribute indirectly to company sales.

The Institute of Public Relations defines public relations as "the deliberate, planned, and sustained effort to establish and maintain mutual understanding between an organization and its public."[25] Public relations is broader in scope than publicity and is aimed not only at present and potential customers, but also at stockholders, employees, government, voters, and other such groups.

In many industrial companies, publicity and public relations are lumped together and assumed to be the same even though there are technical differences. Regardless, this type of promotion can be very productive to the marketing manager believing in the corporate promotion approach. It has been widely used by some industrial companies to create a favorable public image in reaction to charges by environmentalists, and it has also been used to help create a more favorable climate for the company salesmen.

Specialty Advertising

One other area of sales promotion that is not reflected in Table 10.2, but which deserves some mention is specialty advertising. Specialty advertising is defined as "that advertising and sales promotion medium which utilizes useful articles to carry the advertiser's name, address, and advertising message to his target audience."[26] It is distributed without cost or obligation to the prospect and includes such items as calendars, business gifts, and advertising specialties such as ball-point pens, cigarette lighters, and the like. Although the use of this medium in consumer marketing has been understood for some time, its application to the industrial market is not well known.

An example may best illustrate the use of this medium in the overall promotional strategy of an industrial company. Dayton Walther Corporation, a truck equipment manufacturer, wished to introduce a new suspension system, with the goal of 800 sales in the first year and 1,200 in the following year. The company used specialty advertising in conjunction with a direct mail advertising campaign. Accompanying a series of letters to the target audience were a three-minute timer, a candle clock, a wooden historical calendar, and a handsome table clock. These specialties were chosen because of their relationship to the company's promotional theme, "It's about time." The time-measuring specialties and direct mail advertisements in the form of letters were sent to fleet maintenance executives of the top 100 motor carriers in the country. The result of the combined campaign was that in the first four months after the promotion, 882 suspension systems had been sold. The goal was subsequently revised upward, and the promotion was continued to take in another 100 prospects.[27] This is but one example, but it does show that this medium can be integrated into the overall industrial promotional strategy, and it can contribute to the effectiveness of that strategy.

FORMULATING INDUSTRIAL PROMOTIONAL STRATEGY

In the final analysis, the task of the industrial marketing manager is to integrate personal selling, advertising, and sales promotion into an overall promotional mix that communicates effectively with the market being sought. This mix must, of course, be consistent with corporate and marketing objectives, the firm's marketing strategy and marketing plan, the previously discussed substrategies of product and channel and the substrategy of price, which has yet to be covered. In the formulation of such a promotional strategy, the following format might be considered:

1. Define specifically in terms of SIC those customer firms that the manager considers to comprise the market segment or segments that are to be reached by the company's promotional strategy.
2. Define the buying influences that specifically must be reached by the company's promotion if communication is to be achieved. If possible, know these buying influences both by name and position.
3. Determine the size of the market and the number and concentration of customer firms that are to be reached.
4. Discover what factors influence the buying influences in their purchases of such products as the company is selling. This should be accomplished for each buying influence by position, and then the factors should be ranked in terms of their relative importance.
5. Define specifically the objectives for each possible component in the promotional mix. What are the objectives of personal selling? What are the objectives of advertising? What are the objectives of sales promotion?
6. Determine specifically what message is to be communicated to each buying influence by position. What does each of the key buying influences require to make a decision on the product? This information should be discovered, and advertising themes and messages should be formulated accordingly.

7. Select the proper medium or combination of media most capable of registering the intended message with the key buying influences at the most reasonable cost. Fig. 10.2 illustrates a cost and effectiveness spectrum that is involved in selecting media to carry various types of messages. Table 10.3 also illustrates the application of various media in relation to the task being accomplished in McGraw-Hill's basic marketing communication steps.

8. Discover how many buying influences in the target firms already know or are aware of the basic promotional message being communicated. The purpose of this step is to help determine how effective the promotion was–how many new customers or prospects were reached, and so on.

Table 10.3
MEDIA MOST APPROPRIATE FOR ACCOMPLISHING TASKS
IN THE INDUSTRIAL PROMOTION PROCESS

Tasks in the Industrial Promotion Process	To Accomplish This Task, Employ This Medium or Media	
	New Customers	Existing Customers
Making Contact	Trade Publications Direct Mail Trade Shows Industrial Directories	Inside Salesmen Direct Mail Catalogs Specialty Advertising
Arousing Interest	Trade Publications Direct Mail Trade Shows Industrial Directories	Inside Salesmen Direct Mail Catalogs Specialty Advertising
Creating Preference	Field Salesmen Direct Mail Trade Shows	Catalogs Inside Salesmen Field Salesmen Direct Mail
Making Specific Proposals	Field Salesmen	Field Salesmen Inside Salesmen
Closing the Order	Field Salesmen	Field Salesmen Inside Salesmen
Keeping Customers Sold	Field Salesmen Inside Salesmen Direct Mail	Inside Salesmen Direct Mail Specialty Advertising

Note: Tasks in the industrial promotion process reprinted by permission from McGraw-Hill Research Department.

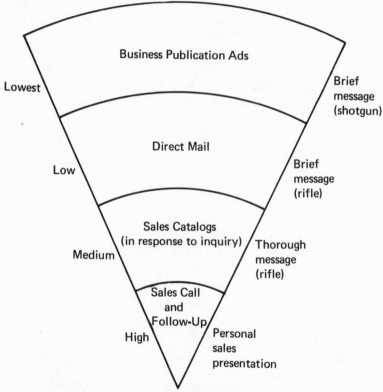

COST PER COMMUNICATION
(increases as sales message
becomes more individualized)

EFFECTIVENESS

Business Publication Ads

Lowest

Brief
message
(shotgun)

Direct Mail

Low

Brief
message
(rifle)

Sales Catalogs
(in response to inquiry)

Medium

Thorough
message
(rifle)

Sales Call
and
Follow-Up

High

Personal
sales
presentation

Fig. 10.2. Cost and effectiveness of industrial promotional media. (Reprinted by permission from William C. Grindrod, "Effective Catalogs: Industry's Silent Salesmen," *Industrial Marketing* 57, November 1972, 136. Copyright 1972 by Crain Communications, Inc., Chicago, Illinois.)

9. Determine the methods by which the promotional efforts will be evaluated. If personal selling is involved, how will its contribution be measured? If advertising is utilized, how will its contribution be measured? If any sales promotion efforts are used, how will they be measured? The key here is to have specific objectives set for each component, as was mentioned in the fifth step of this format, and then have techniques capable of measuring performance against these objectives. There is not much evidence to conclude that industrial marketing managers exert much effort in this area of evaluation. *Industrial Marketing* magazine's annual census of advertising budgets show less than 1 percent being spent in the area of advertising research.[28]

10. Determine the budget required to implement the promotional strategy thus defined, and adjust accordingly to budget constraints and promotional objectives. The methods used by industrial marketing managers to build promotion budgets are revealed in each of *Industrial Marketing* magazine's annual census of industrial advertising budgets. In 1973, 11 percent built advertising budgets with a percent-of-sales method, 36 percent built budgets via the task method exclusively, and the remaining 46 percent used both the task method and the percent-of-sales method in formulating their ad budgets.[29]

CHAPTER SUMMARY

The emphasis of this chapter was to complete the promotional strategy and show how advertising and sales promotion are integrated with personal sales in the formulation of industrial promotion. Advertising's roles in industrial marketing were discussed, and industrial advertising media were analyzed in considerable depth. The formulation of industrial advertising themes or messages was covered, and the controversy between product and corporate advertising was analyzed. Various types of sales promotion media were examined, and a format was developed for the effective integration of personal selling, advertising, and sales promotion into an overall promotional strategy capable of communicating the desired message to the appropriate buyers and buying influences.

QUESTIONS FOR CHAPTER 10

1. The industrial advertiser's task is often complicated by the fact that his product often loses its identity in the end product of his customer. What are the major marketing implications in this statement?

2. Because industrial buyers and buying influences are motivated primarily by rational reasons, emotion plays no real part in industrial advertising strategy. Do you agree or disagree with this statement? If you agree, why do you agree? If you disagree, why do you disagree?
3. How do multiple buying influences in industrial customer firms make the task of industrial advertising strategy more difficult, both in formulating specific advertising appeals and in selecting advertising media?
4. Why are catalogs in the industrial market called industry's silent salesmen? Explain your answer.
5. Because the cost of an industrial advertising call is considerably less than the cost of an industrial sales call, it makes good sense for the industrial marketing manager to substitute advertising for personal selling whenever possible. Do you agree or disagree with this statement? If you agree, why do you agree? If you disagree, why do you disagree?

11

PRICING STRATEGY IN INDUSTRIAL MARKETING

The fourth substrategy in marketing involves the pricing of goods and services in the marketplace. This is not to imply that pricing takes place only after markets have been defined, their potential assessed, products produced, channels selected and implemented, and promotional programs introduced. To proceed through all these phases and then decide upon a price can be tantamount to marketing disaster if the price that will be paid by the market is less than the costs involved to produce and market the product in question. In other words, pricing strategy is not necessarily the last substrategy for the marketing manager to consider in putting together his overall strategy. Pricing should be considered when the product is in the screening stage, and those products whose costs will exceed prices commanded in the marketplace should be screened out on this basis.

In a properly executed marketing strategy, the demand schedule for a product and the prices that can be charged should be known before the product is actually mass-produced. This is, of course, a theoretical construct that is sometimes difficult to implement in the actual business world, but it can be done if managers are willing to make the efforts. Indeed, in the long run, it must be done if the company is to succeed by any means other than sheer luck! The prospects of producing and marketing a product and hoping the price in the marketplace will be high enough to generate required profit objectives leave a great deal to be desired. It makes much better sense to have an idea of what the price will be and then try to control costs within that price, achieving the desired profit in this manner. Therefore, although this chapter will cover the fourth marketing substrategy of pricing, this does not imply that pricing is the fourth in importance in the formulation of overall marketing strategy.

Pricing must be in accordance with the corporate and marketing objectives, and it must be integrated into the overall marketing strategy along with product, channel, and promotion, and this integration must be a continuous process. Price cannot be set and then forgotten as conditions change! Pricing policy must be coordinated with channel decisions, product decisions, and promotion decisions. This coordination must take place through time, not only at a point in time as economic analysis often assumes.[1]

What Is Price?

Price is a relatively simple term, but it is not simple in its interpretation. From a marketing point of view, price is the value placed on a good or service by customers at some point in time. It is important that the word *value* be emphasized strongly. A product or service placed in the market with a price higher or lower than the value perceived by potential customers does not really contain the consumer orientation necessary to market that good or service. This value may be subjective, and it can change at a moment's notice. Nevertheless, not to include customer values into the pricing decision is in error. Yet a great many goods and services are priced with little or no market input or even suspicion of customer perceived value. Many manufacturers take the cost of the product, add on a desired margin, and call that the price. Although this may be a simple way to price, it lacks reality in that it ignores two important factors—customer perceived value and competition. When it is recalled also that in marketing a product or service is a want satisfier, it is most logical to assume that the pricing of that same product or service should be consistent with want satisfaction and thus relevant to customer value. In this text, price will be defined as value to the customer, and pricing shall mean the process of determining this value and then converting it into dollars and cents and then making comparisons in the marketplace.

The Importance of Price

Price can be an extremely critical part of the marketing strategy of many companies. To produce the proper product for a market segment, get it into an effective channel of distribution, and promote it in an effective manner are all for nothing if the product is improperly priced. Moreover, whether or not a product or service gains market acceptance is often determined by price. In addition, price can play a big part in offsetting competitive thrusts when price competition plays a major part in an industry's behavior. Finally, price multiplied by the quantity sold is the major source of revenue in most firms. Thus, improper pricing can affect the financial position of the company involved. All told, there are enough reasons why price cannot be ignored and cannot be handled as a marketing residual activity. Proper or improper pricing strategy can often determine the success of an entire marketing strategy. It is not an area to be taken lightly by the marketing manager, and it requires very specific criteria—criteria much more specific than the other three substrategies. To miss a price by two or three cents can often lead to rejection in the marketplace.

PRICING IN THE INDUSTRIAL MARKET

The role of price in the industrial market is basically similar to the role price plays in the consumer market, although there are some distinct, important differences. For example, many industrial buyers rate price a much less important buying consideration than certainty of delivery, quality of the products, service provisions by the manufacturer, and technical assistance. For these buyers, it makes little sense to buy lower-priced products if the suppliers cannot deliver on time and in the quantity required or if their product quality is lower, and so forth. With a production process, these factors add to cost rather than save money. To illustrate, if a buyer switched suppliers to purchase OEM component parts at a lower price, what has been saved if the new vendor cannot deliver on time and the production line comes to a halt? Similarly, if that buyer switched to a new user product supplier because of lower price only to find the latter's service is poor and down time is increased, what has the buyer gained from the lower price?

Another factor affecting the role of price for some industrial marketing managers is the bidding process. This area will be covered in detail later in this chapter, but it deserves some mention here. In bidding situations, because all bidders must conform to specifications, price may be the deciding factor in a sale. Million dollar orders can be lost because of $50 differences in bids. The bidding process puts tremendous pressure on some industrial marketing managers and their pricing analysts. The bidding process has brought about the use of bidding models and other sophisticated approaches to the pricing of industrial products.

An additional factor involved with the pricing of industrial products is negotiation. Many industrial products are marketed at a price agreed upon by both buyer and seller by negotiation between the two. To understand better how this works, an example might be helpful. Assume that a purchasing director wishes to purchase a line of OEM products. He then contacts appropriate suppliers to bid on the components. RFPs (requests for proposals) are sent to the suppliers requesting unit prices by size and in various quantities in accordance with specifications in the bids. The quotations that come back will almost always vary by unit price and overall price. The buyer can then bargain with the suppliers for a better price. This is what negotiation means, and it is very common in industrial marketing, even in bidding situations. It has been said, "Any buyer who pays the published price for an item when he can negotiate is just plain naive."[2] This type of behavior, common among industrial buyers trying to get the best possible deal for their companies, gives price a very important role in the industrial market.

Derived demand also affects pricing's role in industrial marketing. For example, the manufacturer of a consumer good such as an automobile will only purchase component parts such as batteries, tires, and so on, when there is demand for its product. Thus, when auto sales drop off as they did in 1974 and 1975, the demand for auto OEM component parts also drops off, regardless of price. In other words, derived demand has the effect of making price less influential than it might be. An OEM customer may purchase no more when prices are dropped than it otherwise would when the demand for its final product drops off. What this means is that the industry price elasticity of demand is relatively inelastic, but the demand for the product of each supplier in that industry may well be relatively elastic as the negotiation process has indicated.

Still another factor involved in industrial pricing is that prices charged and prices actually paid may be quite different. In the consumer market, sticker prices and actual prices paid are generally the same. In the industrial market, it is often impossible to determine the actual price paid. To illustrate, many industrial marketing managers start off with their list prices, which are those prices actually printed on their price lists. But none of their customers may eventually pay those list prices! Net prices, or prices actually paid, are determined from list prices minus such factors as cash discounts, trade and quantity discounts, sales rebates, geographic freight differences, and so on. What it all amounts to is that it is often impossible to determine who paid what for what, and thus actual prices paid are often a mystery. Of course, buyers and sellers know the actual price, but often these are jealously concealed, competitive secrets. As has been said, "Owing to hidden discounts and concessions, a company's quoted prices are often very different from the prices that it actually gets."[3] To reiterate, what this means is that there may often be two prices in the industrial market—quoted price and actual price—and both must be considered!

Table 11.1 illustrates some differences between industrial and consumer marketing managers regarding various pricing strategies. The data do not indicate great differences except as regards governmental regulations affecting prices. It appears as though government plays a larger role in the setting of industrial prices than it does in the setting of consumer prices. And the role of pricing as a facet of competitive strategy is about the same in both the consumer and industrial markets as is illustrated in Table 11.1.

Table 11.1

THE PERCEIVED RELATIVE IMPORTANCE OF
VARIOUS PRICING STRATEGIES

	Producers of:		
Pricing Strategy	Industrial Goods	Consumer Durables	Consumer Nondurables
Competitive Level	46.7%	45.0%	46.0%
Certain Percent Above or Below Competitive Level	6.7%	8.1%	11.1%
Cost-Plus	25.1%	28.2%	27.1%
What the Market Will Bear	13.4%	15.8%	14.2%
According th Government Rules and Regulations	8.0%	2.7%	1.6%
Other Strategies	0.1%	0.1%	0.0%
Total	100.0%	100.0%	100.0%

Source: John G. Udell, *Successful Marketing Strategies* (Madison: Mimir Publishers, Inc., 1972), p. 109.

Note: Data are based on the average point allocations of 344 industrial goods producers, 52 consumer durable goods manufacturers, and 89 consumer nondurable goods manufacturers.

All this implies that although pricing plays about the same role in both the consumer and industrial markets, there are differences in the actual practice of pricing in the two markets. This aspect will now be developed in more detail.

FACTORS INFLUENCING INDUSTRIAL PRICING DECISIONS

In setting realistic prices in the marketplace, the industrial marketing manager and the pricing people find their final decision being influenced by six major factors. These factors are (1) customer demand, (2) competition, (3) cost considerations, (4) company pricing objectives, (5) company top management, and (6) government. Prices set without consideration of each of these six factors can be unrealistic and even detrimental to the company. Therefore, a careful look at each factor merits consideration.

Customer Demand

Chapter 2 of this text dealt exclusively with the topic of demand in the industrial market and its many marketing ramifications. Many of the considerations covered in that chapter are appropriate to this discussion, and thus references will be made from time to time to points covered in chapter 2.

Customer demand is a critical factor in understanding any pricing. As any student of elementary economics knows, prices are set in a free market environment where supply and demand intersect. If demand is not known, it is very difficult to understand where price should be set! This is not to imply that the industrial market represents a free market mechanism, but it still impresses the fact that prices set without regard to customer demand lack an essential ingredient.

Yet there is not much evidence to conclude that industrial companies or their marketing managers exert much effort in determining customer demand in their pricing. All indications are that it is easier to feel out such demand by matching competitors' prices. The major reason for this is the difficulty involved in assessing demand for a single industrial product—it is difficult enough to forecast demand for the product of an industry, especially in manufacturing.[4] Many industrial marketing managers assume this statement to be valid to the degree that they do not give much attention to the area of determining customer demand. A study of the pricing practices of 67 Canadian industrial companies found that firms that did attempt to determine demand were frustrated by volatile buyers' preferences and unpredictable reactions by competitors. In addition, the study showed that 46 percent of these companies conducted no research at all to support their pricing, and those that did conduct research in this area focused primarily on their own cost records and on their competitors. Very little research into customer demand was discovered.[5] There is little to indicate that American industrial firms are much different from the Canadian companies in the study.

The determination of customer demand in the industrial market is admittedly difficult, but to ignore it for this reason lacks marketing logic. Any industrial marketing manager attempting to determine the demand for a product for pricing purposes must understand the concept of price elasticity of demand and must discover this concept for each product in each market. To accomplish this, the manager must first understand that the demand curve is but a schedule of prices and quantities of goods or services that will be taken in the marketplace at those prices. In Fig. 11.2, a typical negative sloping demand curve for a single product is illustrated. As can be seen by the coordinates, the curve is simply a series of points depicting quantities demanded at different prices, and it normally slopes downward and to the right. In this case, 5,500 products would be taken at a $30 price; 20,000 would be taken if the price were dropped to $25; 46,000 would be taken if the price were set at $20 per unit; and so forth.

The slope of the demand curve is important and may be explained in terms of price elasticity of demand. Fig. 11.2 illustrates demand curves of elastic and inelastic price elasticities of demand respectively. This is an im-

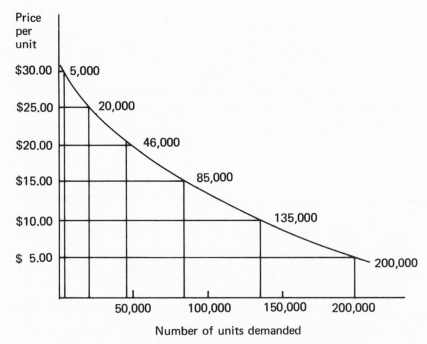

Fig. 11.1. The demand curve for an industrial product.

portant point for the industrial marketing manager. If the price elasticity of demand is not known, the effects of initial pricing and subsequent pricing decisions might not be anticipated. Take, for example, the manufacturer of OEM component parts contemplating a price decrease in hopes of increasing quantity demanded and overall revenue. As can be seen in Fig. 11.2, the decision would be a wise one if the price elasticity of demand were relatively elastic, but unwise if the price elasticity of demand were relatively inelastic. In fact, the marketing manager would lose money in the latter situation. The point being made here is that without some knowledge of the slope of the demand curve, even with all the difficulties involved, the industrial marketing manager can scarcely make the best possible decision.

Constructing the Demand Curve. As in the consumer market, there are a number of methods that may be used to construct a demand curve for an individual product in the industrial market. If the basic format of this text has been followed to this point, a "buildup" method might be applied as follows: (1) determine specifically by SIC those companies that would use the product under consideration; (2) determine how many such firms exist, and locate

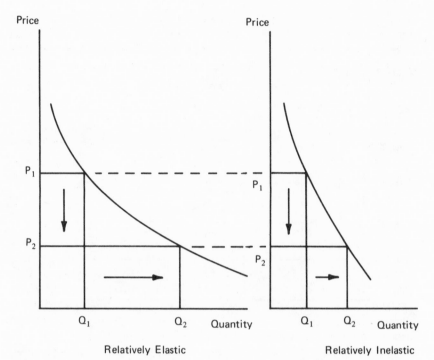

Fig. 11.2. Examples of relatively elastic and inelastic price elasticities
of demand.

them; (3) determine those buying influences having the most influence on the
price that each customer company would pay for such a product; (4) list the
competitive products those companies are now using with which the company's product will have to compete; and (5) through marketing research, go
to the potential users, and find what they would be willing to pay for the
product to replace the products now being used.

This approach is oversimplified, but it does make the desired point. It
is possible to obtain some measure of price-quantity relationships, which is
certainly better than no knowledge at all. On the other hand, the curve derived is apt to be much less than precise owing to factors such as buyers'
sensitivity to other nonprice factors such as company image, product brand
name, service, reputation, certainty of delivery, and the like. In addition,
what an individual buyer claims he will pay for a product or service and what
he actually will pay at a later date may be entirely different. Add to this the
aspect of derived demand, and the job increases in difficulty. Finally, if a
product has multiuse, this procedure must be performed for each market

segment. Nevertheless, intelligent industrial marketing management would dictate attempts being made to determine the level and extent of customer demand even though evidence indicates that the prices of most large industrial firms appear to be inflexible, uncompetitive, and unresponsive to changes in demand.[6]

Competition

Of the six influencing factors affecting pricing, competition appears to command the most attention by pricers of industrial goods. As Table 11.1 illustrates, pricers of industrial goods rated aspects of competitive level pricing above all other factors. And the previously mentioned Canadian survey found that even when the surveyed industrial companies determined prices systematically, they then adjusted those prices in the end to match prices of competitors. If they discovered that they could not match those prices, they would not manufacture and market the product.[7] This behavior appears to be quite common in industrial marketing—the pricer accepts for one reason or another a price set by competition. Then, the industrial pricing decision maker adjusts to that price by trying to obtain a desired profit margin by bringing down costs within the competitive price constraint. This probably happens because of the difficulty of determining customer demand and the assumption that competitive prices reflect this demand.

Such behavior may also be representative of the way in which economic theorists treat pricing in oligopolies. An oligopoly is defined as a market structure with few sellers. *Few* in this sense means such a number that the freedom of any one company to change price is tempered by the possibility of competitive reactions. In other words, any company contemplating a price change must consider the reactions of its competitors. Oligopolies can be pure (where competing products are identical), or they can be differentiated (where competing products are slightly differentiated). Many industrial marketing managers operate in industries that are oligopolistic in nature. To illustrate, steel, aluminum, copper, computers, machine products, and so forth, are all basically oligopolistic in nature at the manufacturing level. It may be argued that an understanding of oligopolistic price theory may well help to understand pricing behavior in the industrial market as regards competition. There has been much written on this topic, but much of it is too complex and too lengthy to use in this text. One aspect, however, that may be used to illustrate why industrial pricers place such great emphasis on competition is the economist's kinked demand curve.

The kinked demand curve, like any part of economic theory, has both its proponents and its opponents. It is outside the scope of this text to comment on those arguments, and the kinked demand curve is used here only for explanatory reasons. Shown here is the kinked demand curve of the oligopolist.

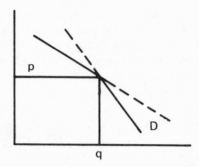

The kink represents the market price, with the company's demand being elastic above the kink and inelastic below. What this means is that unless a company is a price leader, it cannot raise its prices above the kink, for no one will follow, and price will be noncompetitive. To raise price and have no competitors follow is often a very damaging blow to effective marketing strategy. If the company's price is lowered below the kink, its competitors will follow and undercut still further. In other words, a price war occurs, and because industry demand for industrial goods is often inelastic owing to derived demand, market shares are not increased, and company profits suffer. What happens is that the threat of competitive reaction keeps prices relatively stable and at the kink. Because no single company gains by price changes in such situations, the emphasis often shifts to nonprice competition.

The exception to this for the use of a price increase occurs when the marketing manager initiating the increase is in that company that is the industry price leader. Price leaders are quite common in the industrial market, and, therefore, this point deserves some mention here. Contrary to popular belief, the largest firm in the industry is not automatically the price leader, although this can be the case. And the company that is the price leader for one product in an industry is not necessarily the price leader for other products in that industry. Being a price leader is dependent upon the willingness of competitors to follow. Three factors appear to be necessary for a company to be accepted as a price leader in the case of a price increase. These are: (1) the industry must believe that the demand for the product is such that a price increase will not reduce the total size of the market for that product, (2) all major suppliers in the industry must share this belief, and (3) the industry must feel that the price increase is for the good of the entire industry and not just for the good of the company initiating the price increase. If these three factors are not present, the company initiating the price increase will find itself above the kink with a price greater than prices of competitors that did not follow. Many industrial marketing managers have felt the embarrassment of their pricing decisions putting them in this situation. Obviously, this phenomenon causes great risk with the use of price increases if the manager's firm is not the price leader, and the kinked demand example again shows why competition is such a big factor in industrial pricing.

Regarding the competitive effects of a price decrease, the kinked demand curve shows the danger of dropping price below the kink or market price. The use of price decreases as an industrial marketing tool makes sense only when demand for the product involved is relatively elastic and overall revenues will be increased and when competitors will not automatically follow and even undercut. This means that, because of competition, price decreases are very risky and should not be attempted unless the manager is reasonably certain that competition cannot or will not retaliate and knows also that the demand is relatively elastic. But there are times when price decreases can be employed with benefit to the company. Some examples of these instances are as follows: (1) when the cost structures of competitors are known to be higher and when those competitors cannot match price decreases, owing to adverse effects on their desired profit margins; (2) when competitors are operating at a high percentage of production capacity and have ample backlogs of orders, they may not retaliate because they do not need the additional business at that particular time; (3) when competitors cannot immediately react to the price decrease because of required retooling, lack of trained personnel, and so forth—this is a short-run situation, but it may mean increased sales to the marketing manager if competitors cannot match a price decrease until they retool or retrain employees, and so forth; (4) small companies can often use price decreases on their larger competitors because the latter will not retaliate because they, in turn, fear that other large competitors will also retaliate and that a price war will ensue—in such cases, large companies in an industry will allow small competitors to cut prices on them for fear that reacting will only trigger an industrywide price war; and (5) large companies sometimes will not react to price decreases because of fear of antitrust or some other such governmental intervention, thus making it possible for smaller competitors in the industry to use price decreases to advantage.

Examples such as these are dangerous, and miscalculations can have dire effects on marketing strategy. They are illustrated only to show how important competition is when industrial pricing decisions are made. Any pricing decision made without assessment of competitive reaction would appear incomplete and could lead to marketing failure. It is critical that the marketing manager obtain information on each and every major competitor and its pricing behavior prior to making any pricing decisions. Only when this is done can the manager reasonably expect price increases or decreases to result in success. It is, of course, possible to incorporate such information into the company's marketing information system, so that a continuous flow of such data is available. The marketing manager must realize that competition normally sets the upper limit for the pricing decision. Pricing above this limit is virtually impossible unless products can be differentiated enough to increase their value to the buyers and buying influences. Often this is very difficult to accomplish because specifications force product similarity among suppliers.

Cost Considerations

Competition typically sets the upper limitation on the price the industrial marketing manager can charge, and cost normally determines the lower limitation. To price without considering cost makes little sense, and few industrial pricers do so. On the contrary, too many managers use cost almost exclusively as the basis of the prices they will charge. The fixed and variable costs of producing the product are determined, and then a desired profit margin is tacked on for the final selling price. Basically, this type of pricing amounts to total emphasis on the company's supply curve and almost no emphasis on the demand curve. In spite of its almost obvious shortcomings, pricing based on cost is widely used. As Table 11.1 illustrated, about one-quarter of the industrial companies surveyed used a "cost plus" approach to pricing. The previously mentioned survey of Canadian industrial companies discovered that 94 percent of those companies used some type of systematic pricing, and, of these, 55 percent used a "cost plus" system.[8] Cost plus pricing appears to be widely used by those industrial companies that do little research on their pricing. Studies have shown that many firms employ cost plus pricing based on past cost data and future cost estimates plus a recognized profit margin that remains stable over time and is thus considered normal for those operations.

In addition, many industrial companies marketing to the government have used forms of "cost plus" pricing such as cost plus fixed fee, cost incentive contracts, cost plus incentive fee, cost plus award fee, cost only, and cost-sharing contracts. Needless to say, when prices are made under these constraints, cost is the basic element in the prices charged.

The point being made here is not that the industrial marketing manager should price via the "cost plus" method, but rather that cost must be incorporated into the final price with the other elements such as demand, competition, and so on. The most common method for achieving this integration is by break-even analysis. In simple terms, break-even analysis tells the manager how many units must be sold at a given price to break even or to cover total costs. Related back to the quantity of goods that would be taken in the marketplace at those prices, break-even provides a useful tool for gauging the relative feasibility of various prices.

Break-even is a common financial tool and does not require an in-depth analysis in this text. To employ this concept, the marketing manager must know the fixed and variable costs involved with the production and marketing of a single product and also the price under consideration. To illustrate, assume the manager of a company marketing an OEM component part wishes to price that part at $25.00 each. Given fixed costs of $400,000 and variable costs of $10.00 per unit, how many units must he sell to break even? The answer is 26,666 units and is computed as follows:

$$\$25.00x = \$400,000.00 + \$10.00x$$
$$\$15.00x = \$400,000.00$$
$$x = 26,666$$

If the manager drops his price to $20.00 per unit and his costs remain the same, he must sell 40,000 units to break even. Given those same costs and a price of $30.00 per unit, he must then sell 20,000 units to break even. The real value of such analysis becomes apparent when units required to break even at each price are compared with units that will be demanded at each price as determined by customer demand. For example, if we refer back to Fig. 11.1 and assume that the demand curve illustrated is the demand curve for the firm's product and that the $400,000 fixed cost and $10 variable costs still apply, what is the quantity required to break even at each possible price? Table 11.2 illustrates the relationships.

This simple example illustrates well the point being made. Of all six possible prices discovered in the demand analysis and illustrated in Fig. 11.1, only two hold up under the cost constraints. Although the manager could sell 5,000 units at $30.00 per unit, it requires sales of 20,000 units to break even. Moreover, although the market will purchase large amounts of products at $10.00 and $5.00 per unit, cost structure will not permit sales at these prices, as total unit costs exceed each of the two prices. Thus, the manager finds that only two prices are actually feasible—at $15.00 and $20.00 per unit. If the product had been priced at any other prices than the $15.00 and $20.00 figures, it would have lost money unless costs could have been reduced accordingly. Of course, competition and the kinked demand curve may yet dictate whether it could sell at either the $15.00 or the $20.00 price, but the pricing analyst is now in much better position to price than prior to consideration of costs involved. As can now be understood, to price without cost considerations would be in error. But to price solely on the basis of cost makes just as little marketing sense. For proper pricing, cost must be integrated with all other six major factors to be considered.

Company Pricing Objectives
Pricing decisions of the marketing manager must be in accordance with company pricing objectives, and the latter will differ according to company and industry. Probably the best single source of information on corporate

Table 11.2
THE RELATIONSHIP BETWEEN QUANTITY DEMANDED
AND QUANTITY REQUIRED TO BREAK EVEN

Possible Price Per Unit	Quantity That Will Be Demanded at Each Price	Quantity Required to Break Even
$30.00	5,000	20,000
$25.00	20,000	26,667
$20.00	46,000	40,000
$15.00	85,000	80,000
$10.00	135,000	–
$5.00	200,000	–

Note: At the $5.00 and $10.00 price levels, total cost exceeds price, and the company cannot break even at any amount of sales.

pricing objectives is the book *Pricing in Big Business*, published by the Brookings Institution. According to the authors of this book, there are five common pricing objectives used by U.S. companies, and these apply to industrial marketing firms as well as to consumer marketing firms. These objectives are (1) pricing to achieve a target return on investment, (2) stabilization of price and margin, (3) pricing to maintain or improve market position, (4) pricing to meet or follow competition, and (5) pricing related to product differentiation.[10]

Table 11.3 illustrates how selected industrial companies have defined their pricing objectives. As can be seen, all these companies have primary pricing objectives and secondary or collateral pricing objectives. It is interesting to note that price stabilization is quite common as a secondary objective and reinforces the points made earlier in regard to the kinked demand curve. The main point, however, is to realize that the company pricing objectives affect pricing decisions being made because these decisions must be in agreement with the established objectives. To illustrate, both National Steel and U.S. Steel are in the same basic industry, but, as Table 11.3 shows clearly, their pricing objectives differ distinctly. This implies that their prices, even of identical products, may differ, not because of the product or the customer involved, but because the pricing objectives of each firm differ. The pricing decision of the manager or the pricing analyst must integrate these objectives into demand, competitive, and cost considerations. For example, if the marketing manager in the break-even example illustrated in the last section worked for Alcoa, that manager would have to make sure that the prices of $15.00 and $20.00 were compatible with that company's primary objective of 20 percent on investment before taxes. If neither price achieved this return of 20 percent, the product might not even be marketed. If, however, the marketing manager worked for American Can, the product might be marketed at one of those prices if the price were competitive, did not stir up competitive pricing retaliation, and helped maintain the company's market share for that product. Thus, it can easily be seen that company pricing objectives in the industrial market can greatly influence the actual price being charged on the product.

Company Top Management

Top management in many industrial companies exerts great influence over prices attached to their products. Although the actual pricing decisions are often made in the sales or marketing department, it is very common for these prices to be reviewed in some manner by company top management. The Canadian survey of 67 industrial companies revealed that in 52 percent of those firms, the sales or marketing department was responsible for making the pricing decision; in 26 percent of the firms, the finance department made the pricing decision; and in another 19 percent of the firms, the production department made the decision. But all 67 firms affirmed that pricing decisions were reviewed by senior management, and 84 percent of the companies cited a committee decision in such reviews. Moreover, 70 percent claimed that prices once established could only be changed by those people who had initially set them.[11] Although this is admittedly a small sample, it does appear typical of the behavior in many industrial firms. Price is important, and it is something that everyone relates to; thus, top managements tend to get involved in pricing decisions, whereas they may never affect marketing decisions made in channels, sales promotion, and so on. What this means, of course, is that pricing decisions are often affected by top management preferences, desires, expectations, and whims; and the industrial marketing manager must be able to anticipate these and be prepared to react to them if his own pricing convictions differ from those of top management.

Government

Government at all levels, but particularly at the federal level, may have considerable influence on the pricing practices of industrial marketing managers. This is a complex area and cannot be covered in full in a text of this size, but some of the major considerations will be addressed. Basically, government can affect an industrial company's pricing in the following ways: (1) through taxes, which can directly and indirectly affect the price being charged; (2) through legislation or threat of legislation; (3) through sales of stockpiled strategic materials such as copper, aluminum, and so on; (4) as a customer and usually a large one, government can exert influence on the prices of many industrial products; and (5) through the threat of reduced or

Table 11.3

PRICING GOALS OF SELECTED LARGE INDUSTRIAL CORPORATIONS

Company	Principal Pricing Goal	Collateral Pricing Goals	Rate of ROI (After Taxes) 1947–1955 Avg.	Range	Average Market Share
Alcoa	20% on investment (before taxes); higher on new products (about 10% effective rate after taxes)	(a) Promotive policy on new products (b) Price stabilization	13.8%	7.8%–18.7%	Pig & Ingot, 37%; Sheet, 46%; other fabrications, 62%
American Can	Maintenance of market share	(a) "Meeting" competition (using cost of substitute product to determine price) (b) Price stabilization	11.6%	9.6%–14.7%	Approximately 55% of all types of cans
International Harvester	10% on investment (after taxes)	Market share: ceiling of "less than a dominant share of any market"	8.9%	4.9%–11.9%	Farm tractors, 28–30%; combines, cornpickers, tractor plows, cultivators, mowers, 20–30%; cotton pickers, 65%; light and heavy trucks, 5–18%; medium heavy to heavy-heavy, 12–30%
Johns-Manville	Return on investment greater than last 15-year average (about 15% after taxes); higher target for new products	(a) Market share not greater than 20% (b) Stabilization of prices	14.9%	10.7%–19.6%	Not Available

240

Kennecott	Stabilization of prices		16.0%	9.3%–20.9%	Not Available
National Steel	Matching the market price follower		12.1%	7.0%–17.4%	5%
Union Carbide	Target return on investment	Promotive policy on new products; "life cycle" pricing on chemicals generally	19.2%	13.5%–24.3%	See Note
U.S. Steel	8% on investment (after taxes)	(a) Target market share of 30% (b) Stable price (c) Stable margin	10.3%	7.6%–14.8%	Ingots and steel, 30%; blast furnaces, 34%; finished hot rolled products, 35%; other steel mill products, 37%

Source: Reprinted by permission from Robert F. Lanzillotti, "Pricing Objectives in Large Companies," XLVIII *American Economic Review*, (December 1958), 921–940.

Note: Chemicals account for 30% of Carbide's sales, most of which are in petrochemicals, a field that the company opened 30 years ago and still dominates; plastics account for 18%—the company sells 40% of the two most important plastics (vinyl and polyethylene); alloys and metals account for 26% of sales—top U.S. supplier of ferroalloys (e.g., chrome, silicon, manganese) and the biggest U.S. titanium producer; gases account for 14% of sales—estimated to sell 50% of oxygen in the U.S.; carbon, electrodes, and batteries account for 12% of sales—leading U.S. producer of electrodes, refractory carbon, and flashlights and batteries; and miscellaneous—leading operator of atomic energy plants, a leading producer of uranium, the largest U.S. producer of tungsten, and a major supplier of radium.

curtailed purchases if a price increase by a supplier is enacted. Development of some of these may be helpful for better understanding the role government plays in pricing in the industrial market.

The federal government stockpiles reserves of strategic materials such as copper, aluminum, steel, and others. It then uses these reserves at times to counteract rising prices of these commodities by selling the reserves into the marketplace, thus increasing supply and driving price back down. This type of behavior could definitely affect the pricer of such products as are stockpiled. But the government does not actually have to sell its reserves to bring about the desired change—sometimes the threat to do so is enough to influence the manager not to increase prices.

As a customer, government also affects prices of some industrial goods. It does so directly with such contracts as cost plus fixed fee, and so on, where it dictates the price that will be charged! Indirectly, government can also affect prices of some goods in the industrial market. For example, an industrial firm selling the same product to both industrial customers and large government buying organizations such as GSA (General Services Administration) may find that the large governmental purchases allow the firm to take advantage of economies of scale and produce all items at lower unit cost. This, in turn, permits lower prices to its industrial customers. In addition, when government is a present customer, it can react to price increases by threatening to stop its purchasing from the supplier enacting the increase. Obviously, this threat has a definite influence on the pricing decision involved.

Probably the main influence of government on pricing, however, lies in the area of legislation that directly affects the pricing area. Again this is a complex area in itself, but the following are major areas of federal pricing legislation that affect every industrial marketing manager. Sections 1 and 2 of the Sherman Antitrust Act forbid agreements among suppliers to fix prices in their industry, and violations carry fine, imprisonment, or both, as well as triple damages to parties injured by the violation. That price-fixing practices do take place in the industrial market is attested to by a 1974 indictment of nine large chemical manufacturers charged with rigging prices of dyes. The firms involved in this case collectively controlled about 60 percent of U.S. dye sales, and they were accused of conspiring to raise and fix the price of their products: "As a result, the prices of dyes have been raised, fixed, and maintained at artificial and noncompetitive levels; buyers of dyes have been deprived of free and open competition in the purchases of dyes."[12]

Section 2 of the Clayton Antitrust Act and the Robinson-Patman amendment to the Clayton Act are also very important to the industrial marketing manager in that they prohibit price discrimination among similar buyers of identical products. Sections 2(a) through 2(f) of the Robinson-Patman Act (as it is more commonly called) specifically relate to different price and price concessions being offered to customers, distributors, and manufacturers' reps. Because the industrial market makes wide usage of discounts, rebates, commissions, and so on, in arriving at net prices from list prices, the industrial marketing manager had better well be aware of these and how they restrict his pricing decisions. In addition, the Borah-Van Nuys amendment is now Section 3 of the Robinson-Patman Act and specifically prohibits general price discriminations, geographic price discriminations, and the use of unreasonably low prices to drive out competition. Some states also have laws that prohibit the conspiring to fix prices, such as California's Cartwright Act. All told, there is no doubt that government does influence the pricing decisions of many industrial marketing managers, and the astute manager must know these laws.

In summary, industrial prices are generally a compromise between demand or what the market will pay, what competition will allow, what costs will permit, what is consistent with company pricing objectives, what top management will agree to, and what government will allow. It is the task of the industrial marketing manager and those responsible for pricing to integrate somehow all of these constraints into a base price for each of his products.

LIST AND NET PRICES

Much of the difficulty in determining what prices are actually paid by industrial customers is caused by differences between list prices (what is specified on the price lists) and the net prices (those actually paid by the customer). It is very common in the industrial market to discount from the list price to arrive at the net price or prices to be actually charged. This concept is often misunderstood by those not in the industrial marketing area, but it does make sense! The industrial marketing manager prints up one price list for all his products and distributes this list to all customers, regardless of their type or classification. A discount system is then set up whereby each customer type or classification is given certain discounts off that list for the net price to be charged. In most cases, nobody probably ever pays the list price. The advantage to the manufacturer is that it allows the printing up of one list price sheet and the use of it almost forever—any price changes that take place are accomplished by adjusting the discount system. Thus, costs of printing and reprinting price lists are eliminated. This is a considerable saving for firms producing multiple product lines especially when production and marketing costs are changing rapidly, in turn causing price changes. In addition, the list price concept allows competitors to hide their actual prices, at least to a degree. Discounts and net prices are guarded jealously and, although they can be found out, it is often with much effort. Thus, although the list price and net price concept does not appear to make much sense, it does have logic, and its wide application to the pricing of many industrial products bears this out.

Types of Discounts

The example in the preceding paragraph of the discount given to different types of customers is but one kind of discount that is found in the industrial market. A more complete listing of the types of discounts used follows.

Trade Discounts. Trade discounts are those that are given to different classifications of customers and/or middlemen according to their trade or type of business. For example, a manufacturer of industrial equipment sells through distributors into the commercial market and directly to OEM customers and to government. Three types of distributors are used: (1) a "Class A" distributor, who, by contract, purchases equipment from the manufacturer to display on the showroom floor as a promotional device; (2) a "Class B" distributor, who is also authorized to sell the manufacturer's products, but who does not agree to floor-display equipment; and (3) overseas distributors, who operate in foreign countries. The following shows the trade discounts allowed to each type of customer off the basic list price:

Class B Distributor	Class A Distributor	Overseas Distributor	Original Equipment Manufacturer	Government
25%	25+5%	25+5+5%	25+5+5%	25+5+5%

The use of trade discounts must be carefully watched, as different discounts given to basically the same types of customers can amount to violation of the previously mentioned Robinson-Patman Act and are tantamount to price discrimination. In this case, the price discrimination is legal because the customers are not the same—flooring and overseas price requirements permit additional 5 percent discounts to some distributors, and OEM and government customers are not the same. In addition, the discount system is an incentive to distributors to floor-display equipment and for large OEMs and government to buy direct from the manufacturer, providing the discounts are competitive.

Cash Discounts. Cash discounts are those given to encourage rapid payment by customers and to allow faster cash flow for the marketing manager's firm. Typical of these are such as 2/10: n/30, whereby the customer deducts 2 percent if it pays within ten days of invoice and the full amount if it takes longer. Although these are often stated contractual terms between buyers and sellers, they are flagrantly abused and tolerated. If a particularly large customer takes the 2 percent, but does not pay for 60 days, nothing may be said by the seller. On the other hand, a brand new customer who does the same may not be permitted to enjoy such a privilege. Cash discounts are common in the industrial market and do have an impact on the actual price paid by customers.

Quantity Discounts. Quantity discounts are those given for the amount or quantity of goods purchased, either on individual orders or purchases over a longer period of time such as one year. The objective of such a discount is to encourage customers to buy in large volumes. Typically, such discounts accelerate as the volume increases, for example, no discounts if under 25 units are purchased, 2 percent if between 26 and 50 units are bought, 4 percent if from 51 to 100 units are purchased, and so on. Quantity discounts are not in violation of the Robinson-Patman Act as long as they are available to any and all customers. Of course, quantity discounts in the long run permit different prices to the same types of customers dependent upon the volume purchased.

Quantity discounts, though offered to all customers, may still be in violation of the Robinson-Patman Act if the discount granted cannot be proved to be equal to or less than the savings gained by doing business on the increased quantity. In such violations, both buyer and seller can be charged, and the suspected violation can be reported by anyone, and the government will then assume the case against the parties charged.

Rebates. Rebates are a special kind of quantity discount and are quite common in some industries. The basic difference between a rebate system and a longer time period quantity discount is when the buyer actually receives the discount. In the latter, discounts are given off list price on invoices. In the rebate system, the buyer receives an actual cash rebate at the end of the designated time period based on sales volume during that period. A typical rebate system may work as follows. If a customer purchases less than $10,000 in equipment per year, it receives no rebate; if it purchases between $10,000 and $25,000, it may receive a 2 percent cash rebate; if it buys from $25,000 to $50,000 of equipment, the rebate may be 4 percent; if it buys from $50,000 to $100,000, the rebate may be 6 percent; and so on. The rebate is a cash incentive for encouraging larger purchasers and again is not in violation of the Robinson-Patman Act as long as all customers are able to participate in it. Rebates encourage some strange pricing on the part of middlemen, as in the case of a New York distributor of commercial kitchen equipment who sold equipment at cost and made the profit on the rebate. Again rebate systems affect in an indirect sense the actual price paid by customers from the list published price.

Geographic Price Differentials. Price differentials based on geographic location of customers are not strictly discounts, but they do affect the final prices paid by customers. Basically, this amounts to freight considerations, which may increase the actual price paid by the customer, depending on how far the goods must be shipped. The use of geographic price differentials must be watched closely as Section 3 of the Robinson-Patman Act specifically prohibits price discrimination based on geographic considerations.

F.O.B. Considerations. F.O.B. points actually affect the prices paid by industrial customers, although it can be argued that whether a product is shipped F.O.B. Destination, or F.O.B. Shipping Point, it is immaterial inasmuch as the final price paid by the customer will be the same. To illustrate, if the manufacturer ships F.O.B. Shipping Point, it means that the buyer pays the invoice price plus freight. But if the same goods are shipped F.O.B. Destination, it means that the seller ships freight prepaid and the buyer pays only the invoice price. It is, however, highly unlikely that the manufacturer will absorb the freight in the latter case, and the invoice price includes the freight in almost all cases. Differences can arise, however, dependent upon the freight or mode of transportation used—rail may be cheaper than truck, and so on.

What all this means is that the industrial marketing manager must know what discounts and price differentials are common to the industry and adjust prices to adapt to them. Bucking them can be detrimental to the company's marketing program. To illustrate, to refuse to ship F.O.B. Destination when that is the accepted method used in the industry can cause customers to shift to other suppliers. The same logic applies to trade discounts, cash discounts, quantity discounts, rebates, and so forth. The final or net price to be paid by customers must reflect factors such as these.

RETURN ON INVESTMENT PRICING

Return on investment or ROI pricing is common in the industrial market. As Table 11.3 shows, five of the eight industrial firms illustrated have principal pricing objectives based on return on investment. A rough estimate is that about one-half of the industrial companies in the United States use some form of ROI in their pricing. Some firms use it for single-year purposes, and some use it for longer-run purposes. Some use it for single products, and some use it across the board for all products. Some firms use it as a rigid rule for pricing, whereas others use it as a bench mark for their pricing.

There is a lot of controversy over the use of ROI in pricing in American business firms. Much of this controversy centers about the way in which businessmen actually use the concept in their pricing, and much of it centers around the way in which ROI is calculated.[13] There are probably as many methods used to calculate ROI in the actual industrial market as there are firms using the method. For example, ROI has been defined in the following ways: (1) annual benefits divided by the average investment, average investment being computed as one-half the sum of the asset at its institution plus its value at the end of its useful life; (2) the ratio of income before preferred stock dividends to stockholder's net worth, including preferred stock; and (3) the ratio of income before interest payments to total operating assets. Numerous other definitions could be listed here as everyone seems to have his or her own preferred method for calculating ROI, and thus comparisons among firms and among industries are sometimes quite meaningless.

Theoretically, the correct method for computing ROI is to divide the discounted present value of annual future revenues by the initial investment. This method can be adapted to the pricing of industrial products and can be used to provide an estimate of ROI for bench-mark purposes. Evidence indicates that most businessmen use ROI as a screening device or a reference point for their pricing.[14] What this means is that they will define a required ROI and then attempt to determine whether or not various prices attached to their products or product lines will achieve that desired return on investment. If it does, they will accept the product and the price and market it. If it does not and if costs cannot be adjusted favorably, they may decide not to market the product. This is what is meant by bench-mark use of ROI in pricing.

An Example of ROI Pricing. An example of how ROI pricing takes place may help to show what is involved with the use of this method. If reference is made back to Table 11.2 and the example carried through earlier sections of this chapter, it will be recalled that the marketing manager had found that the company could market the product in question only at either $15.00 or $20.00 per unit out of the six possible prices. Assume now that the firm has a principal pricing objective of 8 percent return on investment after taxes. Will both the $15.00 and the $20.00 unit prices, if either, achieve this 8 percent ROI and permit the product to be marketed? Remember that at the $20.00 price, demand would have been 46,000 units, and at the $15.00 price, demand would have been 85,000 units.

Some other assumptions will be made to implement the ROI model. These assumptions are: (1) an initial investment of $25,000 will be required to produce and market the product; (2) the fixed costs are $100,000 per year, and variable costs are $10.00 per unit; (3) at either price, the product can be expected to have a four-year life cycle with 24 percent of its sales in the first year, 26 percent in the second year, 26 percent in the third year, and 24 percent in the fourth year; (4) the firm is in the 48 percent tax bracket; and (5) for the sake of keeping the model simple, no depreciation or salvage values will be included.

Given these assumptions, which are admittedly unrealistic, data can be plugged into the model to show the discounted present value of future revenues from sales of the product at both the $15.00 and the $20.00 prices, so that they may be equated back to the $25,000 initial investment figure.

Table 11.4 shows the entire calculations for both prices and both demand schedules. A figure of 8 percent is used to discount the revenues because the company requires an 8 percent ROI after taxes. In this case, the present value of revenues at the $15.00 price is $10,735, which is less than the required $25,000 initial investment, indicating that at the $15.00 per unit price, the required 8 percent ROI is not achieved. At the $20.00 price, however, a present value of revenues of $25,794 is achieved, which is in excess of the $25,000 initial investment figure and indicates a return in excess of the required 8 percent after taxes. Exactly what ROIs are involved with both prices can be determined from interpolation into present value tables, but, in this situation, the company would accept only the $20.00 price, as the $15.00 price will not permit realization ofthe required pricing objective. This is what is meant by bench-mark use of the ROI concept—it is used to screen among products and prices.

ROI pricing is quite common in the industrial market for a number of reasons. For one thing, it allows the marketing manager to use the principles of capital budgeting in the pricing of products, treating new products as investments rather than as expenses. With ROI, the manager can treat new and existing products just as any other capital investment in which capital funds are expended. ROI also permits managers to compare performances of products, product lines, and so on, by giving them all a common denominator—a required ROI figure! As can be seen in the ROI model described here, ROI is not easy to implement, and its use can be risky if costs are not known precisely or if demand schedules are inaccurate or if improper ROI methods are used. But, as can also be realized, with proper usage, such a model could prevent product losses through poor pricing that does not even permit the recapture of funds expended in the product. In fact, for a price leader, return on investment pricing may be the most feasible method.

There are a number of methods by which industrial marketing managers pick the ROI figures that end up as their pricing objectives. Some of the more common are: (1) what seems to be fair for their industry, (2) a desire for a better ROI than has been achieved in the past, (3) basing the figure on their cost of capital, (4) what they feel they can get in the long run, and (5) the use of a specific ROI figure that will stabilize industry prices. Regard-

Table 11.4
RETURN ON INVESTMENT PRICING MODEL COMPUTATIONS

Product Priced at $15.00 per Unit:

Year	Number of Units Demanded	Gross Sales	Fixed Costs	Variable Costs	Total Costs	Gross Profits	Tax	After Tax Profits	PV @ 8%	Discounted Revenues
1	20,400	306,000	100,000 +	204,000 =	304,000	2,000	.52	1,040	.93	967
2	22,100	331,500	100,000 +	221,000 =	321,000	10,500	.52	5,460	.86	4,696
3	22,100	331,500	100,000 +	221,000 =	321,000	10,500	.52	5,460	.79	4,313
4	20,400	306,000	100,000 +	204,000 =	304,000	2,000	.52	1,040	.73	759
	85,000									10,735

Product Priced at $20.00 per Unit:

Year	Number of Units Demanded	Gross Sales	Fixed Costs	Variable Costs	Total Costs	Gross Profits	Tax	After Tax Profits	PV @ 8%	Discounted Revenues
1	11,040	220,800	100,000 +	110,400 =	210,400	10,400	.52	5,408	.93	5,029
2	11,960	239,200	100,000 +	119,600 =	219,600	19,600	.52	10,192	.86	8,765
3	11,960	239,200	100,000 +	119,600 =	219,600	19,600	.52	10,192	.79	8,052
4	11,040	220,800	100,000 +	110,400 =	210,400	10,400	.52	5,408	.73	3,948
	46,000									25,794

less of the method, return on investment pricing is quite common in the industrial market and should be understood by the marketing manager.

BIDDING MODELS IN INDUSTRIAL PRICING

Many industrial marketing transactions are conducted through the inquiry/ bid system, also called the bidding process. In this process, a purchasing agent in a company desiring to buy certain products may send requests for proposals (RFPs), also called invitations to bid, to those companies believed capable of producing the product involved. Sometimes the RFPs are sent only to selected firms on the buyer's bid list, and at other times open bidding is encouraged whereby any supplier is free to bid. In bidding, the emphasis is placed upon price—the RFP gives all the necessary data regarding the requirements of the prospective buyer. Such factors include the specifications of the product involved, terms, and conditions of the bid. Bids may cover individual products or lines of products, and they may be for a single sale or for term contracts for a longer period of time. Buyers use the bidding system because they feel that it permits them to obtain the most reasonable price in the purchase of required goods and/or services. In accordance with the conditions of the RFP, suppliers must submit bids to the prospective purchaser, stipulating their prices. The bids are then analyzed by the buyer, and a choice is made on the basis of price in awarding the sale contract.

It is not necessarily the lowest bidder that gets the contract in many cases, as some companies and many governmental and institutional customers award contracts on the basis of what is commonly referred to as the "lowest responsible bidder." This term is subject to interpretation by the individual purchaser, but basically it includes an assessment of the bidder's ability to deliver as promised, production capabilities, past record, and so on. In other instances, the purchaser does not automatically buy at the bid price submitted by the winning bidder, but, in fact, negotiates further with that bidder on the actual price. In this type of situation, the bidding process is used to decide with whom to negotiate! In any case, one thing happens in the bidding process—because everything else must conform to the specifications in the RFP, price may become a very important factor and sometimes becomes the sole deciding factor in the award of a contract of sale.

For the bidding process to take place, a number of criteria must be present.[15] These criteria are as follows: (1) the item in question must be capable of being defined specifically so that both buyer and seller are clear on what is involved, (2) there must be enough sellers to allow for bids to compete, (3) the sellers must want the job and be willing to bid competitively, (4) the product's dollar value must be large enough to support the costs to both buyer and seller, and (5) sufficient time must be available for the bidding process to take place.

The bidding process presents a real problem for the industrial marketing manager and the pricing analyst. For companies who price in this manner, decisions as to how many jobs to bid on and how many jobs to win depend entirely upon the pricing mechanism used. This has brought about bidding models that are mathematical methods used to determine prices in a competitive bidding situation that are consistent with corporate objectives such as return on investment, share of the market, and so on. The basis of many bidding models is the relationship of the prices that are bid and their probability of winning the bid. If the industrial marketing manager submits a bid, what is the probability that it will take the job? There are a number of models in use, but space does not permit an in-depth assessment of each of them here. Perhaps a simplified example of how one such model works will make the desired point.

An Example of a Bidding Model. Assume that a manufacturer of commercial dishwashers markets products into a market such as the Army & Air Force Exchange, which purchases the machines for use in military kitchens. The competitive bidding situation is involved with the government awarding contracts to the lowest responsible bidder, and this manufacturer qualifies as being responsible. Invitations to bid are sent to ten to 12 such responsible bidders requesting a price on a rackless type of commercial dishwasher. Assume also that the manufacturer has a principal pricing objective of maintaining a 30 percent share of the market. How does the marketing manager in this company achieve this objective within the constraints of the competitive bidding situation?

The marketing manager in this case knows that the dishwasher involved is purchased continually via the bidding process on a specification that has not changed in two to three years. It is also known that, as in most government bidding situations, it is possible to find out past winning bids of all suppliers who have won contracts on this type of machine from the Army & Air Force Exchange. Through research, the manager then determines how many bids were awarded on this type of dishwasher during the two-to-three-year period and is able to plot the distribution of those winning bids. The plotting of winning bids is shown in Fig. 11.3. This figure illustrates the distribution of the past 120 winning bids awarded to suppliers of the rackless model by the Army & Air Force Exchange. What the manager discovered in this case is that no single price accounted for all winning bids, but rather a range of winning bid prices exists around a mean of all winning bids. To illustrate, of the 120 total winning bids, 19 jobs were awarded at the mean price of all 120 bids, 15 jobs were awarded to prices 2 percent above that mean, and one job was awarded as high as 6 percent above that mean! A distribution of winning bids such as is illustrated here is common in the industrial market owing to plant

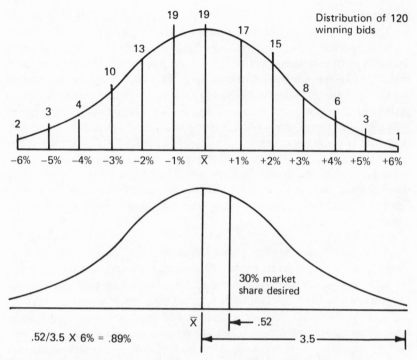

Fig. 11.3. Example of a bidding model. (Adapted from Arleigh W. Walker, "How to Price Industrial Products," *Harvard Business Review,* September–October 1967, 127–132.)

capacity and order backlogs of the bidding companies. When plant capacities are high and suppliers do not need the work, they will bid high—when capacities are low and they need the work, they will bid low. This type of pricing behavior by suppliers is what accounts for the 6 percent spread in winning bids on both sides of the mean of all the winning bids.

At this point, an observation can be made. The distribution of winning bids is very close to the normal curve, at least close enough so that probabilities under the normal curve might have application in determining market shares that could be taken by various bid prices. For example, if the marketing manager had priced in this market at the mean price, the company could have taken a 50 percent share of that market, as its price would have been lower than all those winning bids on the right-hand side of the distribution. Similarly, if the company had priced at the mean bid price plus one standard deviation above that mean, it would have taken 16 percent of the jobs (the mean plus one standard deviation explains 84 percent of the area under the normal curve). If, on the other hand, the company had priced one standard deviation below that mean, it would have taken 84 percent of the 120 jobs awarded during the two-to-three-year time period.

What this means, of course, is that there is a relationship between prices above and below the mean and the shares of the market each could command. Going one step further, the marketing manager refers to a table of Z values for the normal curve to determine where the company would have had to price to obtain a desired 30 percent share of that market. From the table, he defines a Z value of 3.5 as explaining 50 percent of the area under the curve. Then, as Fig. 11.3 shows, by again referring to the table of Z values, the manager finds that .52 explains the 20 percent variation between the mean bid price and the desired 30 percent market share. If .52/3.5 is multiplied by the 6 percent spread, it can be shown that to capture a 30 percent share of the winning 120 bids, the manager would have had to price each job at a price of .89 percent above the winning bid price. If this had been done, the company would have captured the right-hand tail of Fig. 11.3 and achieved its required 30 percent share of that market. Calculating similarly, the manager could determine where to price to capture any share of the market as reflected by the distribution of winning bids. Then, by assuming that the past distribution is representative of how winning bids will continue to range, the manager will price at the mean winning bid plus .89 percent of that mean to achieve the company's desired 30 percent share in the future.

This is a relatively simple bidding model and ignores some big points, such as the manufacturer's varying plant capacities at times RFPs are sent out, and it shows no relationship to costs involved. In addition, it assumes that no competitors are using the same model and that data on past winning bids are available. Also, it only applies to the bids of specific products where specifications do not differ. Regardless, it makes the desired point—by using a bid probability model to determine price, the marketing manager has a better chance of achieving the required pricing objective, in this case a 30 percent share of the market, than without the aid of such a model. Naturally, the company must continue to monitor winning bids to ensure that the distribution does not change and that the mean value stays current. Both of these considerations are relatively easy to accomplish. One thing must be kept in mind—the model is not a decision maker, but only a tool to better pricing decisions. It is only as good as the man or woman using it! Properly formulated, it can simplify pricing decisions to the point where they can be delegated to staff personnel and not tie up management time. In addition, such bidding models can be adapted to other pricing objectives such as return on investment, stabilization of price, stabilization of margin, and so on, when bid prices and relevant costs are integrated. This model is admittedly simple and unrealistic, but it does show the level of sophistication that can be and is being used in the pricing of industrial goods.

LEASING IN THE INDUSTRIAL MARKET

One other area that deserves some mention is leasing in the industrial market. Leasing of capital equipment by industrial companies, as opposed to purchasing that capital equipment, is a trend that has gained great momentum in the past few years. Thus, for any industrial company marketing user type products, the concept of leasing rather than selling is something that should be considered. The argument is made that any product that can be sold can also be leased. This appears to be true—the following are types of products that have been or are being leased to industrial customers: printing presses, metal fabricating equipment, forklift trucks, oil well meter equipment, machine tools, dairy equipment, compressors, warehouse machinery, tallow-rendering equipment, canning and food-packing equipment, kelp-drying ovens, cargo-handling equipment, among others.[16]

For the industrial marketing manager in any company marketing such goods, leasing can be an alternative to selling those products to potential customers, and leasing may allow the company to penetrate markets that might otherwise not exist for that company's products if it had to sell them outright. For example, the full price of a two horsepower Vertimill might be $2,375.00 for each unit, which could be prohibitive for a small, capital-shy manufacturing firm requiring two or three of these machines. But if the same machine can be leased for $125.00 per month, then this same customer firm might well be able to afford the machine and thus can be considered a sound prospect. In simple terms, leasing may allow the customer to acquire something required, and it lets the customer pay for it over a longer period of time. Basically, leasing expands the market base for many high-priced industrial products.

The magnitude of industrial leasing is difficult to determine, but some estimates may help show its usage. In 1973 it was estimated that about 18 to 20 percent of all capital expenditures were financed through leases of various kinds.[17] This figure was up from about 15 percent of all capital expenditures in 1970.[18] And the leasing market in the industrial market has been increasing by about 15 percent for the past few years. The economic crunch in the late 1960s and early 1970s contributed greatly to this growth. Tight money and inflation have made payment of fixed monthly lease payments a popular way for industrial customers to finance capital equipment. In addition, the pollution control standards have had great impact on leasing where companies have been reluctant to make huge capital investments necessary for air, water, or waste treatment facilities. Many firms have preferred to lease such facilities rather than purchase them. All indications are that leasing will become more of a factor in the financing of industrial capital equipment as time goes by.

The marketing manager must understand that leasing has both benefits and disadvantages when viewed from the customer's perspective. On the benefit side, leasing can provide customers with up to 100 percent financing in some instances. It can also help the customer obtain more favorable cash flows, and it can conserve the customer's working capital, giving him more flexibility. Finally, leasing can often help the customer protect himself against loss that could occur if he purchased heavy equipment and that equipment became obsolete. These are general advantages that may or may not apply to specific lease agreements.

There are also disadvantages to the customer's leasing industrial equipment. For one thing, in the long run, leasing usually requires a greater outlay of capital than does debt financing. This means the customer may pay more for the same equipment. In addition, although the customer may view lease payments as operating expenses, they are, in fact, fixed payments that he must meet. Some customers also take great pride in owning their businesses, including their plant and equipment. With such customers, leasing is not seen as advantageous. Finally, lease agreements can be hazardous if the customer is not careful. This is especially true if the equipment leased is subject to rapid obsolescence, as the customer can be tied to a lease agreement whose duration exceeds the useful life of the equipment. Again, these are general disadvantages that may or may not apply to specific lease agreements.

For the industrial marketing manager, there are three possible ways for equipment to be leased rather than sold outright to customers. First of all, the manager's company itself can lease to the customer. This means the company must carry the financing and work out the lease arrangements itself, which is a form of pricing. Secondly, many banks are involved in the leasing of industrial equipment to industrial customers. It is possible for the marketing manager to lease the company's equipment through such a bank leasing arrangement by negotiating with the bank involved. Thirdly, there are companies specializing in the industrial leasing market, such as CIT Financial, Commercial Credit, General Finance Corporation, U.S. Leasing, and U.S. Industrial Tools. For the marketing manager, it is possible to lease the company's equipment through organizations such as these to industrial customers. Again it is important to realize that by leasing, the industrial marketing manager may be able to penetrate markets that otherwise might not be reached.

Although there are many types of industrial leases, they are usually one of two basic types: (1) the full payout lease, which has a lower rate, but is a pure financial mechanism; and (2) the service lease, which costs more to the customer, but includes maintenance, service, and other provisions.[19] Actually, leasing plans are developed to the specific demands of the markets involved. To illustrate, Liberty Leasing Company of Chicago worked out a plan for Keene Corporation's water pollution division. This plan offered two different methods of leasing. The first was an "extended takedown plan," by which equipment was introduced in gradual stages over a ten-year period. The second option was a standard three-to-five-year lease for immediate installation of essential equipment.[20]

A typical industrial lease might look like the following. A piece of industrial equipment has an original value of $100,000 and is leased for a basic five-year term, its useful life being eight to ten years. It is leased at a monthly rate of $22.00 per $1,000 of original value. In this case, monthly lease payments would be $2,200. At the end of the five years, the lessee has the option of returning the equipment and negotiating a new lease on improved or updated equipment or of purchasing the item at a residual value of 10 percent. In this example, the marketing company, instead of selling the equipment for $100,000 is leasing it for a total revenue of $142,000 ($2,200 per month X 60 months = $132,000 + $10,000, the 10 percent residual value). Whether or not this would be profitable would depend upon such factors as company pricing objectives such as return on investment, the cost of capital of the $100,000, the amount of service and maintenance required, and so on. But if these factors are properly considered, the lease could be profitable for the marketing manager and the customer. Although the latter pays more over the five-year period, when cash flows are discounted by the present value of payments, that customer will actually pay less with the lease.

What all this means is that for the industrial marketing manager, there may be an alternative to pricing products and selling them outright. This alternative is to lease them to customers. Of course, leasing cannot be applied by industrial companies marketing OEM products—it is apparently restricted to the manufacturers of capital equipment marketing to user customers.

CHAPTER SUMMARY

Pricing is the fourth major substrategy involved in overall marketing strategy. It is important, however, to realize that pricing decisions must be integrated with decisions regarding products, channels, and promotion through time and not simply at one point in time. Pricing is not something that takes place after products have been manufactured, channels established, and promotional campaigns inaugurated—it must be considered simultaneously along with all the other functional marketing decisions that the manager has to make. The role of pricing in the industrial market was explored, and factors influencing the actual pricing decision were developed in depth. These factors are customer demand, competition, cost, company pricing objectives, company top management, and government. A return-on-investment pricing model and a competitive-bidding pricing model were introduced, and the concept of list and net pricing was explained. Finally, the role of leasing in the industrial market was examined as it relates to pricing and financing of industrial capital equipment.

QUESTIONS FOR CHAPTER 11

1. Why do industrial buyers often rate price as a less important buying consideration than certainty of delivery, quality and uniformity of the products purchased, and service and technical assistance provisions offered by the individual suppliers?
2. Regardless of whether an industrial company is a price leader or a price follower, reaction of competitors to that company's pricing decisions must always be considered. Do you agree or disagree with this statement? If you agree, why do you agree? If you disagree, why do you disagree?
3. What are the differences between list and net prices in the industrial market? Why are both used in industrial marketing?
4. Why do so many large industrial companies use rate of return or return on investment as a basis for pricing their products in the marketplace?
5. The use of bidding models in the industrial market, although theoretically helpful, offers little help to the practicing industrial marketing manager in pricing his product in the actual marketplace. Do you agree or disagree with this statement? If you agree, why do you agree? If you disagree, why do you disagree?

12

INDUSTRIAL MARKETING: PROSPECTS AND PERCEPTIONS

This book has had three main goals, which are as follows:

1. To provide a substantive and complete, yet concise, reference on industrial marketing management for the attention of both the practicing industrial marketing manager and the classroom student of industrial marketing
2. To show that the tasks of the industrial marketing manager are considerably different from the tasks of the consumer marketing counterpart, even though the basic principles are the same
3. To demonstrate that the essence of the industrial marketing management function is to provide the right product at the right time and place and price to the right market segment and to communicate this offering to this segment effectively.

PROSPECTS FOR INDUSTRIAL MARKETING IN ACADEMIA

Until recently, industrial marketing has seemingly been the forgotten child of the parent discipline of marketing. This is especially true in academia, where colleges and universities have given relatively short shrift to industrial marketing in their curricula. Analysis of the marketing course offerings in most collegiate schools of business administration, both large and small, reveals that most college courses in marketing emphasize consumer marketing.

The most widely taught courses include Principles of Marketing, Marketing Research, Marketing Management, Retailing, Advertising, Sales Management, Physical Distribution, International Marketing, and Consumer Behavior.[1] It is true, of course, that many of these courses do at times relate to the industrial market. Principles of Marketing textbooks normally contain a chapter on industrial marketing. Sales Management courses normally relate to that specific aspect of the industrial market. Marketing Management courses may cover various industrial marketing topics as well as consumer marketing topics. The same is true for many other marketing courses that relate to various parts of the overall industrial market.

The point is that relatively few U.S. colleges and universities have required courses in industrial marketing for their marketing majors. One study indicates that in 1972, only eight schools out of a sample of 135 four-year institutions with marketing concentrations required their majors to take a course in industrial marketing. Another 15 schools offered the course in a quasi-required capacity, but, in total, less than 20 percent of the schools sampled required a course in industrial marketing in any form of their majors.[2] Of course, some students do also take the course as an elective, but indications are that the majority of graduating marketing seniors have only a superficial or cursory knowledge of industrial marketing. Generally, they have been exposed to bits and pieces of it in their other marketing courses, but this is not the same as completing a course in the area. Yet many of these same graduating seniors will find jobs in various areas of the industrial market—jobs for which they may lack specific knowledge and training.

It was not very long ago that many marketing professors in U.S. colleges and universities actually believed that there were not enough differences between industrial and consumer marketing to warrant separate considerations of the subjects. Their belief was, and still is, in many instances, that marketing is fundamentally marketing whether it be in the consumer or the industrial market. This being the case, a good background in consumer marketing or in the general area of marketing is sufficient. The student could then adapt those basic marketing principles learned in college to the specific constraints of the industrial market once on the job. Unfortunately, there is evidence to conclude that many marketing professors across the United States still hold this philosophy.

Recently, there seems to be a serious rethinking of this position. There have been some compelling reasons for this change in thought. For one thing, there seems to be a shift in academic marketing away from theory for theory's sake toward more practical applications of the contributions of marketing. Much of this may have been stimulated by the recession that plagued the country in the mid-1970s. During this period, two phenomena stimulated the interest toward more practical marketing. For one thing, the marketplace itself changed. Employers were seeking business school graduates who could apply what they had learned and apply it with a minimum amount of training. Extended training programs for college graduates were many times cut back or even discontinued in many industrial companies as the attempt was made to cut costs to offset decreasing demand in the marketplace. Because industrial marketing is by nature more practical than theoretical, it was one of the marketing course offerings benefiting from this change.

A second phenomenon also renewed interest in industrial marketing. It, too, was related to the recession. As the crunch came in the recession, practicing marketing managers began to look for answers in marketing journals and business periodicals. In attempting to offer substantive articles of value to their readers, many journals switched from publishing abstract and theoretical articles to publishing more pragmatic articles. This switch stimulated research into such areas as industrial marketing, as academicians tried to write materials that journals were publishing. This indirect motive prompted a number of college and university marketing professors to research various areas of the industrial market and to write articles in those areas. This rekindled an interest in industrial marketing that in turn was passed on in terms of curriculum changes, course additions, and the like.

The overall result of these two phenomena, both related to the recession of the mid-1970s, was to stimulate interest in industrial marketing for the marketing curricula. As late as 1972, however, only about 6 percent of schools of business required the course of their marketing students, and only about 29 percent even taught the course.[3] Indications are that the course will become more prominent in U.S. marketing curricula in the future, as there seems to be a rebirth of the value of such a course in marketing education.

PROSPECTS FOR INDUSTRIAL MARKETING IN INDUSTRY

A different implication for industrial marketing relates to its future in American industry. What roles can marketing be expected to play in the future in industrial companies? Will marketing be more or less important in the industrial market in the future? How will marketing management change in the industrial market?

Perhaps the key to understanding what changes may take place in the future for industrial marketing management lies in understanding the manner in which economic difficulties in the mid-1970s affected industrial marketing managers.

During this period of time, many managers faced an environment characterized by (1) enduring inflation, (2) high unemployment, (3) high materials and labor costs, (4) unstable interest rates, (5) low ultimate consumer confidence, (6) an energy crisis, (7) shortages of certain materials required for production, and (8) delays in obtaining materials that were available. These factors and others had a sobering effect on many industrial marketing managers, who previously had not been confronted by such constraints.

Many industrial companies previously experiencing periods of high sales and good profits faced almost the complete opposite. This was particularly true of those companies producing goods for inventory to OEM customers and distributors. The recession of the mid-1970s proved a classic textbook example of the concept of derived demand as covered in this text.

Individual industrial marketing managers reacted in many ways. Some panicked and almost immediately cut off marginal customers, raised prices regardless of impact on customers, reduced product offerings with little real analysis, cut back on sales and advertising programs, and, in general, attempted a variety of stopgap marketing measures in attempts to cope with the situation. Others looked at the recession in a more reasoned and calculated manner. These managers sought out new customer market segments and found new applications for their products in industries that were not adversely affected by the recession. They examined the effectiveness of their marketing programs and analyzed their customers' problems so as to help them, not penalize them in the hard times that they also faced. In short, these latter managers adapted to the situation rather than reacted to it. They did this by utilizing many of the strategic concepts covered in this text.

Whatever directions individual managers took, the discipline of industrial marketing learned much from the recession that will affect it in the future. Some of the more important lessons learned are as follows:

1. The derived demand concept is valid. The recession reminded many managers of the validity of derived demand in the industrial market. Often this concept had been forgotten in the prosperous years preceding the recession. Actually, it took quite a while for many industrial companies to feel the pinch of the recession. This was especially true of those companies not producing to inventory requirements of their customers. Ultimately, however, the decreases in demand for consumer goods affected the sales of most industrial producers. For many industrial marketing managers, it was a rude awakening from the prosperous years that preceded the recession. Sales decreases of this magnitude had never been seen before by many managers who overlooked the basic message of the derived demand concept. The recession made many industrial marketing managers realize that they had better keep abreast of the ultimate consumer market as well as the industrial market.

2. Hard economic times can cause industrial companies to fail. Com-

parison of the 1975 "Survey of Industrial Purchasing Power" data with 1974 data reveals 13,091 fewer manufacturing establishments with 20 or more employees and 1,664 fewer manufacturing establishments with 100 or more employees.[4] Undoubtedly, many of these companies failed because they were unable to adapt to the recession. Such failures had a sobering effect and reinforced the need for sound industrial marketing practices.

3. Market segmentation is imperative for industrial marketing success. As traditional markets became depressed, managers were forced to seek out new markets or suffer the consequences. In doing so, many discovered or rediscovered the value of the standard industrial classification system and other SIC-related data such as were discussed in this text. Innovative industrial marketing managers found new customer target market segments that were not hurt by the recession and converted them into the appropriate SIC numbers. They then assessed their potentials, located individual companies, and marketed goods and services to those companies. In a manner of speaking, the recession reemphasized the value of market segmentation to many managers who previously had not given much thought to the concept.

4. Marketing effectiveness can be increased. When times are good and sales are up, it is common simply to accept what is happening without really questioning its effectiveness. To a great extent, this is what happened in the industrial market prior to the recession of the mid-1970s. But when the economy soured and sales became depressed, many managers found out just how much fat had built up in their marketing programs over time. In attempting to control costs and manage rather than stimulate demand, these managers discovered that they could thin out product lines, increase sales and advertising effectiveness, reconstruct channels of distribution, and readjust pricing mechanisms and, in doing so, market more efficiently. In short, the recession forced many industrial marketing managers to assess present marketing practices and, in doing so, discover new and more efficient methods of performing the same basic tasks. It is illogical to conclude that these methods will be abandoned in the future when times improve.

In summary, the recession of the mid-1970s served to reemphasize, not diminish, the importance of effective marketing in the U.S. industrial firm. American industry's technical capabilities appear to exceed its marketing capabilities. This is something that many had forgotten, yet that was borne out in the recession when large inventories of highly sophisticated goods stockpiled because traditional customers decreased their purchasing of these goods. To survive, companies had to devise new ways of adapting to a changing market environment. The ability to adapt was instrumental in the success of many companies in the recession and reminded companies that marketing is indeed a necessity and not a luxury for American industry. This is not to imply that marketing is important only in a recession. As this text has attempted to illustrate, effective marketing is instrumental in business success in good times and bad. The recession has been emphasized only to show its effect in reminding companies of this fact.

FUTURE TRENDS IN INDUSTRIAL MARKETING

Analysis of the industrial market prior to, during, and after the recession of the mid-1970s indicates a number of trends that may characterize industrial marketing in the future. A brief description of some of these trends follows:

An Increased Use of the Behavioral Sciences

Indications are there will be increased usage of behavioral science contributions in industrial marketing. It is becoming apparent to many industrial marketing managers that if they are to serve the industrial market better, they must have a better understanding of industrial buyers and buying influences. There is a great need to understand better the motivations of those actually making purchasing decisions in U.S. industrial firms. If this is to be done, it is going to be necessary for industrial marketers to apply more and more of the contributions of the behavioral sciences to the industrial market. Consumer marketing, especially in the area of consumer behavior, has been far in advance of industrial marketing in this regard. It is quite logical to conclude that what has worked in the consumer market will find application in the industrial market. This is especially true in those areas where a great deal of interpersonal contact is required between buyer and seller to facilitate the marketing exchange.

References have been made to this point throughout the text. Chapter 4 illustrated how the industrial marketer might better understand buyers in the marketplace by using some of the applications of the behavioral sciences. In particular, references were made to the application of the cognitive consonance principle and projection of the buyer's self-image. But evidence to date indicates that usage of the behavioral sciences is in its embryonic stage of development in the industrial market. Because this is a way to understand buyers and their motivations better, it appears logical to conclude that the future will see more applications of the behavioral sciences to industrial marketing.

An Increased Awareness in Social Issues

There is also a trend toward more social awareness on the part of industrial companies, and this will affect marketing behavior. In the past, many industrial marketing managers have tended to view value changes in America toward quality-of-life considerations as far more pertinent for consumer companies than industrial companies. Many industrial marketing managers reasoned that because they were removed from the ultimate consumer in their marketing of goods and services, the need for social awareness and sensitivity to corporate responsibility was not as great as for their consumer counterparts. Pressures from environmentalists and government, however, are forcing industrial companies to consider their impact on the quality of life both in the immediate and national environments. This pressure has had the effect of forcing industrial companies increasingly to view themselves in the context of corporate citizens having responsibilities to society.

The future will undoubtedly see more and more industrial marketing managers focusing their marketing programs on societal obligations, as well as on customer obligations. This trend can affect marketing programs in many ways. For example, it may require companies to make huge capital expenditures for air, water, or waste treatment facilities to reduce pollution. Such expenditures may well affect the marketing offerings of an industrial company in that the resources for many projects may not be available owing to the added expense of antipollution equipment. In addition, the industrial marketing manager may well have to watch the overall effects of his product offerings on the total environment. In the past, it may have been possible for the manager to add a product to the company's product line with the ultimate consideration being that product's contribution to the product line. Today that manager had better watch the effects of the by-products of adding that product; and if a production process affects the environment adversely, the product may be rejected, even though it could be profitable. And, of course, industrial companies are already heavily using advertising and other forms of promotion to inform the public of their social corporate responsibility. Again indications are that this trend is only in its early stage of development.

A Growing Emphasis on Marketing Research and Marketing Intelligence

Another likely trend involves a growing emphasis on marketing research and marketing intelligence gathering in industrial marketing. As the text has shown, industrial marketing research tends to be piecemeal, and the development of marketing information systems is still in its early stages. However, the recession of the mid-1970s revealed to many industrial marketing managers just how inadequate their market data collection mechanisms were. As more sophisticated research techniques are applied in the industrial market and as data systems are implemented and improved, it is logical to conclude that research will play a much larger role in future industrial marketing decisions than it has in the past.

An Increased Use of Formal Marketing Planning

Still another likely trend is the increased emphasis that will be placed on sound marketing planning to provide better marketing direction. This is not to imply that marketing planning has not been used in the industrial market, but rather that it has not been effectively applied in many instances. For many marketing managers, the economic havoc of the mid-1970s made a deep impression about just how ill-prepared they were for what took place. It again seems logical to conclude that a lesson was learned and that the answer might lie in more thoughtful and realistic marketing planning. Perhaps it is more correct to describe this trend as follows—there will not only be more use of marketing planning per se, but also more use of sophisticated marketing planning in the industrial market.

An Increased Need for Understanding Organizational Behavior

In addition to understanding industrial buyers and buying influences better, another trend likely to be seen is the increased need for better understanding of the behavior of business organizations. Understanding the motivations of individual buyers and buying influences is not the same as understanding the behavior of the companies in which they work. As more and more buying influences become involved in the purchasing of industrial goods and services, there is an increased need to understand how all these influences relate in their own organization. As the text has shown, purchase decision concerning industrial products are usually made on the basis of some kind of interaction among those people in the customer firm responsible for such purchasing.

In addition, business enterprises actually differ in their total behavior as regards the purchasing of industrial goods and services. Some business organizations are innovative and aggressive, whereas others are very apt to remain cautious and maintain the status quo. As can be seen, characteristics such as these affect the manner in which they buy goods and services. There appears to be a genuine need for industrial marketing managers to understand the organizational behavior of each and every customer better. If they are not able to do this, it is questionable that purchasing behavior will be really understood.

An Increased Use of On-line Data Systems between Buyers and Sellers

Finally, there appears to be a trend toward the increased use of on-line data systems, already common among consumer marketers such as large banks and retail chains. It is not inconceivable that, in the near future, on-line hookups between suppliers and customers will be commonplace in the marketing of the more standardized industrial goods and services. Orders would be placed and goods shipped with a minimum of human involvement beyond programming the computer. Once these systems materialize, there could be profound effects on individual marketing substrategies, particularly in the area of sales and distribution. For example, with such a system, economic order quantities could be established for each customer along with an automated mechanism for alerting the purchaser's computer when the point was reached for such products as were required. Through the on-line hookup between supplier and purchaser, the latter's computer would inform the former's computer that goods were to be shipped. The supplier's computer would then ship the required goods from an automated warehouse directly to the customer. The long-run costs savings in such a system make it seem almost a certainty in the industrial market, and, as was pointed out, systems such as these are now in operation in some of the nation's larger retail chains.

This is not a trend that will pervade all of industrial marketing. For example, on-line systems would be difficult to use with some types of industrial products and with some types of customers. It is hard to conceive of their use with highly specialized industrial products produced to individual customer specifications where a great deal of personal interaction is necessary before products are ever even produced. Nevertheless, with established customers and relatively standardized products, the on-line system is but a natural extension of the role of the inside salesman with the computer replacing the phone salesman.

These are but a few of the trends that will probably affect industrial marketing managers in the years to come. They are illustrated to make the point that industrial marketing, just like any other kind of marketing, is not static. For the industrial marketing manager, anticipation and adaptation may be the key to company success. Future trends must be anticipated, and the manager must adapt to them via the marketing strategy and substrategies of product, place, promotion, and price.

CHAPTER SUMMARY

This has been a text in industrial marketing—that branch of marketing specifically devoted to serving the industrial, institutional, and governmental markets. Although most of the text has focused on the industrial market as opposed to the institutional and governmental markets, it should be understood that the three markets are similar and that most of what is contained in this text can be adapted to the latter two markets.

Although the approach of this text may appear very specific in its application, the objective has been to develop a comprehensive understanding of what is specifically involved in industrial marketing management. The intent has been to provide a reference appropriate for both the practicing industrial marketing manager and for the classroom student of industrial marketing. The text is practically oriented and yet contains sophisticated theoretical constructs applicable to the industrial market. It is hoped that the practicing industrial marketing manager may find it useful as a guide in making actual industrial marketing decisions and also stimulating in the suggestion of ways in which marketing management practices may be improved in the marketplace. At the same time, it is hoped that the student of industrial marketing may find the text of value in terms of education about the workings of the industrial market and stimulating in terms of pursuing a career in industrial marketing.

APPENDIX:
INDUSTRIAL MARKETING
MANAGEMENT PROJECTS

The purpose of this appendix is to provide a number of varied industrial marketing field projects so that the principles discussed in this text may be applied to simulated marketing management situations. Through these projects, which apply to many areas of industrial marketing, the points illustrated in the text become more realistic. Some projects require library research, whereas others relate more to stimulating managerial responses. In each project, a suggested approach is provided to point the reader in the proper direction or refer him or her to the appropriate sources of information.

PROJECT 1. Derived Demand in the Industrial Market:
Machine Steel Company

You are the marketing manager for the Machine Steel Company, a manufacturer of steel used in the production of machine tools, both metal-cutting tools and metal-forming tools. At the present time, your company controls 25 percent of the market for steel used in the production of these tools, and it is expected that this 25 percent market share will be maintained in the coming year. According to data published in the *U.S. Industrial Outlook 1975*, the value of shipments in the machine tools industry is expected to increase 10 percent in 1975 over shipments in 1974. This amounts to a $200 million increase in shipments—from $1.9 billion in 1974 to $2.1 billion in 1975. In the machine tools industry, only about one-half of the value of shipments is paid out for materials, components, supplies, packaging, and so forth. Thus, only $100 million of the increase in the value of shipments involves the purchase of materials. The problem you face as marketing manager of the Machine Steel Company is to determine what the increase in shipments of machine tools in 1975 will mean to your company in 1975 sales. To state the problem in another manner, if the industry will purchase $100 million more in materials to produce the machine tools, what effect will that have on your 1975 sales?

Suggested Approach. To forecast the effects of additional purchases of materials by the machine tools industry on sales of steel producers, you need to know what part of a dollar's worth of machine tool sales is represented by steel. To determine this, you should refer to Table 3 of the national input-output model, illustrated in the February 1974 issue of the *Survey of Current Business*, which is carried in the public documents section of most libraries. If chapter 3 of this text is used as a reference, the effect on 1975 sales of the Machine Steel Company can be determined.

PROJECT 2. Media Selection among Trade Publications: The ABC Company

You are the marketing manager for the ABC Company, a firm that markets its products into the chemical industry. Your advertising approach to reaching desired executives in this industry is through the use of trade journal publications. You have determined what journals are appropriate for reaching those executives in the chemical industry, but you are undecided as to which specific journals or how many of those journals would provide optimum advertising impact per dollar spent.

You have obtained data from various rating services regarding trade publications classified by SIC, and these data illustrate the percentage of executives in the chemical industry reached by each of the appropriate journals. Based on average issue audience and net cumulative coverage, the percentage of executives reached by the trade journals is as follows:

1. The top five journals will reach 51 percent of the executives at a cost of $5,680.
2. The top ten journals will reach 64 percent of the executives at a cost of $10,810.
3. The top 15 journals will reach 67 percent of the executives at a cost of $15,870.
4. The top 20 journals will reach 68 percent of the executives at a cost of $19,743.

Because all the journals will reach desired executives in the chemical industry, the problem you face is that of deciding the optimum number of journals in which to place your company's advertisements. Basing your decision on the data provided, would you recommend advertising in the top five, ten, 15, or 20 journals?

Suggested Approach. To determine whether the optimum number of trade journals is five, ten, 15, or 20, you need to compare the cost of adding five more journals at each level with the benefits to be obtained in terms of reaching executives at each level. Then you need to determine at what level the point of diminishing return will be reached.

PROJECT 3. SIC Market Segmentation: Bio-Chem Corporation

You are the marketing manager for the Bio-Chem Corporation, a chemical company specializing in the production of diagnostic reagent chemicals. These chemicals are used in laboratory equipment in hospitals, clinics, and so on, for the diagnosis of human illnesses and other disorders. Preliminary investigation indicates that there are manufacturers of laboratory and scientific instruments who produce laboratory testing equipment and that these manufacturers buy chemicals for test kits to be used with their equipment. Under normal conditions, these manufacturers do not produce their own chemicals, but rather subcontract the chemicals out to their desired specifications. It is this market that your company is trying to enter. Your task is to locate specific customer prospects who are manufacturers of such testing equipment and who would purchase such chemicals as your company produces. You want to locate such specific customers by state and by county. How do you propose to locate specific prospective customer firms of this type throughout the United States? What methodology do you propose to implement?

Suggested Approach. Locating such customer firms requires that you first find the appropriate SIC number for manufacturers of laboratory and scientific instruments using diagnostic reagent chemicals. This number can be found by reference to the *Standard Industrial Classification Manual* and the *Census of Manufactures*, both of which can be found in the public documents section of most libraries. Using chapter 3 of this text as a reference, you will then be able to locate specific customer firms by state and county, using the methods outlined in that chapter.

PROJECT 4. Choosing between Company Salesmen and Manufacturer's Reps: The Delta Corporation

You are the marketing manager for the Delta Corporation, a company that manufactures an off-the-shelf, standardized, low-cost component part that is sold to OEM customers in the industrial market. At present, you are using manufacturer's reps to sell the product to industrial distributors, who, in turn, sell the component parts into the OEM market. Because of control problems with the reps, you are seriously considering replacing these reps with your own salesmen, who will continue to sell to the industrial distributors.

The MRs are currently being paid a straight commission of 8 percent of the sales price of $10.00 per case to the distributor. According to your preliminary estimates, the cost of using your own salesmen will average about 60 cents per case once the sales force is trained. At the present time, the reps are contributing sales of 150,000 cases per year, but you believe this is about the extent of their sales capabilities, and there is little probability of increasing sales through the continued use of manufacturer's reps. You do feel, however, that company salesmen will do better than 150,000 cases per year, once trained, because you will have more control over their selling efforts. Your expected sales from switching to company salesmen are estimated as follows for the first five years:

Year 1 . . . . . .   75,000 Cases
Year 2 . . . . . . 125,000 Cases
Year 3 . . . . . . 175,000 Cases
Year 4 . . . . . . 200,000 Cases
Year 5 . . . . . . 225,000 Cases

It is estimated that the cost of training the salesmen until they are productive will be $150,000, and corporate policy dictates that you must recoup these costs over the five-year period from the savings obtained from switching from MRs to company salesmen.

Ignoring the time value of money in this situation, would you as marketing manager recommend the switch to company salesmen, or would you recommend continued use of the manufacturer's representatives?

Suggested Approach. You, as the manager, would switch to company salesmen when savings in the cost of sales between MRs and company salesmen over the five-year period exceed the cost of training the salesmen.

PROJECT 5. Estimating Market Potential: UMAK Steel Corporation

You are the marketing manager for the UMAK Steel Corporation, a southern California company that is in the automotive salvage business. Your company buys auto wrecks and other such scrap hulks for steel salvage and processes these hulks through a shredder into scrap steel, which is then sold overseas to Japanese steel mills. Your top management is looking for alternative markets for this scrap steel and is seriously considering the purchase of an electric steel "minimill" to melt down the scrap steel and process it into reinforcing bar for construction purposes. Before any such decision is made, however, your top management wants an accurate estimate for reinforcing bar in the southern California market with particular emphasis on the market potential in Los Angeles, Orange, and San Diego counties. As marketing manager, your task is to provide reliable data regarding the market potential for reinforcing bar in this three-county area.

Preliminary investigations indicate that about 95 percent of the production of reinforcing bar goes into construction, and this can be broken down into the following three classifications: (1) residential construction—single unit, two unit, and multiunit; (2) nonresidential construction—industrial buildings, office buildings, schools, hospitals, churches, and so on; and (3) engineering construction contracts—highways and bridges, sewers, waterworks, storm drains, dams and flood control projects, and other similar types of construction.

Secondary research in construction trade journals shows that it is possible to find ratios showing the amount of reinforcing bar per $1,000 of construction in various types of construction. On this subject, your marketing research manager has found the following:

Type of Construction	*Amount of Reinforcing Bar Used*
Single unit housing	$2.70 of rebar per $1,000 of value
Multiunit housing	$28.70 of rebar per $1,000 of value
Industrial buildings	$53.50 of rebar per $1,000 of value
Office buildings	$45.50 of rebar per $1,000 of value
Stores	$28.70 of rebar per $1,000 of value
Educational buildings	5.7% of the material costs, which are 55% of the value
Dam & flood control	$37.90 of rebar per $1,000 of value
Sewers, storm drains	$10.00 of rebar per $1,000 of value
Highways & Bridges.	190 ton used per $1 million of construction @ $250 per ton

Given these data and your assignment, how would you estimate the market potential for the reinforcing bar in the three-county market area?

Suggested Approach. Total market potential in this case can be determined from the government documents section of most libraries. By referring to the U.S. Department of Commerce's *Construction Reports*; the U.S. Department of Commerce's *Construction Review*; and *Daily Construction Reports*, published by the F. W. Dodge Division of McGraw-Hill Systems Company, you can find the dollar value of all three types of construction (residential, nonresidential, and engineering construction contracts) for all counties throughout the United States. With these data and knowledge of how much rebar is used per dollar of construction, you can determine the market potential in the three-county area.

PROJECT 6. Return on Investment Pricing: Machine Tools, Inc.

You are the marketing manager for Machine Tools, Inc., a company that manufactures a line of industrial products that are sold to small machine shops in a localized market area. Your research and development department has developed a new portable drill press that has an expected marketing life cycle of four years. Your company requires an 8 percent return on investment on all capital expenditures, including new products. This required ROI is based on a cost of capital of 4 percent. To produce this product, your company incurs fixed costs of $5,000 per year and variable costs of $10.00 per unit produced. You estimate that the initial investment required to produce and market the new drill press is $100,000.

You are undecided whether to penetrate or skim the market with this product. The skimming price would be $1,000 per unit, and the penetration price would be $500 per unit. On the basis of these two feasible prices, your marketing research department has prepared the following demand schedule for the four-year time period.

Skim @ $1,000 per unit:		Penetrate @ $500 per unit:	
Year	*No. of Units Demanded*	*Year*	*No. of Units Demanded*
1	30	1	90
2	70	2	80
3	50	3	80
4	10	4	70

Assuming the above data to be reliable and given your company pricing objective of 8 percent return on investment, would you, as marketing manager, advise your company to skim or to penetrate, if either? For the sake of simplicity, assume that no salvage values are involved and that the 8 percent ROI required is before taxes. How would you recommend pricing these drill presses?

Suggested Approach. Referring to Chapter 11 in this text and a present value table, you should be able to decide at which price you would achieve your company's desired 8 percent return on investment.

NOTES

Chapter 1 (pages 1-17)
1. Harry L. Hansen, *Marketing Text, Techniques and Cases* (Homewood, Illinois: Richard D. Irwin, Inc., 1967), p. 4.
2. Kathryn Sederberg, "How to Sell to States, Counties, and Cities," *Industrial Marketing* 140 (September 1964): 140.
3. Ibid.
4. Ibid.
5. William M. Diamond, *Distribution Channels for Industrial Goods* (Columbus, Ohio: Bureau of Business Research, College of Commerce and Administration, The Ohio State University, 1963).

Chapter 2 (pages 19-34)
1. *Relative National Accounts: A Statistical Basebook* (New York: The Conference Board, Inc., 1974), pp. 35, 37.
2. U.S. Department of Commerce, *Mini-Guide to the 1972 Economic Censuses* (Washington, D.C.: U.S. Government Printing Office, 1973), p. 25.
3. Ibid., p. 22.
4. "Car Output Fell 4% Last Month From 1973 Pace," *The Wall Street Journal* 91 (September 4, 1974): 2.
5. Arthur H. Dix, "Industry Moving West, South," *Marketing Insights* 1 (January 23, 1967): 10.
6. Ibid.
7. U.S. Department of Commerce, *U.S. Industrial Outlook 1972 with Projections to 1980* (Washington, D.C.: U.S. Government Printing Office, April 1972), p. 308.
8. Ibid., p. 16.

Chapter 3 (pages 35–54)

1. "Input-Output Structure of the U.S. Economy: 1967," *Survey of Current Business* 54 (February 1974): 38–55.
2. Ibid., 34–37.
3. *Dun's Market Identifiers* (New York: Dun & Bradstreet, Inc., 1971), p. 29.
4. "You Scratch My Back and I'll Scratch Yours," *Sales Management* 103 (December 1, 1969): 33–34.
5. *Calling on Cyanamid* (Wayne, New Jersey: American Cyanamid Company, June 1974), pp. 1–16.

Chapter 4 (pages 55–74)

1. "Market Newsletter," *Chemical Week* 114 (April 10, 1974): 23.
2. *Purchasing Magazine Readers Have Something to Tell You about Chemicals, Report Number 10-A* (New York: *Purchasing Magazine*, 1965), pp. 7–8.
3. Murray Harding, "Who Really Makes the Purchasing Decision?" *Industrial Marketing* 51 (September 1966): 76.
4. Ibid.
5. Mary Rita O'Rourke, James M. Shea, and William M. Solley, "Survey Shows Need for Increased Sales Calls, Advertising and Updated Mailing Lists to Reach Buying Influences," *Industrial Marketing* 58 (April 1973): 38.
6. Steve Blickstein, "How to Find the Key Buying Influence," *Sales Management* 107 (September 20, 1971): 52.
7. Charles A. Koepke, *Plant Production Control,* 3rd ed. (New York: John Wiley and Sons, Inc., 1961), p. 60.
8. Blickstein, op. cit., 53.
9. Ibid.
10. Tom Finnegan, "Special Report: Profile of the Purchasing Man," *Purchasing Magazine* 70 (February 4, 1971): 51–56.
11. Howard G. Sawyer, "What Does the Industrial Buyer's Emotional Involvement Mean to You?" *Industrial Marketing* 44 (May 1959): 133–34.
12. Shelby D. Hunt, "Post-transaction Communications and Dissonance Reduction," *Journal of Marketing* 34 (July 1970): 46.
13. Ibid.

Chapter 5 (pages 75–92)

1. U.S. Department of Commerce, *U.S. Industrial Outlook 1972 with Projections to 1980* (op. cit.), p. 350.

Chapter 6 (pages 93–111)

1. *San Diego Union,* 16 July 1974, p. A-9.
2. "Car Output Fell 4% Last Month From 1973 Pace" (op. cit.), 2.
3. U.S. Department of Commerce, *U.S. Industrial Outlook 1973 with Projections to 1980* (op. cit.), p. 344.
4. Ibid., p. 343.

5. *Survey of Current Business* 45 (November 1965): 10–29.
6. "Input-Output Structure of the U.S. Economy: 1967 (op. cit.), 38–55.
7. "Car Output Fell 4% Last Month From 1973 Pace" (op. cit.), 2.
8. "Marketing Definitions, A Glossary of Marketing Terms," compiled by the Committee on Definitions (Chicago: American Marketing Association, 1960).
9. Charles S. Roberts, "How to Apply Research to Industrial Marketing," *Industrial Marketing* 43 (February 1958): 64.
10. "Who Is the Marketing Researcher? Is There a Chance He'll Become Company President?" *Marketing Insights* 4 (March 2, 1970): 4.
11. Ibid.
12. Thayer C. Taylor, "The Survey of Industrial Purchasing Power—What It Is and Why," *Sales Management* 112 (April 22, 1974): 15.

Chapter 7 (pages 113–137)
1. Robert G. Murdick, "Planning New Products," *Industrial Marketing* 48 (August 1963): 92.
2. *Convair Aerospace Division of General Dynamics/Fiftieth Year Anniversary* (San Diego: Convair Aerospace Division, 1973), p. 72.
3. . Rita Warner and Sally Strong, "Out of the Lab and Into the Market," *Industrial Marketing* 56 (December 1971): 20.
4. C. Wilson Randle, "On Profits, Products, and Life Cycles," *Industrial Marketing* 49 (September 1964): 103
5. Arch Patton, "Top Management Stake in the Product Life Cycle," *The Management Review* 48 (June 1959): 68.
6. "A Study in Contrast: The Industrial Product Manager and the Consumer Brand Manager," *Marketing Insights* 3 (March 10, 1969): 16.
7. Theodore Levitt, "Exploit the Product Life Cycle," *Harvard Business Review* 43 (December 1965): 81.
8. Randle, op. cit., 103.
9. "Why New Products Fail," *The Conference Board Record* 1 (1964): 16.
10. *Convair Aerospace Division of General Dynamics/Fiftieth Year Anniversary* (op. cit.), p. 72.
11. *Los Angeles Times,* 24 March 1969, p. 12.
12. Warner and Strong, op. cit., 20.
13. "Why New Products Fail" (op. cit.), 11.
14. Frederick E. Webster, Jr., "New Product Adoption in Industrial Markets: A Framework for Adoption," *Journal of Marketing* 33 (July 1969): 36.
15. Ibid.
16. Ibid.
17. William J. Constandse, "Why New Product Management Fails," *Business Management* 40 (June 1971): 16.
18. Rance Crain, "Profiles of the Product Manager: The Man in the Middle of it All," *Industrial Marketing* 55 (June 1970): 51.

Chapter 8 (pages 139–170)
1. "What Determines the Correct Channel of Distribution?" *Industrial Marketing* 51 (March 1966): 28.

2. "28th Annual Survey of Distributor Operations," *Industrial Distribution* 64 (March 1974): 23.

3. "1973 Census of Industrial Distributors," *Industrial Distribution* 14 (May 1974): 40.

4. Ibid.

5. Ibid.

6. Ibid., 41.

7. Ibid., 39–43.

8. *Laboratory of Advertising Performance Report #8013.2.* (New York: McGraw-Hill Research Department, 1974).

9. *We Could Save You a Few Thousand Bucks* (Cleveland: The Steel Service Center Institute, 1972), pp. 2–10.

10. "The Rep Has to Become a Better Businessman," *Electronic News* 15 (September 14, 1974): 4.

11. Kenneth B. Erdman, "Portrait of a Manufacturer's Representative," *The Agent and Representative* 23 (March 1971): 10.

12. "Taking the Manufacturer's Agent's Pulse," *Chemical Week* 111 (August 9, 1972): 22.

13. "What Manufacturers Want From Their Representatives," *The Agent and Representative* 22 (March 1970): 6.

14. Richard E. Snyder, "Physical Distribution Age," *Distribution Age* 62 (December 1962): 35–42.

15. Wendell M. Stewart, "Physical Distribution: Key to Improving Volume and Profits," *Journal of Marketing* 29 (January 1965): 67.

16. "Selling Expenses as a Percentage of Sales in Major Industries," *Sales Management* 110 (January 8, 1973): 39.

Chapter 9 (pages 171–193)

1. *The Mathematics of Selling* (New York: McGraw-Hill Research Department, 1973), p. 17.

2. Interview with Edward Brady, General Manager of Ducommun Metals & Supply Company, Inc., San Diego Office, October 10, 1972.

3. Robert C. Patchen, "What Drives the Salesman, or . . .the Many Sides of Motivation," *Industrial Distribution* 64 (June 1974): 62.

4. The Editors of Industrial Distributor News, "Women in Industrial Sales: Just the Beginning," *Salesman '75* (Philadelphia: Ames Publishing Company, 1969), p. 18.

5. "Getting Your Money's Worth From Your Salesmen," *Industry Week* 117 (April 16, 1973): 30.

6. "Selling," *Time* 82 (September 13, 1963): 96.

7. *The Mathematics of Selling* (op. cit.), pp. 2–7.

8. Executive Compensation Service, American Management Association, "Compensation," *Sales Management* 10 (January 8, 1973): 43–48.

9. Henry Bernstein, "How To Recruit Good Salesmen," *Industrial Marketing* 50 (October 1965): 70.

10. The Editors of Industrial Distributor News, *Salesman '75* (Philadelphia: Ames Publishing Company, 1969), p. 3.

11. Patchen, op. cit., 62.
12. "The New Supersalesman: Wired for Success," *Business Week* (January 6, 1973): 45.
13. Bernstein, op. cit., 70–71.
14. Ibid.
15. "Rising Cost of Selling," *Marketing Insights* 2 (November 4, 1968): 17.
16. "Sales Calls Continue to Rise," *Marketing Insights* 2 (May 13, 1968): 4.
17. *Laboratory of Advertising Performance Report #8013* (New York: McGraw-Hill Research Department, 1970).
18. Robert F. Vizza, "Managing Time & Territories for Maximum Sales Success," *Sales Management* 107 (July 15, 1971): 31.
19. Ronald Johnson, "Hiring Techniques for Salesmen," *Industrial Marketing* 50 (October 1965): 70–71.
20. "Getting Your Money's Worth From Your Salesmen" (op. cit.), 33.
21. Jesse S. Nirenberg, "What 10 Qualities Make a Top-Notch Salesman?" *Industrial Marketing* 49 (May 1964): 84.
22. Ibid.
23. Bernstein, op. cit., 72.
24. "Getting Your Money's Worth From Your Salesmen" (op. cit.), 31.
25. "Industrial Selling Costs: Now It's $60 a Call," *Sales Management* 110 (January 8, 1973): 14.
26. "Teaching Time Management to Industrial Salesmen," *Industrial Marketing* 50 (April 1965): 131.
27. "Putting More Profit in a Salesman's Time," *Sales Management* 105 (November 10, 1970): 19.

Chapter 10 (pages 195–224)
1. Irwin W. Tyson, Speech given before the Fourteenth Biennial Ohio Valley Industrial Advertising Conference, on board the U.S.S. *Johnston Chaperon*, afloat in the Ohio River, May 9, 1972.
2. Sim A. Kolliner, "Measuring Industrial Advertising," *Journal of Marketing* 29 (October 1965): 53. Reprinted from the *Journal of Marketing*, published by the American Marketing Association.
3. Ibid.
4. *22 Facts That Prove Your Advertising Works Harder in* Purchasing Magazine (New York: Conover-Mast Publications, 1968).
5. *Pick a SIC* (New York: Newsweek, Inc., 1968).
6. *The Story of Direct Advertising* (New York: Direct Mail Advertising Association, Inc., 1959).
7. *Catalog of Mailing & Prospect Lists, No. 67* (Detroit: R. L. Polk & Company, 1970), p. 22.
8. *NBL Marketing Guide* (Chicago: National Business Lists, Inc., 1973), p. 2.
9. "Ads, Direct Mail Double Sales for Biomation," *Industrial Marketing* 58 (September 1973): 10.
10. Fred R. Messner, "Seven Reasons Why You Should Consider a Career in Industrial Direct Mail" (Paper read before the West Coast Conference of the Direct Mail Advertising Association, Los Angeles, March 18, 1970).

11. *How to Increase Your Sales through Industrial Directory Advertising* (Greenwich, Conn.: Conover-Mast Purchasing Directory Research Department, 1969), pp. 2–3.
12. "What Industrial Advertisers Really Think," *Industrial Marketing* 52 (October 1967): 73–74.
13. *How to Build and Distribute Your Next Catalog* (New York: Thomas Publishing Company, 1970), p. 3.
14. Mel Hosansky, "Meeting Activity Profile," *Meetings & Conventions* 7 (December 1972): 92–93.
15. "Speaking Out At Trade Shows," *Meetings & Conventions* 8 (September 1973): 46.
16. Donald Stewart, "Carbide Exhibit Boss Speaks His Mind," *Industrial Marketing* 54 (March 1969): 41.
17. Hosansky, op. cit., 94.
18. "Honeywell Divisions Cut National Shows," *Industrial Marketing* 52 (August 1967): 52–55.
19. "What Happens to Trade Show Leads?" *Sales Management* 99 (July 15, 1967): 85–89. Reprinted by permission from *Sales Management, The Marketing Magazine.* Copyright 1967.
20. Richard K. Swandby and Jonathan M. Cox, "Trade Show Trends for 1973: The Vital Signs Hit a Plateau," *Industrial Marketing* 59 (April 1974): 66.
21. Hosansky, op. cit., 96.
22. Richard K. Swandby, "Trade Show Trends, '67," *Industrial Marketing* 53 (March 1968): 45–48. Reprinted by permission from *Industrial Marketing*, copyright 1968, by Advertising Publications, Inc., Chicago, Illinois.
23. Stewart, op. cit., 42.
24. "Marketing Definitions, A Glossary of Marketing Terms" (op. cit.).
25. Lawrence Fisher, *Industrial Marketing* (Princeton, N. J.: Brandon/Systems Press, Inc., 1970), p. 197.
26. "The Specialty Advertising Association Very Important Professor Program," *Linage* 22 (Spring 1970): 24.
27. *Campaign Bell Ringers in Specialty Advertising* (Chicago: Specialty Advertising Association International, 1973), p. 19.
28. Sally Strong, "Ad Budgets '74: Trend is Still to Spend, Spend, Spend," *Industrial Marketing* 59 (February 1974): 60.
29. Ibid.

Chapter 11 (pages 225–257)

1. Bill R. Darden, "An Operational Approach to Product Pricing," *Journal of Marketing* 82 (April 1968): 30.
2. "Negotiation: Some Tips From Kaiser's Tactics Book," *Purchasing Week* 12 (January 13, 1969): 22.
3. Gilbert Burck, "The Myths and Realities of Corporate Pricing," *Fortune* 85 (April 1972): 88.

4. Alfred R. Oxenfeldt, "Distinction Between Price Theory and Pricing in Practice," in *Economic Principles and Public Issues* (New York: Holt, Rinehart and Winston, Inc., 1951), reprinted in Schuyler F. Otteson, William G. Panschar, and James M. Patterson, *Marketing: The Firm's Viewpoint* (New York: The Macmillan Company, 1964), pp. 454–455.

5. Isaiah A. Litvak, James A. Johnson, and Peter M. Banting, "Industrial Pricing—Art or Science," *The Business Quarterly* (Autumn 1967): 43.

6. Burck, op cit., 88.

7. Litvak, Johnson, and Banting, op cit., 37.

8. Ibid., 41.

9. Burck, op. cit., 86.

10. A. D. H. Kaplan, Joel B. Dirlam, and Robert F. Lanzillotti, *Pricing in Big Business* (Washington, D.C.: The Brookings Institution, 1958), pp. 127–219.

11. Litvak, Johnson, and Banting, op. cit., 42.

12. *San Diego Union*, 19 July 1974, p. B-9.

13. Burck, op. cit., 88.

14. Ibid.

15. Lamar Lee, Jr., and Donald W. Dobler, *Purchasing and Materials Management: Text and Cases* (New York: McGraw-Hill Book Company, Inc., 1965), p. 97.

16. Ray Schuster, "The Plant Engineer and Equipment Leasing," *Plant Engineering* 21 (May 1967): 155.

17. "Tight Money Turning Industry toward Leasing," *Industry Week* 177 (April 16, 1973): 70.

18. Herbert A. Warren, "Leasing Sparks an Old Product in an Old Market," *Industrial Marketing* 53 (September 1968): 59.

19. "Leasing Becoming Sharp Marketing Tool, Zises Says," *Industrial Marketing* 55 (August 1970): 10.

20. Ibid., 20.

Chapter 12 (pages 259–268)

1. Richard T. Hise, "The Marketing Curriculum: Does It Reflect the Recommendations of Marketing Educators?" *Collegiate News and Views* 28 (Spring 1975): 14.

2. Ibid.

3. Ibid.

4. Jay M. Gould, "The Survey—A Useful Monitor of Turbulent Change," *Sales Management* 114 (April 21, 1975): 22.

SELECTED BIBLIOGRAPHY

BOOKS

Cateora, Philip R., and Hess, John M. *The Industrial Marketing Environment.* Boulder, Colorado: School of Business, University of Colorado, 1964.

Corey, E. Raymond. *Industrial Marketing.* Englewood Cliffs, New Jersey: Prentice-Hall, Inc., 1962.

Dodge, Robert H. *Industrial Marketing.* New York: McGraw-Hill Book Company, 1970.

Fisher, Lawrence. *Industrial Marketing.* Princeton: Brandon/Systems Press, 1970.

Hill, Richard M.; Alexander, Ralph S.; and Cross, James S. *Industrial Marketing.* Homewood, Illinois: Richard D. Irwin, Inc., 1975.

Kaplan, A. D. H.; Dirlam, Joel B.; and Lanzillotti, Robert F. *Pricing in Big Business.* Washington, D.C.: The Brookings Institution, 1958.

Lester, Bernard. *Marketing Industrial Equipment.* New York: McGraw-Hill Book Company, 1935.

Messner, Fred R., *Industrial Advertising.* New York: McGraw-Hill Book Company, 1963.

Oxenfeldt, Alfred R. *Industrial Pricing and Market Practices.* Englewood Cliffs, New Jersey: Prentice-Hall, Inc., 1951.

Risley, George. *Modern Industrial Marketing.* New York: McGraw-Hill Book Company, 1972.

Robinson, Patrick J., and Faris, Charles W. *Industrial Buying and Creative Marketing.* Boston: Allyn & Bacon, Inc., 1967.

Vinson, Donald E., and Sciglimpaglia, Donald, eds. *The Environment of Industrial Marketing.* Columbus, Ohio: Grid, Inc., 1975.

Webster, Frederick E., Jr., and Wind, Yoram. *Organizational Buying Behavior.* Englewood Cliffs, New Jersey: Prentice Hall, Inc., 1972.
Williams, L. A. *Industrial Marketing Management and Controls.* New York: American Elsevier Publishing Company, Inc., 1968.

ARTICLES

Alexander, Fred C. "Is Industrial Marketing Ready to Go Consumer?" *Industrial Marketing* 49:74–77, December 1964.
Ames, Charles B. "Marketing Planning For Industrial Products." *Harvard Business Review* 46:100–111, September–October 1968.
——"Trappings vs. Substance in Industrial Marketing." *Harvard Business Review* 48:93–102, July-August 1970.
Barr, Joel J. "SIC: A Basic Tool For the Marketer." *Industrial Marketing* 54: 52–79, August 1969.
Blickstein, Steve. "How To Find the Key Buying Influence." *Sales Management* 107:51–54, September 20, 1971.
Burck, Gilbert. "The Myths and Realities of Corporate Pricing." *Fortune* 85: 85–126, April 1972.
"The New Supersalesman: Wired For Success." *Business Week* 2261:44–49, January 6, 1973.
Cardozo. Richard N., and Cagley, James W. "Experimental Study of Industrial Buyer Behavior." *Journal of Marketing Research* 8:329–344, August 1971.
Claycamp, Henry J.; Boyd, Harper W.; and McClelland, Charles W. "Media Models for the Industrial Goods Advertiser." *Journal of Marketing* 34: 23–27, April 1970.
Crissy, William J. E., and Kaplan, Robert M. "Matrix Models For Marketing Planning." *MSU Business Topics* 11:48–66, Summer 1963.
de Koning, Co. "Effective Techniques in Industrial Marketing Research." *Journal of Marketing Research* 1:57–61, April 1964.
"The Changing Anatomy of Industrial Sales Distribution." *Dun's Review and Modern Industry* 81:37–64, January 1963.
Edelman, Franz. "Art & Science of Competitive Bidding." *Harvard Business Review* 45:53–66, July 1965.
Erdman, Kenneth B. "Portrait of a Manufacturer's Representative." *The Agent and Representative* 23:10–11, March 1971.
Finnegan, Thomas. "Profile of the Purchasing Man." *Purchasing Magazine* 70:51–56, February 4, 1971.
"The Flexible World of Leasing." *Fortune* 90:50–77, November 1974.
Freeman, Cyril. "Growth Perspective for Industrial Advertising." *Journal of Marketing* 28:79–82, July 1964.
Gallop, Norman J. "Manufacturer's Representative or Company Salesman?" *Journal of Marketing* 28:62–63, April 1964.

Henderson, Russell H. "Relating Company Markets to SIC." *Journal of Marketing* 27:42–45, April 1963.

"What Determines the Correct Channel of Distribution?" *Industrial Marketing* 51:28, March 1966.

Karns, E., and McGee, H. T. "Product Planning Aids Industry." *Iron Age* 186:92–94, November 24, 1960.

Kolliner, Sim A. "Measuring Industrial Advertising." *Journal of Marketing* 29:51–53, October 1965.

Lehmann, Donald R., and O'Shaughnessy, John. "Differences in Attribute Importance for Different Industrial Products." *Journal of Marketing* 38:36–41, April 1974.

Levitt, Theodore. "Communications and Industrial Selling." *Journal of Marketing* 31:15–21, April 1967.

Litvak, Isaiah A.; Johnson, James A.; and Banting, Peter M. "Industrial Pricing—Art or Science?" *The Business Quarterly* 36–45, Autumn 1967.

Lotshaw, Elmer P. "Industrial Marketing: Trends and Challenges." *Journal of Marketing* 34:22–24, January 1970.

"A Study in Contrast: The Industrial Product Manager and the Consumer Brand Manager." *Marketing Insights* 3:14–17, March 10, 1969.

Martilla, John A. "Word-of-Mouth Communication in the Industrial Adoption Process." *Journal of Marketing Research* 8:173–178, May 1971.

Messner, Fred A. "A Systems Approach to Industrial Marketing Communications." *Journal of Marketing* 28:64–67, October 1964.

Morrill, John E. "Industrial Advertising Pays Off." *Harvard Business Review* 48:4–160, March-April 1970.

Newman, Richard G. "An Analysis of Competitive Bidding Strategy." *Journal of Purchasing* 5:73–84, May 1969.

Parket, I. Robert, and Rabinowitz, Manus. "The Influence of Product Class Perception on Industrial Buyers' Channel Source Choice." *Journal of Economics and Business* 26:203–208, Spring 1974.

Piersol, Robert J. "Accuracy of Estimating Markets for Industrial Products by Size of Consuming Industries." *Journal of Marketing Research* 6:147–154, May 1969.

Sawyer, Howard G. "How To Sell Through Industrial Distributors." *Industrial Marketing* 45:61–73, May 1960.

Schiff, Michael. "ROI: A New Criterion for Salesmen." *Marketing Insights* 2:14–16, April 29, 1968.

Schuster, Ray. "The Plant Engineer and Equipment Leasing." *Plant Engineering* 21:155–162, May 1967.

Smith, W. N., and McGreight, J. R. "Analysis of Competitive Bids." *Management Services* 5:40–44, May-June 1968.

Thompson, J. W., and Evans, W. W. "Behavioral Approach to Industrial Selling." *Harvard Business Review* 47:137–151, March-April 1969.

Walker, Arleigh W. "How To Price Industrial Products." *Harvard Business Review* 45:125–132, September-October 1967.

Webster, Frederick E., Jr. "Modeling the Industrial Buying Process." *Journal of Marketing Research* 2:370–376, November 1965.

———"New Product Adoption in Industrial Markets." *Journal of Marketing* 33:35–39, July 1969.

———"On the Applicability of Communication Theory to Industrial Markets." *Journal of Marketing Research* 5:426–428, November 1968.

———and Wind, Yoram. "Industrial Buying as Organizational Behavior: A Guideline For Research Strategy." *Journal of Purchasing* 8:5–16, August 1972.

Weigand, Robert E. "Identifying Industrial Buying Responsibility." *Journal of Marketing Research* 3:81–84, February 1966.

———"Why Studying the Purchasing Agent Is Not Enough." *Journal of Marketing* 32:41–45, January 1968.

INDEX